In Idi Amin's Shadow

NEW AFRICAN HISTORIES

SERIES EDITORS: JEAN ALLMAN, ALLEN ISAACMAN, AND DEREK R. PETERSON

*Books in this series are published with support from the
Ohio University National Resource Center for African Studies.*

David William Cohen and E. S. Atieno Odhiambo, *The Risks of Knowledge: Investigations into the Death of the Hon. Minister John Robert Ouko in Kenya, 1990*

Belinda Bozzoli, *Theatres of Struggle and the End of Apartheid*

Gary Kynoch, *We Are Fighting the World: A History of the Marashea Gangs in South Africa, 1947–1999*

Stephanie Newell, *The Forger's Tale: The Search for Odeziaku*

Jacob A. Tropp, *Natures of Colonial Change: Environmental Relations in the Making of the Transkei*

Jan Bender Shetler, *Imagining Serengeti: A History of Landscape Memory in Tanzania from Earliest Times to the Present*

Cheikh Anta Babou, *Fighting the Greater Jihad: Amadu Bamba and the Founding of the Muridiyya in Senegal, 1853–1913*

Marc Epprecht, *Heterosexual Africa? The History of an Idea from the Age of Exploration to the Age of AIDS*

Marissa J. Moorman, *Intonations: A Social History of Music and Nation in Luanda, Angola, from 1945 to Recent Times*

Karen E. Flint, *Healing Traditions: African Medicine, Cultural Exchange, and Competition in South Africa, 1820–1948*

Derek R. Peterson and Giacomo Macola, editors, *Recasting the Past: History Writing and Political Work in Modern Africa*

Moses E. Ochonu, *Colonial Meltdown: Northern Nigeria in the Great Depression*

Emily S. Burrill, Richard L. Roberts, and Elizabeth Thornberry, editors, *Domestic Violence and the Law in Colonial and Postcolonial Africa*

Daniel R. Magaziner, *The Law and the Prophets: Black Consciousness in South Africa, 1968–1977*

Emily Lynn Osborn, *Our New Husbands Are Here: Households, Gender, and Politics in a West African State from the Slave Trade to Colonial Rule*

Robert Trent Vinson, *The Americans Are Coming! Dreams of African American Liberation in Segregationist South Africa*

James R. Brennan, *Taifa: Making Nation and Race in Urban Tanzania*

Benjamin N. Lawrance and Richard L. Roberts, editors, *Trafficking in Slavery's Wake: Law and the Experience of Women and Children*

David M. Gordon, *Invisible Agents: Spirits in a Central African History*

Allen F. Isaacman and Barbara S. Isaacman, *Dams, Displacement, and the Delusion of Development: Cahora Bassa and Its Legacies in Mozambique, 1965–2007*

Stephanie Newell, *The Power to Name: A History of Anonymity in Colonial West Africa*

Gibril R. Cole, *The Krio of West Africa: Islam, Culture, Creolization, and Colonialism in the Nineteenth Century*

Matthew M. Heaton, *Black Skin, White Coats: Nigerian Psychiatrists, Decolonization, and the Globalization of Psychiatry*

Meredith Terretta, *Nation of Outlaws, State of Violence: Nationalism, Grassfields Tradition, and State Building in Cameroon*

Paolo Israel, *In Step with the Times: Mapiko Masquerades of Mozambique*

Michelle R. Moyd, *Violent Intermediaries: African Soldiers, Conquest, and Everyday Colonialism in German East Africa*

Abosede A. George, *Making Modern Girls: A History of Girlhood, Labor, and Social Development in Colonial Lagos*

Alicia C. Decker, *In Idi Amin's Shadow: Women, Gender, and Militarism in Uganda*

Rachel Jean-Baptiste, *Conjugal Rights: Marriage, Sexuality, and Urban Life in Colonial Libreville, Gabon*

Shobana Shankar, *Who Shall Enter Paradise? Christian Origins in Muslim Northern Nigeria, c. 1890–1975*

In Idi Amin's Shadow

Women, Gender, and Militarism in Uganda

Alicia C. Decker

OHIO UNIVERSITY PRESS ～ ATHENS, OHIO

Ohio University Press, Athens, Ohio 45701
ohioswallow.com
© 2014 by Ohio University Press

To obtain permission to quote, reprint, or otherwise reproduce or distribute
material from Ohio University Press publications, please contact our rights
and permissions department at (740) 593-1154 or (740) 593-4536 (fax).

Printed in the United States of America
Ohio University Press books are printed on acid-free paper ∞ ™

24 23 22 21 20 19 18 17 16 15 14   5 4 3 2 1

Earlier versions of chapters 4 and 6 appeared as "An Accidental Liberation:
Ugandan Women on the Frontlines of Idi Amin's Economic War," in *Women's
History Review* 22, no. 6 (2013): 1–17, and "'Sometimes you may leave your
husband in Karuma Falls or in the forest there': A Gendered History of
Disappearance in Idi Amin's Uganda, in *Journal of Eastern African Studies*
7, no. 1 (2013): 125–42, respectively; http://www.tandfonline.com. Some material from chapter 1 also appeared in Italian in "Militarismo, nazionalismo e
matrimonio . . . " in *Afriche e Orienti* 14, no. 3–4 (2012): 124–38 (Aiep Editore
& Afriche e Orienti).

Library of Congress Cataloging-in-Publication Data

Decker, Alicia Catharine, author.
 In Idi Amin's shadow : women, gender, and militarism in Uganda / Alicia C.
Decker.
     pages cm. — (New African histories)
 Includes bibliographical references and index.
 ISBN 978-0-8214-2117-8 (hc : alk. paper) — ISBN 978-0-8214-2118-5 (pb : alk.
paper) — ISBN 978-0-8214-4502-0 (pdf)
 1. Uganda—Social conditions—1971-1979. 2. Women—Uganda—Social
conditions—20th century. 3. Violence—Uganda—History—20th century. 4.
Women and the military—Uganda. 5. Women and war—Uganda. 6. Amin,
Idi, 1925-2003—Political and social views. 7. Militarism—Uganda. 8. Sex
role—Uganda. I. Title. II. Series: New African histories series.
 HN794.A8D32 2014
 967.61042—dc23

2014020779

For my mom,
who never stopped believing in me
(and who kept sending the "Beetlejuice")

Contents

Illustrations

Acknowledgments

This book would not have been possible without the collaboration of the many Ugandan women and men who generously gave me their time and trusted me with their stories. I cannot thank you enough for sharing your memories of a very difficult period and helping me to better understand the complexities of life under military rule. Every time that I read your words on the page, I am awed by your strength and resilience, not only as individuals but as a people. I also acknowledge the tremendous energy and enthusiasm of my research assistants in Uganda. Your contributions to the project went beyond translating and transcribing interviews. You introduced me to your friends, your families, and your communities. You put up with my incessant questions and interruptions. And you kept me in good humor when things did not go according to plan. For all of these things I am eternally grateful. Special thanks to Jane Nabasirye, Innocent Tumwebaze, Denis Kakembo, Sam Suubi, George Peter Ngogolo, Godfrey Adia, and Lindsey Siegel. Many thanks also go to Kasirye Mayanja, the archivist at the headquarters of the Uganda People's Congress, who helped me gather many valuable materials, to Medi Nsereko of CBS Radio Uganda for providing me with an audio recording of his interview with Madina Amin, and to the late Bob Astles for welcoming me into his London home in 2011. I also wish to thank Betty Nakabiito Musoke of the New Vision Printing and Publishing Company for helping me secure permission to reproduce some of the photographs in this book.

It is always difficult to spend significant time away from loved ones, but my dear friends in Uganda have become my second family. My deepest respect and admiration go to my Rotary host family, Tusu, Dorcus, Angela, Brenda, and Yo. Your friendship over the years has meant a great deal to me. Thank you for inviting me into your home and adopting me as one of your own. My love also goes out to my dear friend Herbert and his entire family. I always feel welcome at your home in Kireka. Please know that you are always welcome at mine. To my other close Ugandan friends—Cornelius Mukiibi, Florence Masu, Sarah Adero, Willy Ateng, Anzua, Lucy Olama, Kate Katama, Teo Walusimbi, Consolata Kabonesa, Arnold Bisase, and the dozens of women in Wandegeya Market—you are the reason I keep returning to Africa. And to my American "partners in crime," Emily Bass, Kristen Fleschner, Jessica Munson, Kathryn Barrett-Gaines, Lindsey Siegel, and Suzanne Wint, thank you for all of the laughter.

I owe a great intellectual debt of gratitude to the numerous scholars who have taught me such a vast amount about the complexities of Uganda and East Africa in general. In particular, I would like to thank Holly Hanson, Derek Peterson, and Aili Mari Tripp for mentoring me in various ways over the years. I am a much better scholar because of the insights that I have gained from your work. I must also acknowledge the members of my doctoral dissertation committee at Emory University. Julie Shayne, Pamela Scully, Edna Bay, and Layli Maparyan provided tremendous support and guidance as I worked my way through many of the ideas that undergird this book. Thank you for providing me with a powerful analytical toolkit.

I could not have traveled to Uganda to conduct this research without generous financial support from the U.S. Department of Education (Fulbright-Hays Doctoral Dissertation Research Abroad Fellowship), the American Historical Association (Bernadotte Schmidt Grant), Emory University (University Fund for Internationalization Research Grant), and Purdue University (Research Incentive Grant, Library Scholars Grant, and Purdue Research Fund Summer Grant). Thank you for providing me with this opportunity.

In Lafayette, special thanks go to Julie Knoeller, Rebecca Gwyn, Fay Chan, Nancy Cramer, Leslie Barnes, and Nancy Hughes, all of whom helped me with many of the logistical aspects of this project. Thank you for answering my frantic e-mails from the field, for processing the endless stream of travel receipts, for photocopying and scanning countless documents, and for making sure that the correct paperwork got filed so that my students could graduate on time! I appreciate all of you tremendously.

I am fortunate to have had the opportunity to work with two of the most fantastic graduate students on the planet: Jacqueline-Bethel Mougoué and Adrianna Ernstberger. The two of you have provided me with great support and encouragement over the years. I thank you both for kindly offering to read numerous early drafts of this book, even when you had plenty of your own work to keep you busy. I also appreciate your willingness to guest lecture to my classes over the years. You are both excellent teachers and scholars. I am so proud of you!

I am also grateful to have such terrific mentors in my life. Valentine Moghadam, you introduced me to many people who have critically shaped my thinking about global feminisms. Thank you for bringing me into the UNESCO Network. I am very happy that I had the opportunity to work with you during my first five years at Purdue. TJ Boisseau, you have been a wonderful addition to the Women's, Gender, and Sexuality Studies Program. I have learned a lot from you over the last two years and have enjoyed our travels together immensely. You cannot imagine how much I appreciate your willingness to read countless drafts of this manuscript. I am not sure that I would have gotten through the revisions without you. Whitney Walton, you have been a great mentor to me in the History Department, and I appreciate all of your guidance over the years. Thank you for helping me and all of the other female junior faculty members succeed.

I recently made the difficult decision to leave Purdue in order to pursue an exciting new opportunity at The Pennsylvania State University. Although I am leaving behind dear friends and colleagues, I know that our paths will cross again in the future. I am grateful to have amazing women like Michele Buzon, Carrie Janney, and Ayşe Çiftçi in my life. You are more precious to me than you will ever know and I will miss you all so very much. I am proud that I could be part of the NPG with Jennifer Freeman Marshall, Cheryl Cooky, and Marlo David and feel lucky to have worked with such dear friends. I am also glad that I could participate in a book club whose members did not chastise me when I showed up without doing the reading! Anu Subramanian, Susan Lopez, Jana Chapman Gates, Antonia Syson, Kathy Schroth, Rebecca Bryant, and Ayşe, thank you for understanding! In the History Department, I must give special thanks to Yvonne Pitts, Stacy Holden, Melinda Zook, Dawn Marsh, Rebekah Klein-Pejšová, and Neil Bynum for your ongoing friendship and support. To my dear friends in the Anthropology Department, especially Kory Cooper, Ellen Gruenbaum, Evie Blackwood, and Laura Zanotti, thank you for bringing me into your fold. Jay O'Brien, rest in peace. You will be sorely missed. And finally, many thanks go to Kirk Hoppe, Dave Kiser, and Ivan Brumbaugh—quite possibly the city's greatest restaurateur—for all of your encouragement.

In the course of researching and writing this book, I have fallen out of touch with many of the friends who are most special to me. Now that I have this important milestone behind me, let me hope that I can reconnect with each of you: Emily Rosenau, Maggie Goetze, Dorey Butter, Peri Klemm, Jeremy Pool, Julie Dorn, Tiffany Worboy, K. C. Prakiti, Veronica Setzke, and Mark and Paul Bringardner. Here's to the future!

My dear friend Patrice Rankine, I thank you for always pushing me to make my work better, for knowing when to offer encouragement, and for celebrating the victories with me along the way.

I am grateful to have had my closest friend, Andrea Arrington, by my side throughout this entire process. Over the past twelve years, I have learned a great deal from you. I respect you tremendously and cannot wait for your book to come out so that we can celebrate together. There is no one else with whom I would rather travel the world and share the adventures. Thank you for being such a loyal friend, honest critic, and ardent supporter. I love you dearly.

My family knows that writing this book has been the hardest thing that I have ever done. They also know that completing it is now my proudest accomplishment. I could not have done it without their constant love and support. Dad and Pat, thank you for all of the encouraging phone calls. Jeff and Lisa, thank you for all of the flowers and care packages. Sam and Mason, thank you for being such a wonderful source of happiness in our lives. Les, thank you for the Friday morning conversations and for helping me during the various moves and surgeries. Mom, thank you for being my greatest cheerleader. And Mr. Waffles, thank you for continuing to fight until the very end. You will always be my sweet boy.

And to the man who has become my Rock, Rahman Dorsey, I love you so very much. Thank you for being you.

Special thanks go to Allen Isaacman, Jean Allman, and Gillian Berchowitz for believing in this project. Your constructive feedback, as well as that of the three anonymous reviewers, has allowed me to strengthen this manuscript considerably. I also wish to thank Nancy Basmajian and her editorial team at Ohio University Press for cleaning up "a number of" awkward sentence constructions and grammatical errors. (May I never use that phrase again!) Any remaining mistakes are my own.

Abbreviations

CID	Criminal Investigations Division
CORE	Congress of Racial Equality
IBEAC	Imperial British East Africa Company
ICJ	International Commission of Jurists
IGP	Inspector General of Police
IWY	International Women's Year
KAR	King's African Rifles
KY	Kabaka Yekka
NCC	National Consultative Council
NEC	National Executive Committee
OAU	Organization of African Unity
PSU	Public Safety Unit
SADF	South African Defense Forces
SRC	State Research Centre
UCW	Uganda Council of Women
UNLF	Uganda National Liberation Front
UPC	Uganda People's Congress

A Note on the Use of Names

Throughout the book I refer to most people by their first names unless they are public figures and known primarily by their last names. I have used pseudonyms for everyone I interviewed unless they spoke with me in an official or professional capacity. Pseudonyms are clearly marked in the list of oral interviews that is included in the bibliography.

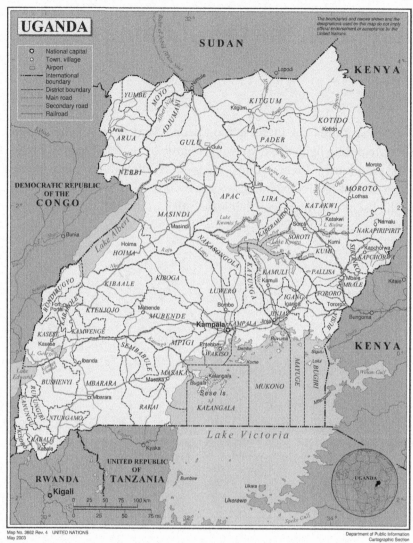

Uganda. *Source: United Nations Department of Public Information, Cartographic Section, Map No. 3862, Rev. 4.*

In Search of Amin's Women

"DURING AMIN'S time, there were not many problems apart from our people disappearing and being killed," explained Namuli Kasozi, a sixty-year-old market vendor from the outskirts of Kampala. Namuli is my pseudonym for this robust, spirited Ugandan woman, one of the many people I interviewed who lived through the harrowing years of Idi Amin's reign. "Big Daddy," as he was affectionately known, the so-called father of the nation, was president of Uganda from January 1971 until April 1979. While others experienced his rule as a time of terror, Namuli suggests that there was relative quiet for those in the shadow of the many reported kidnappings, disappearances, and killings. "I was not a person who used to move a lot because that regime affected so much people who could move from one place or one bar to another bar. But for me, I was not among those people."

This brief statement, which echoes many that I recorded of women living through this period, reveals a great deal about Amin's military dictatorship and how some Ugandan women experienced his rule. While Namuli acknowledges the violence that is commonly associated with the regime, she insists that it did not have a major impact on her life because she was not one of "those" people. She carefully sets herself apart from those who moved "from one bar to another bar," implying that such people were morally debased and perhaps even got what was coming to them. The fact that she says "there were not many problems apart from our people disappearing and being killed" also suggests that her life had some degree of normalcy despite the violence. This tells us something very different from what the scholarly and popular literature would suggest, namely, that people managed to survive the chaos and sometimes, as I argue throughout this book, were even able to thrive.

The voices of ordinary women provide insight into the ways in which age, religion, and social class mediated their experiences, among other factors. Because many of the "disappeared" under the regime were men, the women left behind often had to serve in multiple social roles—father, mother, laborer—in the shadows of the regime. That is, Amin's militarism, his efforts to seize and reinforce power through military means, was deeply gendered. Men fought in his armed forces, protected the state, and, in more cases than not, raped women. Violent, terrible things happened to them during the regime, but women were not merely victims. They continued to live their lives heroically and represent the other side of this militarism. Was Amin their father too? What types of social, political, and historical spaces did these women carve out for themselves?

This book examines Ugandan women's complex and sometimes paradoxical relationship to Amin's military state. I argue that the violence of his regime resulted in opportunities as well as challenges for women, which varied according to one's relationship to the military state. Some women assumed positions of political power or taught themselves to become successful business entrepreneurs, while others experienced the trauma of watching their brothers, husbands, and sons be "disappeared" by the state's security forces or lived through violent sexual assaults. In most cases, however, women had a mixed relationship to Amin and his military government, one that was complicated and uneven. While they appreciated many of the policies that he put into place, they feared and resented the violence of militarism. For this reason, many women sought refuge in the obscurity of the shadows.

This book is not only about women's experiences during Amin's rule but also about the complex and contradictory ways that gender informed (and was informed by) the ideology and practice of militarism. Scholars have seriously underestimated the degree to which Amin utilized gendered discourse to consolidate political hegemony and to maintain a certain performance of power. They have also overlooked how militarism shaped his own gender identity, as well as many of his actions. Indeed, as I argue throughout the book, new constructions of masculinity and femininity emerged from militaristic practice, which in turn profoundly influenced gender roles and relations. By exploring the dialectical relationship between gender and militarism, this book offers a more nuanced interpretation of Amin's dictatorship than most scholarly treatments and popular histories have presented. This allows us to make better sense of Amin's Uganda and the lives of the women who lived through it.

MAKING SENSE OF AMIN

To appreciate the nuances of women's lives as lived in the shadow of Amin, one must first understand the nature of Amin's regime and consider the implications of Amin's deployment of gender and use of gendered violence. This consideration entails putting aside the shibboleth that Idi Amin was an aberrant character with no underlying rationale animating or unifying his political strategies that can be studied and understood. Idi Amin was not crazy. He was not suffering from syphilis, nor did he have any other type of degenerative mental illness that caused him to act "psychotic" or "psychopathic."[1] Far from the ignorant brute who has been caricatured in literature, music, and film, Amin was a calculating military man who made choices about violence. He performed masculinity in strategic ways and deployed irrationality as a performative tactic, one based largely on hypermasculinity and gendered violence. Gender analysis provides us with the tools to better understand Amin and his seemingly inexplicable behaviors. This, in turn, helps us to better understand women's experiences of military rule. In this section, I briefly analyze some of the most popular rhetoric in circulation about why Amin used violence. This is important because, as I argue throughout the book, Ugandans frequently appropriated many of these reductive discourses, using them to talk about and make sense of the violence.

Most popular and scholarly explanations of Amin's violent and erratic behavior fall into three general categories—mental illness, sadism, and culture. The first is perhaps the most common, because it seems to make sense cross-culturally. After all, every society has its share of "crazy" people. One of Amin's former physicians, John Kibuka-Musoke, said that the military strongman had been suffering from hypomania, "a condition bringing about a rapid succession of other contradicting ideas expressed in confused verbal outbursts and fits of anger alternating with spells of extreme optimism and a sense of the grandiose."[2] He thought that this disease was the result of advanced syphilis or a symptom of schizophrenia. M. S. M. Semakula Kiwanuka, one of Uganda's most prominent historians, agreed that Amin was probably schizophrenic, although he did not think Amin had a venereal disease.[3] George Ivan Smith, a prominent Australian diplomat, also thought that the former dictator was psychotic. He did not, however, believe that Amin was the "schizophrenic type." Instead, Smith imagined him as a clever and cunning "psychopath."[4] Most observers seem to agree that even if Amin had been suffering from some sort of mental illness, he was not so "unhinged" that he did not know what he was doing.[5]

Others have tried to explain Amin's violence through the lens of sadism.[6] In *Lust to Kill*, Joseph Kamau and Andrew Cameron suggest that Amin learned to demonstrate his anger using an array of "painful methods." They said that by the age of twelve, "he was well established as the leader of the village children—a domineering, resourceful, brute-strong youth with a pronounced streak of sadism. In the sundown hours of play, he would overcome any opposition by simply grasping his opponent's genitals and crushing them in his great bear paw of [a] hand."[7] Loyal Gould and James Leo Garrett Jr. referred to Amin as the "Eichmann of the British army" because of his habit of "torturing to death by choking" suspected Mau Mau insurgents.[8] Maurice Rogoff agreed with their scholarly assessment. In the early 1960s, while he was working as a pathologist for the Kenyan government, he investigated a village massacre that Amin allegedly perpetrated when serving in the King's African Rifles. He also observed Amin in the boxing ring when he worked as a volunteer medical advisor to the Kenyan Amateur Boxing Association. "I was seriously concerned," he told George Ivan Smith during an interview shortly after the fall of Kampala. "He was hitting with all his force. Too much. I feared he would kill someone."[9] While these accounts certainly confirm Amin's propensity toward violence, they do not explain *why* he acted in the ways that he did. Instead, they suggest that Amin was simply a "bad seed."

There are still others who have explained Amin's violence as a reflection of an ancient "warrior tradition," a resurrection of "those early warriors in Bunyoro, Acholi, as well as West Nile, who reached for their spears to strike a blow, however weak, against European imperialism."[10] As a warrior, Amin represented a hero of sorts, someone who was self-reliant and would not be cowed by his former colonial masters. According to Ali Mazrui, a preeminent Kenyan political scientist who was dean of the Faculty of Social Sciences at Makerere University until Amin forced him into exile in 1973, Amin was the embodiment of "political masculinity." Mazrui explains,

As a personal quality political masculinity is a powerful image of manliness in a political leader, which tends to affect his style of leadership and his impact on his followers. . . . . The political masculinity of the General does not lie merely in his size, though he is impressively tall and broad. Nor does it lie merely in his insistence that he fears no-one but God. Yet these factors are part of the story, combined with the additional factor that an affirmation of fearlessness and an athletic build have indeed been part of the total picture of martial values within African political cultures.[11]

Mazrui's attempt to connect Amin's political masculinity to a resurrected warrior tradition is interesting, but a partial explanation at best. Because Amin spent all of his life in and around army barracks, any innate warrior traits would have been overlaid by years of military training and service. While I agree that gender had a profound impact on Amin's leadership style, my research shows that his understandings of masculinity and femininity were not linked to a primordial warrior tradition. Instead, they reflected many of the values that he learned in the military, namely, to equate masculine virility with violence and martial valor.[12] This book explores the deadly repercussions of these deeply gendered lessons.

THEORIZING GENDER AND MILITARISM IN AFRICA

To understand the complex relationship between gender and militarism within Amin's Uganda, we must step back to consider how scholars have defined and theorized these concepts within broader contexts, including Africa. Throughout this book, I argue that gender was a crucial organizing factor within Amin's military state, indelibly shaping who he was as a man and how he governed as a ruler. It also profoundly influenced women's (and men's) understandings and experiences of military rule. But what exactly is gender? Among Western feminists, gender is frequently conceptualized as the socially constructed counterpart to biological sex. According to Joan Wallach Scott, gender is "the social organization of sexual difference." It does not reflect "fixed or natural physical differences between women and men; rather gender is the knowledge that establishes meanings for bodily differences."[13] Like many other scholars from the West, Scott exhibits an understanding of gender that is closely linked to ideas about the body and therefore follows a particular type of "bio-logic."[14] This does not mean that gender is biologically determined but instead suggests that it is a function of sexual difference. Various African scholars, in contrast, argue that gender should be entirely divorced from biology or sex. They maintain that masculinity is not necessarily linked to maleness, nor is femininity necessarily linked to femaleness. Ifi Amadiume, for instance, suggests that among the Igbo peoples of Nigeria, biological females could become "husbands" or "sons" because one's sex did not determine one's gender. Women could take on masculine gender roles, just as men could take on those deemed feminine.[15] However, as Nwando Achebe's study of female kingship in colonial Igboland demonstrates, female masculinity had limitations and was not the same as (biological) maleness.[16]

Even if we acknowledge that gender and sex are slippery concepts and that one cannot be easily mapped onto the other, we can still construct a provisional framework that allows us to begin making sense of gender within Amin's Uganda. Building off of the definition of masculinity provided by Lisa Lindsay and Stephan Miescher in their path-breaking book, *Men and Masculinities in Modern Africa*, I conceptualize gender as "a cluster of norms, values, and behavioral patterns expressing explicitly and implicitly expectations of how men [and women] should act and represent themselves to others. Ideologies of masculinity—like those of femininity—are culturally and historically constructed, their meanings continually contested and always in the process of being renegotiated in the context of existing power relations."[17] Because this definition is flexible enough to capture the fluidities that encompass "gender" in Africa, it serves as a useful starting point.

Like Lindsay and Miescher, I see great value in exploring gender as discourse, identity, and practice. Throughout the book, I analyze how Amin and other state actors utilized gendered ideologies and rhetoric to consolidate and maintain power, as well as the gendered ways that ordinary women articulated their experiences of military rule. I also pay attention to gender as an identity that shapes and is shaped by military practice. And finally, taking my inspiration from Judith Butler, I look at gender as performance, as an expression of social practice that reflects and simultaneously constitutes the larger social order. I see gender not only as an intentional act that illuminates the agency of social actors but also as a performative act that creates identity.[18] Amin and the Ugandan women whose lives are at the heart of this book performed gender in strategic ways. In so doing, they produced new understandings of gender in a hypermilitarized social world.

Militarism can also be analyzed in terms of discourse, identity, and practice. Unlike gender, however, the ideology of militarism is remarkably similar across cultures. According to Jacklyn Cock, it is an ideology that accepts "organized state violence as a legitimate solution to conflict."[19] It is a system of beliefs that glorifies war and celebrates so-called military values—hierarchy, discipline, obedience, and the centralization of authority. Even though militarism flourishes in many different types of societies, it is particularly common within those that have experienced military coups. "Once the military constitutes the ultimate source of formal state power and politics," suggests Amii Omara-Otunnu, "its policies, priorities and values begin to affect social relations among the citizenry and it is likely to circumscribe the scope for internal politics."[20] The population therefore has little choice but to acquiesce to the values and priorities of the military. As a result of militarism, there is "a whole spectrum of socio-political interactions [that] become informed by a cultural ethos that values military force over rational and moral persuasion."[21]

Amina Mama and Margo Okazawa-Rey argue that militarism should be conceptualized as "an extreme variant of patriarchy, a gendered regime characterized by discourses and practices that subordinate and oppress women, as well as non-dominant men, reinforcing hierarchies of class, gender, race and ethnicity, and in some contexts caste, religion and location."[22] Out of militarism come militarized versions of masculinity and femininity, those that support or are dependent on military values. A militarized masculinity might place emphasis on physical strength, courage, endurance, discipline, and heterosexual competency, among other traits. A militarized femininity, in contrast, might emphasize patience, nurturance, and support. Gender dispositions vary according to the needs of the particular military structure, as well as the cultural and historical context. In Amin's Uganda, militarism promoted a variety of new and old gender constructions, which are explored throughout this book.

Feminist scholarship demonstrates important linkages between gender and militarism in Africa.[23] Jacklyn Cock's work, for example, teaches us that although militaries are predominantly male, women make significant contributions to the militarization of society. In apartheid South Africa, white women provided material and ideological support to the military. On a material level, they joined support organizations that sent care packages to soldiers, they participated in civil defense and commando units, and they engaged in armament production. On an ideological level, they socialized men into a militarized version of masculinity by encouraging their husbands to join the military and by providing their sons with war toys. White women also directly participated in the militarization of society by joining the South African Defense Forces (SADF) as nurses, intelligence officers, secretaries, and administrators. They were not, however, allowed to participate as soldiers, because combat was central to the construction of masculinity. In this way, women supported militarism without threatening the patriarchal social structure.[24]

Black South African women also supported militarism in similar ways. They, too, socialized men into violent forms of masculinity and participated in Umkhonto we Sizwe, the armed wing of the African National Congress. And they too were excluded from combat roles, although black women seemed to have a slightly wider range of opportunities within the guerrilla army than did white women within the SADF. Nonetheless, their participation did not challenge dominant notions of masculinity and femininity, so the larger gendered power structure remained intact.[25] Cock's work is important in that it also demonstrates how South African women resisted militarism, often through multiracial nonviolent women's organizations. It alerts us to the fact that there is still a great deal of information that we do not know about gendered patterns of support for and resistance to militarism in other African contexts.

Feminist scholarship also highlights the ways in which African military states have used women to advance their own political agendas. Nina Mba's comparative study of political regimes in postcolonial Nigeria, for instance, demonstrates that military governments often promote limited rights for women because of political expedience.[26] However, because they do not tend to appoint women to prominent political or military positions, their "commitment" to women's liberation can be seen as shallow at best. Amina Mama makes a similar point in her research. She suggests that the Nigerian military state used women, particularly the wives of high-ranking military officers, to normalize and legitimate military rule. During the regimes of Ibrahim Babangida (1985–93) and Sani Abacha (1993–98), the state "improvised a banal game of gender politics which became a key mechanism through which the tentacles of militarism were extended, legitimized, and consolidated at a time when internationally, military rule had become an unacceptable form of government."[27] First ladies, in particular, played a crucial role in convincing the public that army officers were "responsible and familial" and that people could feel "at home" with the military in charge.[28] As we see throughout the book, Amin's wives functioned in much the same manner, thereby presenting the nation with a softer side of military rule.

Moving beyond the military state, feminist scholars have also highlighted the gender politics of militarism in Africa more generally. Yaliwe Clark, for instance, examines security sector reform in postconflict societies as an opportunity to deconstruct, understand, and transform militarized masculinities. She suggests that unless these processes seriously question the value of militarism, as well as the cultures of masculinity that undergird military institutions, there is little possibility for meaningful reform.[29] Her work is useful in helping us to think about security in more complicated ways than the dominant "national security framework," which emphasizes the security of the nation-state and not necessarily its citizenry. Throughout the book, I consider the gendered repercussions of Amin's (often futile) attempts to bring "security" to the military state.

Patricia McFadden suggests that we need to reconceptualize the African postcolonial state as a militarized construction that excludes women and limits their citizenship potential. She argues that militarism has been central "to the deployment of the state as a site of accumulation by various ruling classes throughout history, as well as a vehicle of repression, surveillance, and exclusion of the majority of people, particularly women, the young, and the elderly in working communities."[30] Furthermore, she demonstrates that those who control the state often violate women's bodily and sexual integrity as an expression of "reclaimed" African masculinity, a reassertion of manhood that colonial rule undermined.[31] They use rape, and other forms of violence, to humiliate women, as well as the men who are unable to protect them. We certainly see this pattern play out in Uganda during Amin's rule when poorly educated soldiers, members of what Ali Mazrui calls the "lumpen militariat," terrorized women (and civilian men) to bolster their own masculinity.[32]

Women are not simply victims of militarism, however. They employ various strategies to mediate the violence. Mama and Okazawa-Rey remind us that even in highly militarized settings, women demonstrate tactical and strategic agency. They suggest that "tactical agency refers to the individual negotiations of survival that occur even in the context of extreme disempowerment or overwhelmingly negative options."[33] For example, a woman might start smuggling or sleeping with a soldier to gain access to precious resources. This contrasts with more strategic forms of agency, which can be found in collective mobilization by women for peace. While Ugandan women demonstrated tactical agency as a way to survive Amin's military dictatorship, they did not engage in collective forms of resistance. Such a move, as this book demonstrates, was far too dangerous.

This study builds off of the theoretical scaffolding sketched above by analyzing the ways in which gender informs the ideology and practice of militarism. Throughout the book, we see how Amin utilized gendered discourses and performances to consolidate and maintain power. He fashioned himself not only as the "father of the nation" who would provide guidance, protection, and discipline but also as a "man's man," a hypermasculine tough guy who "feared no one but God."[34] He gendered the security apparatus of the state by referring to the police as the "mothers of the nation" and the soldiers as the "fathers," a rhetorical strategy that significantly undermined the authority of the former, while reinforcing the power of the latter. And he tapped into global discourses about gender equality and women's emancipation to increase his popularity both at home and abroad. We also see how women utilized gendered rhetoric and performances to support or resist militarism. As "mothers of the nation," they penned congratulatory messages to Amin when he banned miniskirts and other forms of "indecent" dress. As mothers, sisters, and wives, they also testified before a commission of inquiry about the disappearance of their loved ones at the hands of the military state. By reexamining Amin's Uganda through the lens of social history, this book allows us to see the myriad ways that gender informed militarism as both ideology and practice.

This book also demonstrates the ways in which militarism informs gender. It carefully analyzes how military rule produced, maintained, and positioned differences between men and women. For instance, because the state placed national security in the hands of military men, many women (and civilian men) experienced greater violence and insecurity. And because the government labeled certain men as enemies of the state, thus forcing them to flee into exile, many women gained greater power and autonomy within the household. In these ways, military rule reified gender differences between men and women. New constructions of masculinity and femininity also emerged from militaristic practice, which significantly influenced gender roles and relations in Amin's Uganda. We see how the proliferation of "security" agencies led to the emergence of hyperviolent masculinities. These can be juxtaposed with the more feminized versions of masculinity that simultaneously emerged, such as the emasculated police officer or the "weak" man who left his family and fled to Tanzania. Militarism also produced a variety of new femininities. There were masculinized femininities that could be found among "tough" women leaders or "fierce" security operatives. There were disreputable femininities, such as the "loose" women who migrated to town and the "immoral" schoolgirls who refused to shed their miniskirts. And there were respectable femininities, such as the "mothers of the nation" who served as the arbiters of moral rectitude, as well as the grieving widows who found work in the informal sector to provide for their families in times of economic crisis. As this book clearly demonstrates, these gendered identities were informed by, and therefore a product of, military rule.

FINDING AMIN'S WOMEN

Namuli Kasozi, the vibrant market woman whom we met at the beginning of this introduction, spent much of her adult life living in Idi Amin's shadow. While he was in power, she kept her head down, minding her own business and living a somewhat normal existence. Once he had been forced into exile, she remained in the shadows in an effort to survive the culture of violence that had become Amin's most enduring legacy. To provide a better understanding of the experiences of women like Namuli who lived through this harrowing time, this book ventures into the shadows. One of my major arguments is that Ugandan women were not irrelevant to the state (nor was the state irrelevant to most women). Although women were important historical actors, they have been virtually absent from most popular and scholarly accounts. It is striking that despite the abundance of literature about Amin's rule, including at least two annotated bibliographies, there is very little scholarship about women's experiences.[35] By putting women at the center of my analysis, I am able to unpack the complexities of their relationship to the state, which, in turn, allows us to make better sense of Amin's Uganda.

I have been able to find Amin's women largely through memory. By interviewing more than one hundred Ugandan women from all walks of life, as well as several dozen men, I have been able to reconstruct the experiences of those who have been left out of the historical record. Oftentimes their memories are partial, disjointed, or even inaccurate, but this does not render them useless. Instead, these elisions or errors allow me to map out the ways in which certain women experienced and remembered particular historical events. They help me to move away from "history as fact" and toward "history as meaning." Unlike most documentary evidence, memory enables me to explore the subjective aspects of history, to investigate what it might have felt like to live through this tumultuous period of time. I therefore read memory as an archive of the past and of the present, a rich cultural repository that reveals individual and collective truths.

Memory works in different ways throughout this book. In the first chapter, I utilize a variety of published memoirs to examine the early years of Amin's life as a military recruit in the British colonial army. Although these texts do not tell us much about Ugandan women, they do provide important clues about gender. Through these memoirs, as well as a host of other primary and secondary source materials, I am able to tease out the historical relationship between militarism and masculinity that so profoundly shaped Amin and his fellow soldiers. Memoirs written by Amin's contemporaries clearly demonstrate that his propensity toward violence was not random or accidental. On the contrary, the British cultivated a militarized version of masculinity in their soldiers, one that produced fierce warriors who did not question authority and were not afraid to use violence. Amin was a product of this deeply gendered training. After independence, he continued to understand and perform masculinity in similar ways, thus setting the stage for his eventual military coup.

In the second chapter, I use memory to investigate how Amin and his henchmen utilized violence to consolidate and maintain political power. Using transcripts from the fifteen-volume report of the Commission of Inquiry into Violations of Human Rights, which examined violations from the time of independence until the current government took power in 1986, as well as interviews, newspaper articles, and military decrees, I offer a gendered reading of state violence during the early years of the regime. I maintain that narratives of torture are not simply macabre descriptions of sadism and depravity but instead useful texts that clearly reveal the performative aspects of the regime's violence. Memory allows us to see violence as a gendered performance, in other words, as a reiterative demonstration of hypermasculine military power. As I argue throughout the chapter, these performances were a crucial mode of governmentality that allowed those in power to mask the fragility of the military state.

Memory is often rife with contradictions. No two people remember the same event in quite the same manner, nor do their memories of the event remain static. This presents several interesting challenges for the researcher, particularly when it comes to interpretation. Which version is "correct"? Whose "truth" is more authentic? In the third chapter, which examines Amin's attempts to establish political legitimacy through the regulation of women's dress, I begin grappling with these issues. Women repeatedly told me that they dared not resist Amin's ban on miniskirts and other forms of "indecent" dress, and yet the state newspaper regularly published articles threatening those who wore miniskirts. Arrest records at the Central Police Station confirm that many women continued violating the ban, despite the apparent risks. In an effort to make sense of this apparent discrepancy, this chapter uses women's narratives and archival evidence to examine the internal contradictions and contested meanings of this highly gendered campaign.

The meanings that people attach to the past are always mediated by the present. Because memory is a constantly shifting terrain, I had to consider the ways in which daily life influenced how women remembered and forgot the past. In the fourth chapter, I use memory to analyze women's experiences of the "economic war." When, in late 1972, Amin expelled most of the Asian population, a group that had for many years been the nation's primary entrepreneurs, he inadvertently opened up a new economic space for Ugandan women. Whether they were forced to engage in petty trade out of necessity or because they received a shop "abandoned" by the departing Asians, numerous women remembered Amin as the one who "taught us how to work." For the first time, many gained access to economic resources and decision-making power. Despite the violence and hardship that ensued, most women looked back on this era with some degree of fondness. I argue that this nostalgia was less about their admiration for Amin and more about their mounting frustration with the current president.

In the fifth chapter, I utilize the memoir of Uganda's first female cabinet minister, Elizabeth Bagaya, to unpack Amin's surprising "commitment" to women's rights. Her memories confirm and disrupt popular and scholarly understandings of this turbulent historical era. Through a close reading of this text, as well as a wide variety of newspaper articles, political cartoons, documentaries, and public speeches, I examine some of the more performative aspects of military rule. I suggest that Amin was not genuinely interested in empowering women but instead used women's issues to consolidate political hegemony and maintain a certain performance of power. He appointed women to important political positions and espoused rhetoric about women's empowerment because it bought him political capital, both at home and abroad. By tapping into global discourses about women's liberation, he was able to demonstrate, at least in theory, that he was a progressive political leader despite his military pedigree. Although Amin was not genuinely interested in empowering women, this does not mean that certain women did not benefit from military rule. Instead, as this chapter clearly demonstrates, the politics of empowerment were complex and resulted in various opportunities and challenges for Ugandan women.

Memory projects are often contested in public spaces. Using transcripts from the commission of inquiry that investigated disappearances in Uganda during Amin's first years in power, chapter 6 compares women's memories of "enforced disappearance" with those of the state. More than just a tragic litany of devastation and loss, these testimonies reveal important details about the workings of Amin's security apparatus. Most significantly, they confirm that the regime's use of violence was far more calculated and strategic than has been previously imagined. Disappearance was not simply an unfortunate consequence of military rule but instead a deliberate ruling strategy that was designed to spread fear and stifle opposition. By analyzing disappearance as a performance of hypermasculine military violence, we can better understand the logic of political terror. When we read women's interpretations of the past alongside the official findings of the commission, we also see that their understandings were very different from those of the state, just as their experiences of military rule were very different from those of men.

Women's memories confirm that state collapse, much like military rule more generally, was also deeply gendered. Chapter 7 uses narratives of Ugandan women, gathered primarily from oral interviews and testimony before the Commission of Inquiry into Violations of Human Rights, to map the gendered terrain of violence and harassment that fomented state collapse. I argue that as threats to the military state intensified in the mid- to late 1970s, soldiers lashed out in violent displays of hypermasculinity to demonstrate that they were still strong and powerful. Security forces continued to abduct, or disappear, "enemy" men at an alarming rate, which brought tremendous pain and hardship to the families that were left behind. They also began targeting women for rape and physical assault on a level that was unprecedented. These gendered acts of violence were about humiliating the men who were unable to protect "their women" as much as about demonstrating male dominance and punishing women for their perceived "indiscretions." As a result of this brutality, those women who had supported Amin, who once considered him the "father of the nation," began referring to him as *kijambiya,* or the machete. By failing to rein in his security forces, Amin lost one of his largest bases of support, thus setting the stage for the war that would eventually oust him from power.

In chapter 8, I use memory to critically reexamine the eight-month liberation struggle that toppled Amin's regime on April 11, 1979. These narratives demonstrate that Ugandan women were not simply victims of a violent conflict but instead dynamic historical actors who engaged in complex decision-making processes to protect their families during the war. Stories about women gathered from human rights reports, newspaper articles, and various popular sources confirm the centrality of gender to the larger war effort by highlighting the ways that Amin invoked and deployed masculinity and femininity throughout the con-flict. By feminizing the enemy through various performative gestures, he attempted to bolster his own masculinity, thus confirming, at least in theory, that the military state remained powerful.

The book concludes with an exploration of the gendered legacies of violence that Amin's militarism produced. More than thirty years after the military ruler's fall from power, Ugandans continue to live with a deeply embedded culture of militarism. This militarism is re-flected in the armed conflict and civil unrest that has thoroughly en-veloped the nation, as well as the pattern of heavy military spending that has been justified on the basis of this political instability. Although Ugandan women have struggled with the violent legacies of militarism, they have also played an important role in promoting military norms and values. Whether they have been empowered by their actions or simply militarized by them remains to be seen. I suggest that we still have much to learn about and from the women who continue to live in Idi Amin's shadow.

1 ↬ Violence, Militarism, and Masculinity

The Making of Idi Amin

Sᴀʀᴀʜ Mᴜᴛᴇsɪ Kibedi never imagined that her "kind and compassionate" husband would become such a tyrant.[1] The Idi Amin that she fell in love with as a young woman was "gentle and passionate," not the "strutting, arrogant, womanizing killer" who emerged in later years. Sarah first met Amin in November 1961 when she was just twenty-two years old and working as an apprentice dressmaker at the Singer Sewing Machine Company in Jinja. She remembered looking up from her work and catching the eye of a handsome young soldier who was standing across the room. After flashing a broad smile, he strode over to introduce himself. The two soon fell in love and decided to get married. Their only problem was religion. Amin was a Muslim, but Sarah was not. If their marriage was going to work, she would need to convert to Islam. Sarah knew that her family would be opposed to the decision, but she was determined to marry the man she loved. She thus began a course of Islamic instruction and changed her name to Malyam. Despite her parents' bitter opposition, the couple wed in March 1962, just eight months before Uganda gained independence.

After three or four years of "blissful" marriage, their relationship began to deteriorate.[2] Malyam (née Sarah) heard rumors that her husband was seeing another woman, and she crafted a plan to catch him in the act. She told Amin that she was going away for a few days to visit her parents in Busoga. Instead of ordering her to stay home with the children, he encouraged her to take a holiday and to stay as long as she liked. That afternoon, Malyam drove to her parents' house and told them of

FIGURE 1.1. Amin and his first wife, Malyam (*second from right*), attend an official state gathering, ca. 1971–73. *Source: New Vision Printing and Publishing Company, Kampala, Uganda.*

her plan. After dark, she secretly returned home in a hired taxi. When she walked into the house, she found Amin in the living room chatting with a senior air force officer. Instead of exchanging customary greetings, she marched straight into the bedroom and found a naked woman lying on their bed. Malyam flew into a rage, grabbing the woman by the hair and hitting her as hard as she could. If the air force officer had not intervened, she would have "half killed" the startled stranger. Amin did his best to calm his wife, apologizing profusely and promising never to be unfaithful again. Less than four months later, however, the mysterious woman had become Amin's second wife.

Kay Adroa was hardly a stranger to Amin. Both hailed from the same West Nile region and probably knew each other as children. One source suggests they may have been related—distant cousins along Amin's maternal line.[3] This could have been the reason why Kay's father, a well-respected clergyman, disapproved of her relationship with Amin. It could also have been a result of the significant educational differences between the two. Kay had always attended the best schools, becoming one of the first Lugbara women to study at Makerere University. Amin, in contrast, had completed only four years of primary school and was barely literate. Despite opposition from Kay's family, the couple wed in May 1966.[4]

FIGURE 1.2. Kay Amin gives Christmas gifts to children at Nakasero Lodge, 1973. *Source: Photographic Section, Ministry of Information and Broadcasting, Kampala, Uganda.*

Malyam knew nothing about the wedding until it was broadcast on national television. Although she was deeply humiliated, she was in no position to leave her marriage. She was pregnant with her fourth child and taking care of four additional children from Amin's previous relationships. She was determined to make things work, even if it meant sharing her husband with another woman. The first months were difficult. Over time, however, the women became close friends and allies. Amin expected them to work on a rotational basis, each taking turns running the house, instructing the servants, preparing the menus, and entertaining the guests. They also shared his bed, spending one week alone in the spare room and the other in the main bedroom with their husband.

In early 1967, Amin moved his family to his "Command Post" on Prince Charles Drive in Kampala. Soon rumors began to circulate about a new mistress named Norah. Because both wives were unwilling to share their husband with another woman, they decided to confront Amin about his infidelities. Malyam remembered telling him, "You are degrading yourself and us, your wives, in front of our people." Then he went berserk. "He lashed out with his fists and knocked me over," she recalled. "Then he turned on Kay, smashing his fist into her face. For several minutes as we reeled about the room trying to avoid him, he continued to batter us. He raged at us as he beat us." He chastised them for questioning his authority and then walked out of the room, leaving them lying on the floor, "bruised and bleeding."[5]

The battle over Norah came to a violent conclusion several weeks later when Amin invited all three women to the same party. Neither wife realized that Norah would be there until they saw her gliding across the dance floor on Amin's arm. Malyam remembered that Kay was so angry that she grabbed Norah and threw her across the floor. The room instantly fell quiet. Amin said nothing but led them away. Once they reached home, he unleashed his rage, brutally beating the women for disgracing him in public. Malyam was eight months pregnant and nearly lost her fifth child. One week later, she learned that Amin had married his third wife. Shortly thereafter, Norah Aloba Enin joined the marital rotation at his Command Post.[6] Although Amin continued to have numerous affairs, he did not marry his fourth and fifth wives until after he had seized power.

Malyam's story foreshadows much of the violence that soon became associated with Amin's military dictatorship. In addition, it provides important clues about gender, in terms of not only how Amin saw himself as a man but also how he interacted with women. This chapter uses memoir, as well as other primary and secondary source materials, to tease out the historical relationship between militarism and

FIGURE 1.3. Norah Amin chats with guests at her birthday party, 1972. *Source: Photographic Section, Ministry of Information and Broadcasting, Kampala, Uganda.*

masculinity that so profoundly shaped Amin and his fellow soldiers. It simultaneously tells the story of a place (West Nile), a people (the Nubians), and a person (Amin), all inextricably linked by violence. Through this telling, I make the argument that the military ruler's propensity toward violence was not random or accidental but instead a product of historical circumstance. To effect and maintain colonial rule, the British cultivated a militarized version of masculinity in their soldiers, one that produced fierce warriors who did not question authority and were not afraid to use violence. Amin was a product of this deeply gendered training. After independence, he continued to understand and perform masculinity in similar ways, thus setting the stage for his eventual military coup.

THE MILITARIZATION OF AMIN'S ANCESTRAL HOME

There is a beautiful place in central Africa where the geographical borders of Uganda, southern Sudan (now the independent country of South Sudan), and the Democratic Republic of the Congo intersect, forming a rich tapestry of peoples, cultures, and histories. This remote hub of global commerce has long been a site of colonial fascination and intrigue. Shortly after the Egyptian army established a military outpost in Khartoum in 1820, Sudan's new rulers began sending troops southward in search of cattle and slaves. By the 1850s, they had reached the northwestern reaches of what is now Uganda. Once there, they raided countless Kakwa, Kuku, and Madi villages, setting up administrative posts throughout the region.[7] Shortly thereafter, they began targeting neighboring peoples. Oral histories collected from Lugbara elders in the early 1970s provide important details about these brutal encounters:

> The Arabs usually made surprise attacks on villages at day-break. They would first shoot their guns into the air to frighten the villagers, who would panic and run off into hiding, leaving behind their cattle and children. The Arabs would kill all the children of tender age but would take away the older children as slaves. They would capture all the able-bodied men who were not able to run away in good time or were discovered in their hiding places. They killed all senile people. They drove away all the abandoned cattle, and either ate or took away a lot of the abandoned food and foodstuffs. Lastly, they set houses and granaries on fire leaving the place completely desolate. The captured

slaves were tied together by their necks and were taken into the Sudan. To help them to identify their run-away slaves, the Arabs marked their captives [*sic*] cheeks by making three deep vertical cuts on each cheek. The slaves walked the whole distance to the Sudan and were forced to carry heavy loads including ivory. However, children were allowed to ride cattle as they were too young to walk such a long distance. Any slave who became too weak to continue the journey was either left in the wilderness to die a slow death or was shot down.[8]

In an effort to stabilize the region and pave the way for legitimate commerce, the Egyptian Khedive sent British explorer Samuel Baker on a military expedition to the equatorial regions of the Nile in 1869. After he established a series of military garrisons along the river, the British appointed Baker as the first governor of Equatoria Province. Several years later, in 1874, they replaced him with another British officer, Colonel Charles Gordon. Gordon served as provincial governor for four years until he was appointed governor general of the Sudan. Emin Pasha, born Eduard Schnitzer, took his place as the provincial governor in 1878.[9]

In September 1882, a young Sudanese man named Mohammed Ahmad ignited a massive rebellion in the north. Calling himself the Mahdi, or "redeemer," he promised to liberate his people from colonial oppression. As the uprising spread south, Emin and his troops had little choice but to retreat to the southern end of the province. Many Egyptian and Sudanese officers subsequently deserted, and the British replaced them with local soldiers from lower ranks. The violent insurgency came to a head on January 26, 1885, when a group of Mahdists stormed the governor's palace, beheaded Colonel Gordon, and seized control of Khartoum. Fearing further loss of life, Egyptian authorities evacuated Equatoria Province and left Emin stranded with several hundred soldiers and their families.[10]

News of Emin's desperate plight spread rapidly throughout the British Empire, and soon several rescue groups were established. William Mackinnon, the founder of the Imperial British East Africa Company (IBEAC), chaired the Emin Pasha Relief Expedition. He hoped that in return for rescuing Emin, the beleaguered governor would act as the company's agent in Equatoria Province. Mackinnon approached Henry Morgan Stanley, one of the foremost explorers of the time, and asked him to lead the expedition. At the time, Stanley was working for King Leopold II, carving out the Congo Free State for the Belgian monarch. The king agreed to let him participate as long as he led the expedition up the uncharted Congo River, instead of taking the shorter overland route from the east. Stanley eagerly agreed. His journey, however, was no easy feat. After innumerable delays and significant casualties, Stanley's team finally "rescued" Emin along the banks of the Albert Nile in 1888.[11]

Emin never wanted to be rescued, nor did any of his soldiers. It took several months to convince the embattled governor to abandon his post. Most of his soldiers remained behind under the leadership of two rival commanders—Selim Bey and Fadl el Mula Bey.[12] The former stationed his troops at Kavallis near Lake Albert, while the latter posted his to Wadelai along the Albert Nile. In the autumn of 1891, Captain Frederick Lugard arrived at Kavallis in search of army recruits for the IBEAC. As the company's official representative, he was assigned the mandate to secure Buganda on behalf of the British government. Given that the kingdom was on the brink of another religious war, he needed to recruit an army that could maintain peace.[13] Emin Pasha's former soldiers, he believed, would be the ideal recruits. Although they were initially reluctant to join Lugard's forces, primarily because of their loyalty to the Khedive, Selim's followers eventually agreed to accompany him back to Buganda.[14]

Shortly after Lugard's recruits began their southward journey, Belgian troops moved into the province in an effort to establish control over the upper reaches of the Nile. Because they were the first European forces to arrive after the departure of Emin Pasha, they were able to negotiate an agreement with Fadl el Mula, the remaining military commander.[15] Under King Leopold's control, the region became known as the Lado Enclave, a veritable playground for ivory hunters and poachers of big game. After Leopold's death in 1909, the Belgian government transferred the enclave back to the Sudan, this time under the Condominium government of Egypt and Britain.[16]

Over the next three years, Sudanese authorities administered the Lado Enclave from afar. The region had earned a reputation for being a rough-and-tumble place, largely because of the former Belgian monarch's "hands-off" approach to governance. Condominium authorities enlisted the help of Major Chauncy Hugh Stigand to determine an administrative strategy. The young British officer recommended that the southern portion of the enclave be transferred to the Uganda Protectorate, which had been formally established in 1894. Colonial officials ultimately agreed and on January 1, 1914, the British integrated southern Lado into Uganda.[17] From this point forward, the region became known as West Nile, the ancestral home of Idi Amin.[18]

THE MILITARIZATION OF AMIN AND HIS ANCESTORS

In 1889, just one year after Henry Morton Stanley famously "rescued" Emin Pasha, Amin's paternal grandfather, Nyabira Tomuresu, nearly started a clan war after repudiating his wife Atata and forcing her to abandon their homestead in Koboko, just days after she had given birth to their second son. According to family lore, the young woman was so angry at being rejected by her husband that she purposely knocked over the cradle of her newborn baby before marching off. If her eldest son, Rajab Yangu, had not been there to save the frightened infant, history might have been very different. But as it happened, the thirteen-year-old boy kept a close watch over his younger brother, Andreas, safely guarding him until a delegation of uncles from their mother's clan could come to the rescue. The boys were then taken to live with their maternal kin. The eldest son eventually joined the army of Sultan Ali Kenyi, a prominent Kakwa chief who worked for the colonial government, while Andreas went to live with his aunt, a childless woman named Yasmin Asungha.[19]

When Andreas was twenty-one years old, he followed in his brother's footsteps and joined the sultan's army. He then converted from Catholicism to Islam and changed his name to Amin (Andreas) Dada.[20] Several years later, in 1913, he joined the colonial police force. Once World War I broke out, the British forcibly conscripted him into the King's African Rifles (KAR). Life as a soldier was difficult, although it brought some tangible rewards. Andreas was able to earn enough money to get married—not once, but twice. After his first wife, Mariam Poya, suffered an unfortunate string of miscarriages, he decided to remarry.[21] His second wife, Aisha Chumaru Aate, gave birth to a son in 1919. Shortly thereafter, Mariam gave birth to a daughter. Years later, Andreas took a third and a fourth wife, Iyaya and Amori, a practice that was common among relatively wealthy Muslims.

Andreas received an honorable discharge from the army in 1921. In appreciation for his service, the government allotted him a plot in Arua, a bustling colonial outpost thirty-four miles south of Koboko.

The retired soldiers christened the area "Tanganyika Village" after their successful tour of duty in the neighboring protectorate. After the war, most of their neighbors had little choice but to move south in search of employment on the sugar plantations. Andreas decided that he would rather reenlist with the colonial police force than become a migrant laborer. He and Aisha moved to Kampala, where they lived with their son in Nsambya Barracks. Mariam remained behind at the Arua homestead, which was reportedly a bitter source of contention for years to come.[22]

Aisha made the most of life in the city. As an expert in holistic medicine, she developed an extensive network of clients, both within and beyond the barracks. So renowned was her ability to deal with fertility and pregnancy complications that she attracted the attention of the royal family of Buganda.[23] King Daudi Chwa and his wife, Irene Druscilla Namaganda, are said to have consulted with the young Lugbara woman after failing to conceive for many years. Within a short period of time, the queen became pregnant, thus cementing a firm friendship between the two women that would last throughout their lives. In 1925, Aisha gave birth to her second child, a daughter who did not survive beyond toddlerhood. Three years later, the colonial government transferred Andreas and his wife across town to Shimoni Police Barracks in Nakasero. It was there, on the day of Eid, that Aisha gave birth to her third and final child.[24]

The details surrounding Idi Amin's birth have been shrouded in mystery. Very few scholars or observers have agreed upon where or when he was born. Amin complicated matters by claiming several different locations as his "official" birthplace: Koboko, Bombo, Semuto, Luwero, and Kampala.[25] The most compelling evidence seems to suggest that he was born on May 30, 1928, in Shimoni Barracks on the outskirts of Kampala. Within three years, the family moved to a new post at Kololo Hill. Shortly thereafter, Andreas retired from the police force and took a job at the district commissioner's office in Arua. Instead of moving back to the north, Aisha separated from her husband.[26] She then went to live with relatives in Semuto, a community of former KAR soldiers that was located thirty-four miles northwest of Kampala. Amin remained with his father and spent the next four years studying at Arua Muslim School.

In 1937, at the age of nine, Amin went to live with his mother and her new husband, Mzee Ibrahim, in Semuto. Although he was just a boy, he engaged in a variety of odd jobs to supplement his mother's income.[27] As her reputation as a midwife and practitioner of holistic medicine continued to grow, she began spending more time on the road. In 1940, she relocated to another ex-KAR community called Buikwe, just on the outskirts of the Lugazi sugar plantation. While there, Aisha met a new man, Corporal Yafesi Yasin, a clerk in D Company of the KAR. Although he was in his early twenties and nearly half her age, the two became intimately involved. In 1954, she moved with him to Jinja Barracks. His friends laughed at him for living with an "old" woman. Yasin eventually tired of the rebuke and sent her back to Buikwe. Several days later, the corporal fell sick and died. Aisha's reputation as a powerful "healer" simply increased.[28]

Meanwhile, Amin had gone to live with a maternal uncle in nearby Bombo. From 1941 until 1944, he attended Garaya Islamic School. Although he was barely literate, Amin had a knack for memorization and won high honors for his skills in Koranic recitation.[29] After finishing his religious education, Amin moved to a Kampala suburb and got a job as a bellboy at the Grand Imperial Hotel in Kampala. There he impressed a British military officer, who recruited him into the army on December 20, 1946.[30]

Amin began his life in the military as an assistant cook at Magamaga Barracks in Jinja.[31] After he completed his basic training in 1947, his commanding officers transferred him to Kenya, where he spent two years serving in the Twenty-First Infantry Battalion in Gilgil.[32] In 1949, they deployed his unit to Somalia to pacify a band of cattle-raiding militiamen. After successfully quelling the insurgency, his unit returned to Kenya. In 1952, Amin's battalion deployed to the Aberdare Mountains, where they attempted to put an end to the Mau Mau rebellion. Because of his success on the battlefield, the British promoted Amin to corporal. Over the next two years, Amin developed a reputation for violence and ferocity. One of Amin's former commanding officers, Major Iain Grahame, recalled that the insurrection "served to accentuate the innate cruelty and ruthlessness of many of Uganda's northern warriors."[33] Instead of facing censure, however, the British sent Amin for further training at a Kenyan military academy in Nakuru. After he completed the course in 1954, they promoted Amin to sergeant despite his difficulties with English, most likely because he was highly respected by his peers and always willing to follow orders.[34]

Amin spent the next several years engaged in various domestic operations in Uganda. In 1958, his superiors promoted him to warrant officer platoon commander, even though he barely passed his written exam.[35] Although Amin had purportedly reached his "intellectual ceiling," his commanding officers selected him for an effendi training course in 1959.[36] This was a significant honor, because it was the highest rank that an African soldier could attain.[37] At the completion of the course, Amin won the Sword of Honor in recognition of his stellar performance.[38] Then, on February 3, 1960, British prime minister Harold Macmillan gave his famous "winds of change" speech, which signified the beginning of the end of colonial rule. With little time to prepare for independence, Britain needed to promote senior African warrant officers and noncommissioned officers.[39] Despite Amin's penchant for violence and his poor educational qualifications, the British commissioned him as a lieutenant on July 15, 1961.[40] Shaban Opolot was the only other Ugandan to receive such a high honor.

After becoming commissioned as an officer, Amin continued to be implicated in violent atrocities. In late 1961, for instance, he participated in a mission to disarm the Turkana in Kenya's Northern Frontier District. The gun-toting pastoralists had been terrorizing their spear-wielding neighbors in an effort to steal their neighbors' cattle. The British ordered the military to intervene by blocking access to local watering holes, thus forcing the Turkana to trade in their weapons for water. Although the exercise was largely successful, Amin's platoon was the only one to return empty-handed. He was deeply humiliated and immediately redeployed his unit in an effort to reassert his masculinity. A few days later, a group of Turkana elders complained that Amin's platoon had tortured and killed numerous pastoralists to speed up disarmament. Officials collected several bodies from a shallow grave nearby. Postmortem investigations verified the disturbing allegations.[41]

The governor of Uganda, Sir Walter Coutts, remembered receiving a phone call from the deputy governor of Kenya, Sir Eric Griffith-Jones, in early 1962: "He rang me and said some pretty fearful things had been going on in Turkana and it looks as though there is some evidence apparently that one of your Ugandan army people has so brutally beaten up a complete Turkana village, including killing them, that I think I shall have to take criminal proceedings against him."[42] Although Coutts was deeply concerned about the massacre, he told the deputy governor that it would be "politically highly disastrous to bring one of the only two black officers in the Uganda army to trial for murder on the eve of independence." He thought it would be better to deal with Amin at home. Griffith-Jones eventually capitulated and sent Amin back to Uganda.

The rogue officer's case troubled Coutts, and eventually he decided to consult the former commander of the Fourth Battalion of the KAR, Colonel Bill Cheyne. The colonel, who was well acquainted with Amin and the case against him, believed that he should be court-martialed. Coutts agreed but thought it would be best to first discuss the matter with the newly elected prime minister, Milton Obote. Given that Amin was one of only two African officers in the army, Obote suggested that nothing more than a "severe reprimand" was in order. Coutts argued that Amin was "unfit" for military service and should be imprisoned or dismissed at the very least. "I warn you," the governor told Obote, "this officer could cause you trouble in the future."[43] Yet no one could have predicted the trouble that would ensue.

MAKING HISTORICAL SENSE OF AMIN'S VIOLENCE

It is difficult to imagine why Obote would have ignored such a powerful warning, given Amin's demonstrated propensity toward violence. He must have believed that a court-martial would be more detrimental to the security of the nascent state than allowing Amin to carry on with his normal duties. Because he needed to maintain his alliances with the military elite, he naively agreed to turn the other cheek. He can hardly be faulted, since the military has always played an important role in politics, starting with the early days of the Uganda Protectorate in the late nineteenth century. On December 31, 1891, Captain Lugard marched into Kampala with a "motley" band of men, women, and children from Kavallis in Equatoria Province.[44] Although less than one-quarter of the 8,200 migrants were soldiers—poorly armed and even more poorly trained at that—they helped to bring the religious wars to a close, firmly entrenching political power in the hands of Protestants. Lugard's mission may have been successful, but it was costly, nearly bankrupting the Imperial British East Africa Company and forcing their withdrawal on March 31, 1893. The following day, the British government assumed provisional responsibility for the territory and established a formal protectorate eighteen months later.

To fulfill their mandate as guardians of empire, the British needed to develop a more permanent military presence in the protectorate. In 1895 they established the Uganda Rifles, a standing army composed largely of Emin Pasha's Sudanese recruits.[45] Although the Sudanese played a vital role in the Ugandan military, they felt unappreciated and mutinied in September 1897. According to Amii Omara-Otunnu, "the troops' awareness of the part they played in the political development of the country, exacerbated by poor conditions of service, . . . emboldened them to think that since they were the only troops in the country, they would encounter little or no opposition if they revolted."[46] The British quelled the rebellion in seven months, largely as a result of additional troops from India, Kenya, and Somalia. Although both sides suffered casualties, the Sudanese emerged victorious. Those who returned after the mutiny received a fivefold pay increase. They hanged only twelve of the mutineers.[47]

To prevent the outbreak of future rebellions, the British began deploying soldiers far from their home areas. This, they hoped, would prevent troops from allying with local populations. This strategy was already in effect elsewhere, particularly in India, where many officers of the Uganda Rifles had served. The British also recognized that they would need to diversify their forces. Toward this end, they passed the Uganda Military Force Ordinance of 1898, which incorporated Indians and Kenyans into the army on a permanent basis. By increasing the size of the army, the military could expand its presence throughout the protectorate. And by ordering military officers to carry out civilian administrative duties, the protectorate could keep its costs down.[48]

The military administration of government was short-lived. Once the army eliminated final pockets of resistance, the protectorate began moving toward civilian rule. The Baganda played a crucial role in this transition, not only because they were the original inhabitants of the region but also because they had a highly centralized political structure.[49] The British formalized their relationship with the Baganda in March 1900 with the promulgation of the Uganda Agreement.[50] This agreement determined the rights and responsibilities of both parties. Although the British eventually signed similar agreements with other local rulers throughout the protectorate, the Baganda became the chief functionaries of colonial rule. This created lasting political tensions, particularly with peoples from the north who were left out of these agreements. By the time that the British incorporated West Nile into the protectorate in 1914, political power had been firmly entrenched in the hands of the Baganda. The north had become little more than a reserve for migrant labor and military recruitment.

In 1902, the British integrated the Uganda Rifles into the newly established colonial army, the KAR, which included forces from Kenya, Nyasaland, and British Somaliland. They divided the Ugandan contingent into two battalions—one African (Fourth) and one Indian (Fifth). Although the majority of Africans in the Fourth Battalion were Sudanese, indigenous Ugandans eventually came to outnumber them. The number of Indians in the Fifth Battalion also began to decline, and by 1913, the British had disbanded their battalion altogether.

Ethnicity formed the basis of military recruitment. According to Timothy Parsons, "the British officers preferred soldiers from groups they judged to possess 'natural' militaristic qualities, and in most cases, the value of the recruit was determined solely by his ethnic origins."[51] Army recruiters preferred men from the impoverished regions of the north because of their brawn and ferocity. According to 1908 KAR regulations, "such men are, as a rule, capable of undergoing prolonged exertion without regular food, and have a natural aptitude for observing and tracking."[52] Recruiters also believed that they had innate fighting abilities. The following chorus from a KAR marching song demonstrates how race and gender came together in an ideal military recruit:

It's the Sudi, my boy, it's the Sudi,
With his grim-set, ugly face;
But he looks like a man and he fights like a man,
For he comes of a fighting race.[53]

The gendering within this song is striking. The Sudi "looked" like men and "fought" like men because of their inherent martial qualities. In other words, "real" men were those who embraced militarism. Although the Sudanese were the original "fighting race," the British needed to expand their pool of potential recruits. In 1941, they sent a questionnaire to native commissioners in East Africa asking them to supply the names of "tribes" in their districts that possessed the following traits: adaptability, reaction to discipline, steadiness under bombing, stamina and staying power, powers of leadership, intelligence, *esprit de corps*, cleanliness and turnout, capacity for hard living, general health, ability to fraternize, and fighting qualities.[54] As the KAR expanded, particularly during World War II, the British designated new martial races on the basis of these qualities.[55]

Army recruiters also preferred soldiers with little to no education because they were more likely to follow orders without question. Peter

Jermyn Allen, a colonial police officer and High Court judge in Uganda, recalled a conversation he had once had with a British army recruiter:

> "What we want," he said, "are big chaps, good sportsmen and fighters. The sort of splendid fellers that we can rely on. Can't stand these mission-educated types—wet weaks. We really prefer our recruits to be uneducated—the more ignorant they are the better so that we can mould them into the army way of doing things and have absolute control over them. . . . You've got to remember that your police chappies are there to use their heads and to keep the peace whereas our fellers are trained to be aggressive and to use their weapons to fight in a war. We need a different sort of chap—the bigger the better. We don't want a lot of semi-educated types each thinking for himself and acting independently. What we need are fellers who work together as a unit and do exactly what they're told to do without thinking and arguing about it first. They don't need school education for that—we'll teach them all they need to know ourselves."[56]

Given the qualities sought by military recruiters, it is no surprise that Idi Amin was the perfect candidate. He was a Kakwa man with cultural links to the economically impoverished north. Like many men from this region, he had few employment options outside of the military. Given his relative lack of education, military service represented an excellent opportunity to earn a living. Amin's family closely identified with the Nubian military communities, which loyally served the colonial government and celebrated military service. He understood and respected military discipline because of these cultural links and because many of the men in his family had been soldiers. Furthermore, his large physique and his willingness to follow orders made him an ideal recruit. Indeed, for all of these reasons, the British considered Amin a "splendid chap."[57]

AMIN, THE MILITARY, AND THE POSTCOLONIAL STATE

After Uganda gained independence on October 9, 1962, they redesignated the Fourth Battalion of the KAR as the Uganda Rifles.[58] Many Africans were surprised to find that political independence did not necessarily translate into additional opportunities within the military. Save for Amin and several of his colleagues who had been promoted to the rank of captain at independence, most of the top positions remained in the hands of expatriates.[59] This was a source of great contention for the African rank and file, who felt that the time for change had come. Inspired by the Zanzibar Revolution and military uprisings in Tanganyika and Kenya, the First Battalion of the Uganda Rifles mutinied on January 23, 1964. The mutineers had two primary goals—to remove British officers from key positions within the army and to compel the government to increase their salaries. Once news of the mutiny reached the prime minister, Milton Obote, he sent the minister of internal affairs, Felix Onama, to Jinja to try to quell the disturbance. The soldiers were not in the mood to negotiate and immediately took the minister hostage. They told him that unless he agreed to their demands, he would never leave the barracks alive. Meanwhile, the British high commissioner, Sir David Hunt, convinced Obote to request the assistance of British troops that were stationed in neighboring Kenya. The prime minister acquiesced, but by the time reinforcements arrived, Onama had capitulated to the mutineers' demands.[60]

In addition to confirming the significant financial concessions brokered by Onama, Obote recommended that Amin and Opolot—both majors by this time—be immediately appointed commanding officers of the First and Second Battalions, respectively.[61] The prime minister's actions ushered in an era of rapid promotion within the military. By September 1964—just nine months after the mutiny—Opolot had been promoted to brigadier and was commander of the army, while Amin served as his deputy at the rank of colonel. The latter quickly established a loyal following within the army by reenlisting all soldiers who had been dismissed after the mutiny.[62] With this move, he not only increased his popularity with the rank and file but also articulated a strong message about the utility of violence.

The turmoil within the ruling party rivaled that of the military. In February 1964, the Uganda People's Congress (UPC) ousted John Kakonge as secretary-general and replaced him with a conservative Munyoro man, Grace Ibingira. After securing a parliamentary majority in August 1964, Obote abrogated the political alliance that had brought him to power, namely, that between his own party, the UPC, and the Kabaka Yekka (KY), a consortium of Baganda nationalists. He then announced that he would hold a referendum on the controversial "lost counties" of Bunyoro, which had been transferred from Buganda to the central government at independence.[63] Despite objections from Baganda loyalists, Obote held the referendum on November 4, 1964.

Buyaga and Bugangazi Counties voted to return to Bunyoro, much to the chagrin of the Baganda. After rioting broke out at the Buganda Parliament, Obote called in the military to intervene. The Baganda never forgave him for the loss of "their" counties.

During the latter half of 1964 and early 1965, the army was also engaged in military operations along the border with Congo in West Nile Province.[64] Obote was supporting a group of Congolese rebels who were trying to topple President Joseph Kasavubu's government. He sent Amin and his troops into the Congo to trade arms and equipment for gold, ivory, and coffee.[65] As a result of these incursions, the military experienced its first external threat in early 1965. On February 13, the Congolese military bombed two villages in West Nile, injuring a platoon commander in the Uganda army.[66] Obote called upon all Ugandans to defend the nation against foreign incursion. He also ordered all ex-soldiers to report to army headquarters in Kampala to reenlist. The crisis prompted a rapid expansion in the size of the army. Some of these men fought in the newly established Third and Fourth Battalions, while others infiltrated Obote's intelligence organization, known as the General Service Unit. Due to his success in the Congo, Amin's popularity among the rank and file soared.[67]

Rumors about Amin's illicit dealings soon began to circulate. In March 1965, Daudi Ochieng, the deputy leader of the opposition, produced copies of Amin's most recent bank statement, which showed several large deposits. The minister of state for defense, by then Felix Onama, dismissed the allegations but promised a full investigation. None was ever forthcoming. In January 1966, Ochieng tabled a motion in parliament to suspend Amin until an investigation of the Congo scandal was complete. He alleged that Amin had acquired $30,000 in looted gold, ivory, and coffee. He proposed "[t]hat this House do urge Government to suspend from duty Col. Idi Amin of the Uganda Army, forthwith, pending the conclusion of police investigations into the allegations regarding his bank account, which should then be passed on to the appropriate authority whose final decision on the matter shall be made public."[68] On January 31, cabinet ministers held a meeting to determine how to deal with the proposed motion. Obote attended and spoke at great length. At the end of the session, the ministers decided to reject the motion. Obote thought the issue had been concluded and left for a tour of the north. On February 4, the minister of justice convened another meeting, asking ministers to reverse their earlier decision. Ochieng made another speech in support of the motion, in which he alleged the involvement of several other high-ranking officials. This included the prime minister (Milton Obote), the minister of state for defense (Felix Onama), and the minister of planning and community development (Adoko Nekyon). He also alleged that Amin and the others were planning a coup to overthrow the constitution. Later that day, the motion passed parliament with only one dissenting vote, from John Kakonge, the ousted secretary-general of the Uganda People's Congress. This vote of no confidence should have obligated Obote and his government to resign. They did not.

Once Obote returned to Kampala, he convened an emergency cabinet meeting on February 15, asking those ministers who had agreed with parliament's decision to resign. No one did. He held an additional meeting on February 22 to appoint a commission of inquiry into the scandal. After appointing three of his own judges, Obote ordered the arrest and imprisonment of five cabinet ministers from the opposition bloc of the UPC (Grace Ibingira, Mathias Ngobi, Balaki Kirya, George Magezi, and Emanuel Lumu). The following day, he gave Opolot a linear "promotion," making him chief of defense staff.[69] In reality, this was a ceremonial position that stripped him of all authority. He then appointed Amin as chief of staff of the army and the air force.

On February 24, Obote announced that he was amending the constitution to reorganize the rights and powers of the president. Shortly thereafter, he eliminated the position of prime minister and assumed executive control over the state. The following month, on April 15, he abrogated the constitution altogether, forcing parliamentarians to pass a new version that they had not yet seen. The document that they found waiting in their mailboxes *after* the session became known as the "pigeon-hole" constitution. Obote was then sworn in as president under heavy military guard.

The erosion of democracy affected all Ugandans, but the Baganda felt particularly compelled to intervene because of their historical relationship to the state. Because they had agreed to serve as the functionaries of colonial rule, the British rewarded them with land and significant political positions. Once Obote began taking away their "traditional" rights, the Baganda fought back. On May 20, the Buganda Parliament sponsored a motion ordering the central government out of Buganda within ten days. Obote saw this as an act of treason and declared a state of emergency. Three days later, he ordered the arrest of three county chiefs who were close to the king. Mobs formed in protest. In response, Obote ordered Amin to attack the palace at Mengo. The assault took place at 5:30 in the morning on May 24. After twelve hours of intense fighting, the king escaped unharmed, fleeing over a palace wall under the cover of heavy rain.[70] Over the next several days, Amin's troops looted the palace and destroyed all royal regalia. They also ransacked the king's other palaces at Bamunanika and Masaka. Although government estimates put the death toll at forty, the Baganda claim that as many as four thousand may have died during the siege.[71] Expatriate Peter Jermyn Allen remembered seeing canvas-covered army trucks coming down the road from Mengo loaded with bodies, blood dripping from the tailboards.[72] There is little doubt that the 1966 crisis institutionalized violence as the main instrument of political control in Uganda.

The following year, the government took additional measures to destroy the polity of Buganda once and for all. In September 1967, parliament enacted a new constitution, abolishing the kingdoms and establishing a republican system of governance. In 1968, the military seized the Buganda Parliament as the new headquarters of the armed forces. They also converted the king's palace into a military barracks.[73] Henry Kyemba, who served as Obote's principal private secretary and later became a minister in Amin's government, described Uganda at this time as "very close to a military dictatorship."[74]

The militarization of the state intensified dramatically over the next few years. Obote recognized that he was highly dependent on the military to maintain power. He wanted to keep the soldiers happy, but at the same time, he also needed to create an external base of support. Toward this end, he began relying more heavily on paramilitary organizations such as the General Service Unit and the Special Forces. These units had been designed to increase security and to reduce government reliance on the army. The General Service Unit was originally established in April 1964 under the leadership of the prime minister's cousin, Akena Adoko. The unit posted nearly one thousand security agents and operatives throughout the country and in embassies abroad.[75] The Special Forces was also created in 1964. Like the General Service Unit, they were controlled by the President's Office and not by the military, although they worked with the army and the police on various occasions. Their mandate focused less on intelligence gathering and more on paramilitary operations (such as riots, armed robbery, and so forth). More than three-fourths of this elite force consisted of Obote's ethnic kin, the Langi.[76]

In addition to the General Service Unit and the Special Forces, Obote established a Military Police Force in January 1967. He designed this unit to combat lawlessness and indiscipline among the army rank and file. It was under the command of two of Amin's close associates from West Nile—Lieutenant Mustafa Adrisi and Second Lieutenant E. Anguduru.[77] Most of those who served within the military police were from the same region, which meant that they were fiercely loyal to Amin, who by this time had been promoted to brigadier.

Over the next year, Amin bolstered his support within the army and the military police by recruiting heavily from his home region. He seemed increasingly concerned that Obote was planning to replace him. His most significant rivals were Suleman Hussein and Pierino Okoya, both of whom had been promoted to brigadier on the same day that Amin was promoted to major general (April 1968). Amin perceived their promotions as a threat and once more began heavily recruiting from West Nile. In fact, between 1968 and 1969, the ratio of Sudanic speakers in the army increased by 74 percent. This was twice the rate of Luo speakers, in other words, those sharing Obote's ethno-linguistic heritage.[78]

The precariousness of Amin's position was confirmed on December 19, 1969, when an unknown assailant shot Obote as he was leaving a Uganda People's Congress meeting in Kampala.[79] Instead of rallying the troops to protect the president from further harm, Amin was nowhere to be seen. Because he had been noticeably absent the entire evening, many suspected that he had planned or even carried out the attempted assassination. One of Obote's closest military advisors, Major David Oyite-Ojok, went to Amin's home to brief him on the shooting. Instead of coming to the door, Amin ran out the back, climbed over a barbed-wire fence surrounding his compound, and took off down the road. After flagging down a passing car, he made his way to a nearby military base.

Oyite-Ojok had little choice but to call in the next most senior officer, Brigadier Okoya, who was the commanding officer at Masaka Barracks. As Okoya made his way to Kampala, the minister of defense, Felix Onama, chaired an emergency meeting of the cabinet. Although Onama wanted to declare martial law, the ministers decided to put the country under a state of emergency instead. One month later, at a meeting of high-ranking military commanders, Okoya confronted Amin about his absence following the assassination attempt. He said that the army lacked discipline and was poorly organized. He chastised Amin for his cowardice and asked him to explain his disappearance.[80]

Instead of putting the outspoken junior officer in his place, Amin coolly responded to the accusation, stating that he had run away because he thought that the soldiers wanted to kill him. Okoya's temerity surely signified to Amin that his own days were numbered.[81] Nonetheless, Amin announced that he would be holding a meeting with senior officers so that they could air their grievances. This meeting was to take place on January 26, but it never occurred. Okoya and his wife were murdered at their home in Gulu on January 25, 1970. Amin was the primary suspect.[82]

Instead of arresting Amin for murder, Obote kept a close eye on his adversary, waiting until the time was right to make his move.[83] He decided to strike in September 1970 when the Egyptian president, Gamal Abdel Nasser, passed away. Obote realized that by sending Amin out of the country to attend the funeral, he would have the opportunity to reorganize the security forces once and for all. Indeed, once Amin was gone, Obote appointed Brigadier Suleman Hussein as his new army chief of staff and Colonel Juma Musa as commander of the air force.[84] He named Amin as chief of defense forces, a demotion that paralleled the ouster of Shaban Opolot several years before. Those officers who were loyal to Amin were then seconded to the civil service. But Amin was not stupid. He kept abreast of domestic affairs, returning home unannounced, just in time to rescind Obote's orders and curtail the new commanders' powers.[85] He was not about to be outmaneuvered.

AMIN'S COUP

Obote's decision to attend the Commonwealth Conference in Singapore was a grave mistake. He understood that the country was becoming increasingly ungovernable, yet he felt it was important to take a stand against Britain's decision to continue selling arms to apartheid South Africa. The day before leaving Uganda, Obote informed Amin that upon his return, Amin would be expected to account for numerous military improprieties. The auditor general had recently informed the president that a substantial amount of money had disappeared from the army budget.[86] There was evidence to suggest that Amin had been illicitly supplying arms and equipment to Anya Anya rebels in southern Sudan—ethnic kin who were fighting against the Arab government in the north. Amin was also said to be recruiting many of these individuals into the Uganda army. These details might have remained a secret if not for Rolf Steiner, a West German mercenary who was arrested in

Kampala on January 8, 1971. Steiner was providing clandestine military training to the rebels on behalf of Amin, much to the embarrassment of Obote, who had become an ally of the Sudanese government.[87] When Steiner refused to implicate Amin, Obote ordered his arrest and deportation. Among his personal effects were diaries discussing Amin's activities in the Sudan. By the time Obote left for Singapore three days later, Steiner was languishing in a Khartoum prison awaiting trial.[88]

Shortly thereafter, a rumor began circulating that Amin was planning to assassinate the president and take over the government. Once Obote learned of the plot, he ordered the inspector general of police, Erinayo Oryema, to arrest the army commander.[89] The inspector refused, arguing that a police officer was unable to arrest the head of the army. He insisted that the minister of defense, Felix Onama, should instead be the one to do so.[90] On the night of January 24, Obote called Jinja Barracks with the message that Amin was to be arrested. Sergeant Major Musa intercepted the call and then mobilized a group of West Nile soldiers to begin the coup.[91] As Musa made his way to Lake Kioga in search of Amin, who at the time had been duck hunting, fighting broke out among the Malire Mechanized Regiment at Lubiri Barracks (that is, the king's former palace).[92] Amin loyalists quickly defeated Obote's men. By the time Amin and Musa returned to Kampala in the early morning hours of January 25, the soldiers had formed a ring around parliament and seized the radio station, the post office, the railroad depot, banks, and other important buildings. They made it clear that they wanted Amin to lead them.

The perpetual drone of martial music finally came to a halt at 3:45 in the afternoon when an unfamiliar voice came over the airwaves.[93] Sergeant Major Aswa, a semieducated Lugbara soldier, announced, "It has been necessary to take action to save a bad situation from getting worse." He then proceeded to read out a list of eighteen grievances that had left the people "angry, worried, and very unhappy."[94] These included the unwarranted detention of many people without a trial, the lack of political and social freedom, and the frequent loss of life and property as a result of *kondoism,* or armed robbery, among other things. Because of these reasons, he concluded, "we men of the Uganda Armed Forces have this day decided to take over power from Obote and hand it to our fellow soldier, Major-General Idi Amin Dada, and we hereby entrust him to lead this our beloved country of Uganda to peace and goodwill among all."

The inspector general of police then took to the airwaves to confirm that the army had indeed taken power and that the police supported their decision.[95] The last to speak was Amin:

> The men of the Uganda Armed Forces have placed this country in my hand by entrusting me with its government. I am not a politician, but a professional soldier. I am, therefore, a man of few words and I have been very brief throughout my professional life. I have emphasized that the military might support a civilian government that has the support of the people and I have not changed from this position. Matters now prevailing in Uganda forced me, however, to accept the task that has been given me by men of the Uganda Armed Forces. I will accept this task, but on the understanding that mine will be a caretaker administration, pending an early return to civilian rule. Free and fair elections will soon be held in the country, given a stable security situation. Everybody will be free to participate in this election. For that reason, political exiles are free to return to this country, and political prisoners held on unfounded charges will be released forthwith. All people are to report for work as usual. Further information and direction will be made as the news arrives. Long live the Republic of Uganda.[96]

In hindsight, we now know that most of Amin's promises never came to fruition. His was not a caretaker administration but instead a violent military dictatorship that devastated the nation. It resulted in the death of thousands — if not hundreds of thousands — of innocent Ugandans.[97] For every person who was killed or disappeared by agents of the military state, there were countless others who mourned their loss, who struggled to survive the innumerable challenges presented by Amin's rule. This book tells the stories of those who survived.

⤚

Although Sarah Kibedi fell in love with a "kind and compassionate" man, she ended up married to a tyrant who used violence and fear to manipulate those around him. Her husband was not an evil man but instead someone who had learned at an early age that violence was an effective strategy of social control, that it made one powerful and manly. The military taught Amin that he could earn power and respect through the use of brutal force. And because his superiors never punished him for his excesses, he continued to utilize violence in his personal and professional relationships. He was largely following a pattern of governance that had been put into place many years before.

This chapter clearly demonstrates that Amin was not a historical anomaly. Instead, he was a product of a much larger history of violence and militarism that had shaped the lives of countless men (and women) before him. He came from a region that had long been the site of military incursion and intrigue. It was a region that had been plundered for slaves and then used as a recruiting ground for various colonial militias. Amin's ancestors learned that military service was a valiant and lucrative career for men, and they took great pride in their service to the state. It is hardly surprising that he, too, would choose this career path or that he would eventually govern the country according to the same hypermilitarized gender logic. In the chapters that follow, I map out the violent repercussions of the militarism-masculinity nexus that was Amin's Uganda.

2 ∽ Gender, Performance, and Pain
The Rise of Amin's Dictatorship

WINNIE MUGENYI remembered hearing the crackling pop of sporadic gunfire on the night of January 24, 1971. Although she and many other Kampala residents had become accustomed to the sound of nocturnal shelling—a disturbing reminder of the violence that had recently plagued the nation—this felt like something different. It was much louder, much more intense. She had heard rumors of an impending coup but never expected it would happen so soon—not when she was heavily pregnant and home alone with two frightened young children. With her husband out of town, who would protect them if they needed to escape? How would he know where to find them? Winnie felt consumed by fear and "almost had a miscarriage because of those strong gunshots."[1] For the twenty-six-year-old Muganda schoolteacher, it was a long, long night.

When the sun crested the horizon at 7:00 the following morning, Winnie's tension began to abate. The world outside her door appeared very much the same—the familiar swishing of homemade brooms, the fragrant aroma of fresh *mandazi* wafting through the air, the soothing embrace of an equatorial dawn. Everything seemed the same, although the drone of somber military music on the radio suggested something quite different. Later that day, she learned that Idi Amin had taken power in a coup d'etat. When this news hit the airwaves, jubilant masses began crowding the streets, singing and dancing. "We were so happy when he had taken over," recalled Winnie. "We knew we had gotten a leader who was good. People liked him so much. They were so happy about his overtaking." She remembered seeing "scarecrows" or effigies of the former president made out of dried banana leaves. People affixed them to the back of their cars and bicycles and pulled them around, crying "crocodile tears" and pretending they were dragging Obote through the streets. They were crying "tears of joy" because Amin had saved them from a "terrible person."

Winnie's experience was far from unique. During interviews, many women from Buganda shared similar stories of excitement and joy. Many said that they celebrated the coup not because they loved Amin but because they hated Obote and his oppressive policies.[2] It was Obote, after all, who had abolished the royal kingdoms, thereby taking away an important source of power and meaning for many Ugandan women. It was Obote who had promoted the infiltration of nearly every trade union, student organization, and women's group with government spies. And it was Obote who had suspended the constitution, imposed a permanent state of emergency, and detained hundreds— if not thousands—of loved ones. By getting rid of a common enemy, Amin had become a "friend" of many Ugandan women.

In the early days after the coup, women expressed their appreciation through various letters of support.[3] The president of the Uganda Council of Women, Rebecca Mulira, thanked Amin for "saving" the country.[4] Thereza Mulindwa sent a similar message on behalf of the Uganda Association of University Women, as did Sugra Visram of the Uganda Muslim Women's Society.[5] A women's group in Kyaddondo expressed their "profound gratitude to Major General Idi Amin for having liberated us from Dr. Obote's terrorist regime." Their message went on to say that "we as mothers of the nation, are particularly happy about your action, for we can now rest in the hope that we and our children can live in freedom and peace."[6] By identifying as "mothers of the nation," these women embraced a collective identity that was meant to signify their importance, indeed their value, to the military state.

Although many Ugandan women may have welcomed Amin's coup, as it turned out, military rule was not good for most women (or civilian men). Instead of liberating the nation from authoritarianism, his regime promoted greater violence and instability. By consolidating power in the hands of military men, the state privileged a violent form of masculinity that had a devastating impact on women and their households. Agents of the state used extreme violence not only to spread fear and stifle political opposition but also to demonstrate their strength and manhood. They "performed" violence in ways that confirmed and reiterated hypermasculine military power. Amin utilized the same type of "tough guy" posturing in front of his soldiers, as well as the larger international community. As I argue below, these gendered performances were a crucial mode of governmentality, allowing those in power to disguise the fragility of the military state. Using transcripts from the Commission of Inquiry into Violations of Human Rights, as well as interviews, newspaper articles, and military decrees, this chapter offers a gendered reading of state violence and torture during the early years of the regime.

MASCULINITY, THEATRICALITY, AND THE MILITARY STATE

After the military seized power, Amin played the role of the reluctant "caretaker." During his first radio address to the nation, he assured the public that prevailing matters had "forced" him to accept a leadership position. He insisted that he was not a politician and that he would organize free and fair elections as soon as the security situation stabilized. Within a short period of time, however, he demonstrated that he had no intention of relinquishing any of his newfound power. Just one week after the coup, Amin dissolved the parliament and assumed all executive and legislative powers.[7] His first administrative order—the Armed Forces Decree—confirmed his position as military head of state, commander in chief of the armed forces, and chief of defense staff. The decree also provided for the establishment of a Defense Council, which would be responsible for the "control and administration" of the armed forces.[8] Besides Amin, the only permanent members of the Defense Council were the army chief of staff and the chief of air staff—positions that Amin eventually assumed as well. Other likely members included high-ranking military officers, although the composition of this supreme policy-making body was fluid and remained secret.[9]

Amin also appointed an all-male Council of Ministers, which, like the Defense Council, served as an important advisory body. The cabinet included one military officer, one police officer, one prisons officer, and fifteen civilian technocrats. Appointees hailed from various regions of the country and represented Christian and Muslim faiths. On the surface, Amin's first cabinet seemed to represent a broad range of diverse, albeit masculine, interests. On a deeper level, however, the regime's chief beneficiary clearly was the military. At the first cabinet meeting on February 10, for instance, Amin swore all ministers into the army as officer-cadets. As such, they became subject to military discipline.[10] Less than two weeks later, he announced that the military government would remain in power for five years, thus breaking his promise to return the country to civilian rule as soon as possible. He also said that the soldiers had appointed him to the rank of general (versus major general) and wanted him to serve as president (versus head of state).[11] The cabinet had little choice but to accept his proposals.

Over the next several months, Amin promulgated a series of decrees that quickened the pace of militarization. On March 13, 1971, he passed the Detention (Prescription of Time Limit) Decree, which allowed the state to continue detaining, for an additional six months, anyone who had been arrested during the coup or who was associated with Obote's General Service Unit.[12] The decree also provided the government with immunity from prosecution for any "act, matter or thing" that was or would be done to any person detained as long as it was done in "good faith."[13] On the same day, Amin passed the Armed Forces (Powers of Arrest) Decree and the Suspension of Political Activities Decree as well.[14] The former gave soldiers and prison officers the right to arrest any person suspected of committing (or about to commit) an offense. In addition, it gave them the right to search and take possession of any property or vehicles linked to a crime.[15] The latter suspended all political activities for two years and made it illegal for groups of three or more persons to assemble. Taken together, these three decrees significantly disrupted the lives of countless families, particularly among the Acholi and Langi. The state detained so many of Obote's former soldiers and security agents that the guards at Luzira Prison began calling them "lodgers."[16] In other words, they were there to stay.

During the early days of military rule, those perceived as enemies of the state were men. Given that the chief enforcers of the regime's repressive policies were also men and that military service was historically associated with maleness, one could argue that the coercive arm of the military state was gendered masculine.[17] This does not mean that women, or ideas about women, were not important. Instead, it suggests that the state maintained power, at least in part, by invoking and celebrating violent displays of masculinity. Soldiers learned to articulate their excitement, their fear, and their hatred through torture. They administered pain to others not only to demonstrate their power and manhood but also to emasculate their enemies, both literally and figuratively. Unfortunately, this also meant that these soldiers, as agents of violence, were also victims of the same militarism that they felt would secure their power.

These gendered acts of violence tell a powerful story about ethnic identity and belonging. In many cases, the state determined who was a friend or a foe based on one's ethnicity or home region. Amin's closest allies came from the northwestern districts of West Nile or Madi, while his main opponents hailed from the north-central districts of Lango and Acholi. Because agents of the state viewed the latter as "Obote's people," they were thought to pose a significant threat to the regime and needed to be "eliminated." Strategic winnowing began in the armed forces on the night of the coup. In military barracks across the country, Amin loyalists rounded up hundreds of Acholi and Langi soldiers and took them to various detention centers. Many of them were massacred along the way, their mutilated bodies dumped carelessly into lakes, rivers, and forests.[18] Others died a more slow and tortuous death, languishing for days, even months, in prisons within the putrid bowels of the earth.

One of the most notorious prisons was located at Makindye Barracks on the outskirts of Kampala. There, at the headquarters of the military police under the leadership of Major Hussein Marella, agents of the regime committed some of their most heinous offenses. On March 5, 1971, for instance, government soldiers transferred a group of thirty-seven Acholi and Langi soldiers from Luzira to Makindye Prison. They detained the men in "Singapore," a death cell named in honor of the former president's fateful journey abroad.[19] Joshua Wakholi, one of Obote's former ministers, watched helplessly as Amin's security agents brutally murdered the soldiers in an adjoining cell. Several months later, he described the macabre scene to a group of human rights investigators in Tanzania:

> The prisoners started shouting and wailing and then the cell door was thrown open and we saw three or four soldiers move into it. They started shooting and when they stopped after a couple of minutes there was no sound except for the groans of the wounded. Then they started dragging the bodies out and those who were still alive were killed with pangas (an African long knife like a machete) or shot. They did not seem to be able to kill one officer whom we thought was a military chaplain. He kept

groaning and they kept shooting and slashing him. The bodies were loaded into an armored personnel carrier and as they drove away we could hear the man still shouting Halleyluyah. . . . The next morning, that was Saturday the 6th of March . . . everyone [sic] of us was handed either scrubbing brushes or a pail for carrying water and were told to go inside the house where these people were killed. When we entered the house the place was full of worms and old blood. In fact, I think the dried blood that was on the floor was almost a quarter of an inch thick, and the whole place was full of pieces of skull bones, teeth, brain tissue and many other pieces of flesh from human beings.[20]

The scene that Joshua described can be likened to a highly orchestrated performance. When the cell doors slammed open, the brutal drama began to unfold. In the first act, the soldiers peppered the cell with gunfire. As the injured writhed on the ground in pools of their own blood, the blows of the soldiers' machetes silenced the groans, thus signaling the end of what might be considered the second act. And finally, as the denouement, the soldiers dragged the fallen prisoners out of the cell, leaving only shards of bone and a massive river of blood. The soldiers wanted Joshua to witness the massacre, to participate in the drama both as a spectator and as an actor. They forced him to wade through the remains with a brush and pail and then, several months later, released him so that he would share the story with others. Terror was most useful to the regime when its results were publicly known, since it paralyzed protest and silenced opposition.[21] Less than one year after Joshua returned to his home in Bugisu District, he received word that he was about to be "disappeared," so he decided to flee. Once he reached Tanzania, he became actively involved in an underground movement to topple the regime. Sadly, he died in September 1972 during a failed attempt to overthrow Amin's government.[22]

At first, few people outside of the military knew about the murders that accompanied Amin's rise to power. By mid-1971, however, it was obvious that many Acholi and Langi soldiers had simply "disappeared."[23] To disguise the losses within the military, Amin moved inexperienced soldiers and junior officers into senior positions of command. By the end of April, he had retroactively promoted all twenty-two of the original coup participants, some of whom jumped six to eight ranks.[24] Not surprisingly, this resulted in a rapid erosion of discipline within the armed forces. Amin also began significantly expanding the size of the military. Within one year, the army had recruited 19,742 new soldiers. Combined with the 7,431 soldiers and officers already serving, the army should have numbered 27,173 by December 1971. Instead, it had only 11,409, which left a deficit of 15,764 persons. Because the army reported only 3,083 desertions during this period, there were 12,681 soldiers or officers "missing." These figures imply that new recruits had also "fallen foul" of the regime.[25]

Military historian Amii Omara-Otunnu suggests that approximately four thousand of the new recruits were former rebels from Sudan or Zaire, while the rest came from West Nile.[26] This important base of support narrowed considerably throughout Amin's first year in power, which likely explains the "missing" soldiers. As relations soured with his Lugbara, Alur, and Madi colleagues, Amin began to rely more heavily on the Nubians and the Kakwa, especially those who practiced Islam. Religion became increasingly important, and by the end of the year, Muslims constituted nearly 40 percent of the army. Most of these new recruits had little education or experience, yet many of them managed to enlist as officers at the rank of second lieutenant or above. There is little doubt that Amin's coup was nothing short of a revolution by the *lumpen militariat*, a group that Ali Mazrui describes as "that class of semi-organized, rugged and semi-literate soldiers which . . . claim[ed] a share of power and influence in what [was] otherwise . . . a heavily privileged meritocracy of the educated."[27] This was significant because it meant that the colonial power structure that privileged the educated elite, particularly those from Buganda, had been turned on its head. Furthermore, it was a revolution that was clearly gendered masculine, in other words, one that was in the hands of violent military men.

Unlike the military units, the police force included both men and women. This had been the case since January 1961, when a female officer from Britain began training the first group of Ugandan female recruits. All eight women completed the course in November 1961, thus becoming the first female officers in the country.[28] Additional recruitment took place during the following years, but as more women joined the force, police work became less prestigious. Once the military seized power in 1971, the soldiers began chastising the police officers as "women" or the "wives of the army."[29] Amin also emasculated the force by publicly ridiculing them for misbehavior. He suggested that they were "like the mothers of the country," while the soldiers were

Figure 2.1. Amin attends a police and prisons shooting competition at Bombo, 1973. *Source:
Photographic Section, Ministry of Information and Broadcasting, Kampala, Uganda.*

"the fathers."[30] V. Spike Peterson argues that "casting a subordinated group as feminine devalorizes not only the empirical gender category of women but also sexually, racially, culturally, and economically marginalized men."[31] By feminizing the police force, Amin clearly reinforced the masculine supremacy of the military. This process reflects a historical pattern of mutual antagonism. During the colonial era, police officers were highly educated but poorly armed. Soldiers, in contrast, were poorly educated but highly armed. This disjuncture caused a great deal of tension but did not reach a breaking point until after the coup,[32] when agents of the military state began eliminating those with leadership potential, arguing that they had little need for a police force that was "weak" or "effeminate."[33] There is no doubt that Amin and his henchmen used gendered rhetoric to justify their actions and to mask their fear of subversion.

Nearly thirty years after the collapse of Amin's regime, many women continued to recall the period in these explicitly gendered terms. Joyce Ondoga, a middle-aged Lugbara woman, said that "the police were like women. They were just underrating them. They didn't respect them much." She explained that "since it was [a] military government, they just felt these police were just nothing. They were the ones who were in power. They were more important. They didn't care about the officers."[34] Patience Arube, a forty-five-year-old Kakwa businesswoman, agreed with this assessment. Her brother had been a high-ranking military officer, so she knew Amin and his henchmen well. She explained that "they did not even respect the police people because they said they are just women because they don't go for war."[35] Because the police engaged in "women's work" by protecting the home front, the soldiers did not respect them. By utilizing idioms of gender in this way, the state naturalized the violence and domination of militarism.

The police force gradually became so weak and ineffective that police officers became little more than "tragic bystanders" watching helplessly as the military destroyed the nation.[36] Because of the soldiers' bullying, the police had little power to do their jobs or to carry out investigations. As one police officer explained, "there is nothing an ordinary policeman can do. He will be sacked or arrested if he intervenes and will later be branded with an allegation that he's corrupt, or a politician, or deadwood, or inefficient. So policemen just watch and say it could happen to anybody anytime."[37] In other words, it was safer *not* to intervene. Consequently, the police investigated very little violence, particularly if it involved anyone from the army or the various security units. Instead, they focused on petty offenses, which kept them out of the way while maintaining the appearance of law and order.

The real power lay in the hands of the State Research Centre (SRC), which served as the government's chief intelligence agency. It was established in June 1971, two months after Amin disbanded the General Service Unit. Amin wanted to create a clandestine security organization that would function as a military intelligence unit within the President's Office—one that would be accountable to no one but himself.[38] Toward this end, he contacted Major Leone Ozi, one of the original coup participants, and ordered him to begin training soldiers in intelligence gathering.[39] Ozi wasted no time in recruiting an elite group of men who possessed integrity, character, and O-level qualifications.[40] After being transferred to Mbuya Barracks, the recruits underwent an intense program of training in three primary areas: intelligence gathering, counterintelligence, and interrogation. Intelligence officers from Israel, Britain, and the United States provided the bulk of the training, with each instructor supervising thirty students.[41] By the end of the course, the ninety new intelligence agents were well prepared to safeguard the security of Amin and the military state.

If Amin had not interfered in the development of the military intelligence unit, it might have become a very different organization. Within a short period of time, however, he assigned forty members of his Presidential Escort Group to the unit. These were his closest allies, men who represented the Kakwa and Nubian communities of West Nile, as well as ethnic kin from Zaire and Sudan. The Escorts had no minimum qualifications and very little education. Their subunit fell under the leadership of Farouk Minawa, a fellow Nubian from West Nile.[42] This faction became increasingly powerful and soon dominated the State Research Centre.

Confirming the actual size of the organization is difficult, because looters destroyed most official documents after Amin's government collapsed. However, most sources seem to suggest that there were between 1,500 and 2,000 personnel at any given time.[43] Most of the agents were young men, ages eighteen to twenty-five, although a significant number of women also worked for the center as spies and informers.[44] These women played an important role in the organization but did not threaten the masculine power structure, since they did not assume leadership positions. Most SRC agents served a one-year tour of duty with the center and then received a posting within the army, the government, or one of the embassies abroad.[45] Several of Amin's closest allies remained in the organization as permanent employees who oversaw the various units. During Major Ozi's tenure, the center had approximately twenty permanent officers and staff. By the time Lieutenant Colonel Francis Itabuka took over in 1974, this number had grown to fifty.[46]

The State Research Centre may have been a covert intelligence organization, but the identities of its agents were hardly a secret. Performing the role of "secret agent" in a very obvious way, these men proudly wore flamboyant flowered shirts, bell-bottom Kaunda suits, high-heeled Bongo shoes, and the all-important dark sunglasses.[47] They drove around in fancy vehicles, easily recognizable by their UVS license plates. SRC agents enjoyed lavish lifestyles with ready access to cash, weapons, and international travel. Not only were they on the government's payroll but also, because of the nature of their jobs, they were at liberty to loot property and extort money from citizens at will. Many agents also committed murder as a way of enriching themselves, throwing the bodies of kidnapped persons where they could not be found. If a friend or relative wanted access to a loved one's body, she or he needed to pay a ransom to an agent.[48] Because of these reasons, they developed a reputation as a "terror gang" that "kidnapped, killed, tortured, extorted, terrorized and looted with impunity."[49]

The State Research Centre was located in a three-story pink stucco building on Kyaggwe Road in Nakasero, one of Kampala's posh neighborhoods. The center had an underground tunnel connecting it to nearby State House, which served as an escape route for the president.[50] This tunnel, known as Cell 1, also doubled as a convenient dungeon for housing minor criminals. It was directly adjacent to Cell 2, a former General Service Unit armory that held death row prisoners. In addition to the two major dungeons, the center also had an execution and torture room located on the first floor directly above.[51] One of the main administrative offices displayed a small but forbidding sign: "Secret what you do here; Secret what you leave here."[52] Although SRC agents were supposed to keep their work a secret, they could not disguise the tortured screams that came from the cavernous depths below. Neighbors reported hearing the cacophony of pain night after night but could not intervene. Violence was a public secret that served an important performative function, namely, to stifle opposition by spreading terror. George William Ssentamu, the former commissioner of prisons, had an opportunity to confront the realities of this violence when he toured the facility after the fall of the regime. In 1989, he testified before the Commission of Inquiry into Violations of Human Rights about what he saw during his visit:

> The tools and the things I found at Nakasero State Research, the first one was the cold room which could be [frozen] when the prisoners are locked in. It was known as *barafu* [ice]. So one could be locked there and die after freezing. Another one was a swimming pool [that] could be filled with water and . . . heated gradually by electricity up to boiling point. Now, if a prisoner was sent there, gradually he would die as water gets heated. . . . I saw one of the gadgets they were using, the weight for men's private parts. . . . [T]his was a stone, [a] very very heavy stone with a [string] which they tie on the men's private parts and by that weight, it pulls the private parts until the man dies. There was a saw, which they used to cut off anywhere they wanted. And they had a gas-welding flame, and they were keeping salt which a prisoner was forced to eat until he dies. And they had pincers which they used to break men's private parts and also to cut off the ears and lips and breasts if there was a woman. And there was also a bag of sand which was used in the same way as salt. And of course guns.[53]

It is difficult to imagine why government agents utilized such horrific forms of torture to extract information or to punish so-called dissidents. However, if we think about the military state as a coercive institution that performed violence as a strategy for maintaining power, then it begins to make sense. If Amin and his henchmen could ensure that the citizenry was too frightened to speak up or to act out, a process that Elaine Scarry refers to as the "unmaking" of the social world, then they could fleece the nation indefinitely.[54] Indeed, that is exactly what they did for more than eight years.

The Public Safety Unit (PSU) was another paramilitary organization that performed spectacular violence. Established in November 1971, this "security" unit focused primarily on *kondoism*, or armed robbery.[55] Like its predecessor, the Special Forces, the PSU was initially attached to the civilian police force. However, as the unit became increasingly militarized, its operatives stopped cooperating with the regular police. Instead, they worked with the military police and the State Research Centre to ensure the safety of their own positions—not that of the general public. In the name of maintaining order and security, PSU operatives committed great violence, both in public and at their headquarters in Naguru Barracks. According to former U.S. ambassador Thomas Melady, torture was rife:

> Prisoners at Naguru are forced to put their heads in a metal truck wheel rim. One of the guards then stands on the neck of the prisoner and beats the metal rim with an iron bar so that the sound reverberates in the victim's head. At the same time, the prisoner is flogged with a *kiboko*, a whip made of dried hippopotamus skin. Others are forced to crawl back and forth on stones in the courtyard on their hands and knees. One person testified that he saw a prison guard tie a string around one testicle of a prisoner and pull while the victim was being interrogated.[56]

The sexualized nature of torture committed within these institutions is important to consider, since it represents a violent attack on masculinity or femininity. It symbolizes the power of the torturer to destroy or "unmake" that which is frequently perceived as central to gender identity (that is, one's reproductive capacity). Within the Public Safety Unit, both men and women worked as torturers. Mathias Ntambi, a police officer and former prisoner at Naguru, recalled that the unit employed a woman who "specialized in whipping." Her role in the macabre production was to beat the female prisoners.[57] By transgressing normative feminine behavior and engaging in extreme acts of violence, such a woman would have likely been masculinized. Because she was acting "like a man," however, she would not have represented a threat to the masculine power structure.

On May 8, 1972, Amin enacted the Robbery Suspects Decree, which gave every security officer the right "to use any force he may deem necessary to prevent the escape" of persons suspected of robbery.[58] By empowering government agents to shoot suspects at will, the decree condoned summary executions, thus giving the state complete sovereignty over life and death. On the same day, Amin also passed the Proceedings against the Government (Protection) Decree, which allowed agents of the state to use violence with impunity. According to the decree,

> No court shall make any decision, order or grant any remedy or relief in any proceedings against the Government or any person acting under the authority of the Government in respect of anything done or omitted to be done for the purpose of maintaining public order or public security in any part of Uganda or for the defense of Uganda or for the enforcement of discipline or law and order in respect of or anything relating to, consequent upon or incidental to any of those purposes, during the period between the 24th day of January, 1971, and such date as the President shall appoint.[59]

By absolving the armed forces of any responsibility for violence, arrests, and murders, Amin pounded the first nail into his own coffin. But his would be a slow and painful death—painful, that is, for the nation. The main problem was that although the military remained in control of the state, the state could not maintain control over the military or the paramilitary organizations. As Amin's ability to rein in his security forces diminished, he began looking outward, desperately searching for new enemies to blame and new allies to befriend.

MILITARISM, MASCULINITY, AND FOREIGN POLICY POSTURING

Although violence and coercion were defining features of the regime, the military state could not have functioned without significant international support. Amin's foreign policy was militarized because it focused solely on the cultivation of allies who would provide him with financial backing and military hardware. It was gendered masculine in that it was designed to protect the men who were in charge of the military state. By allying with countries that supported the regime's bellicosity and aggression vis-à-vis armaments and training, Amin bolstered masculine power and privilege. These relationships are important to our story because they profoundly influenced gender relations. Many of Amin's ideas about women, as well as his policies toward them, were a reflection of his shifting foreign policy orientation. His interactions with global leaders also highlight the more performative aspects of his regime.

During his first year in power, Israel and Britain provided Amin with substantial financial and technical assistance.[60] In fact, there is strong evidence to suggest that both countries aided in the coup itself. Israel needed Uganda's backing to maintain a base for rebel fighters in southern Sudan who were waging war against the Arab government in the north.[61] The British government, in contrast, supported Amin because of their discomfort with the deposed president's embrace of African socialism. Because neighboring Tanzania was already socialist in orientation, the British wanted to protect the rest of their political and financial interests in East Africa. They attempted to meet these goals by backing Amin. They quickly became Uganda's chief trading partner.[62]

If Israel and Britain were Amin's first major allies, Tanzania and Sudan were his first adversaries. Tanzania provided refuge for Obote after the coup, allowing the deposed president to reside at State House in Dar es Salaam. President Julius Nyerere had been a close friend of Obote's and refused to recognize Amin's government for many months. Sudan's president, Gaafar Nimiery, assisted Obote because he thought that Amin's rule would further destabilize the south. He allowed the former president to establish a training camp at Owiny Ki Bul, ten miles from the Ugandan border, with two hundred Sudanese soldiers providing a perimeter guard.[63]

Less than six months after the coup, Amin's relationship with the West began to sour. In July 1971, he traveled to Israel and Britain in search of financial and military support. Realizing that his grasp on power remained tenuous, he wanted to expand the size of the military as quickly as possible. Although pleased by Israel's promise to provide military training for several hundred soldiers, Amin was angered by their refusal to cancel Uganda's debt and ignoring his request for ten million dollars in armaments. When his subsequent visit to Britain left him similarly empty-handed, Amin began to seriously reconsider his political alliances.[64] Lieutenant Colonel Valentine Ochima's attempted coup further spoiled Amin's first diplomatic mission abroad. Even though the high-ranking military officer did not succeed, his actions permanently damaged political relations with the Alur and marked the beginning of the breakup of the West Nile conglomeration that had been so important in Amin's rise to power.[65]

Evidence of a more permanent break with Israel surfaced several months later. After brashly asserting that Uganda was "not in Israel's pockets," Amin began reallocating Israeli military instructorships to Ugandans.[66] Shortly thereafter, in mid-February 1972, Amin made his first state visit to Libya. He needed a new source of aid and found a willing ally in Muammar Gaddafi, who thought that Uganda would be a good investment.[67] Gaddafi believed that Amin would help to promote his political and ideological goals, namely, the struggle against "Western imperialism" and "Zionist expansion."[68] The Libyan strongman liked Amin not only because he was a Muslim but also because he had toppled a "Zionist agent" (that is, Milton Obote).[69] At the end of Amin's visit, both countries signed a joint communiqué formally establishing diplomatic relations.[70]

One week after Amin returned to Uganda, a ten-man Libyan delegation visited Kampala.[71] On February 28, 1972, both sides signed a formal agreement regarding economic, cultural, and trade relations.[72] Three days later, Amin threatened to close the Israeli embassy if its personnel continued to engage in "anti-government activities."[73] Several weeks later, in late March, he refused to renew their military contracts and cut their embassy staff down to four, while warning Ugandans to watch out for Israeli "agents of imperialism."[74] At the end of the month, he closed the embassy altogether, giving officials ten days to vacate the country.[75] By April 10, he had severed all ties with Israel.[76] The day after this momentous geopolitical shift was complete, Amin joined Gaddafi in condemning Israel, pledging his support in the epic "struggle against Zionism and imperialism."[77] Gaddafi rewarded Amin's over-the-top display of loyalty one week later by promising to build two hospitals, to train Ugandan technicians, and to provide instructors for the air force.[78]

Meanwhile, Uganda's relationship with Sudan had completely changed. On February 27, 1972, the Sudanese Central Government signed a peace accord with the Anya Anya rebels, thus ending the seventeen-year civil war. This agreement prohibited either side from providing military facilities to any group for underground activities, which meant that Obote's training camps had to be closed forthwith. It also enabled Amin to adopt a pro-Arab policy without alienating his Anya Anya kin, many of whom became willing recruits for the military state's rapidly expanding army. Diplomatic relations soon normalized, and in June 1972, Amin signed a defense pact with his northern neighbor.[79]

At the same time that Amin was moving toward the Arab world, he was also developing an important relationship with the Soviet Union. Given that Libya and the USSR had been closely aligned through-out the Cold War—especially from the mid-1970s onward—it is not surprising that Amin also gravitated in that direction. Indeed, by the end of his rule, the Soviet Union had become Amin's primary trading partner and his chief arms supplier, making Uganda the most heavily armed state in East Africa. The Soviets were interested in Uganda for three major reasons. First, they were committed to strengthening their position in the country more generally, furthering Obote's previous efforts to challenge both Western and Chinese interests in the region. Second, they supported Amin's decision to cut ties with Israel. And third, they wanted to take advantage of the economic, political, and strategic vacuum that had been created by the withdrawal of other na-tions.[80] Given these factors, the Uganda-Soviet alliance made sense. In fact, when Amin sent a high-powered delegation to Moscow to negoti-ate for arms with the Defense Ministry in July 1972, the Soviets were nothing but accommodating.[81]

On August 5, just days after receiving promises of increased mili-tary aid from the Soviet Union, Amin made the shocking announce-ment that he was expelling 80,000 Asians from Uganda for "sabotaging the economy" and "encouraging corruption." It was time, he claimed, to put the economy back into the hands of black Ugandans.[82] There is little doubt that Libya's caustic rhetoric about Western imperialism spurred Amin's egregious decision. As part of what he dubbed an "eco-nomic war," Amin gave all non-citizen Asians three months to leave the country.[83] Anyone claiming citizenship was to report to immigration by the tenth of September or lose his or her status.[84] One week after mak-ing this announcement, however, Amin ordered all Asians—including Ugandan citizens—to leave. He claimed that this decision reflected the "sabotage and arson the Asians had started or were planning to carry out."[85] Two days later, he changed his mind again, announcing that citizens could stay in the country provided that their paperwork was in order.[86] Because proving one's citizenship was quite difficult, most Asians chose exile.[87]

Following Amin's pronouncement about the Asian expulsion, Britain abruptly halted all financial assistance to Uganda.[88] Amin retaliated by accusing Britain of plotting his assassination. Posturing before the media, he warned that British troops would make good target practice and gave military aides less than one week to leave the country.[89] Several days later, on September 17, a group of Ugandan guerrillas invaded the country from Tanzania in an ill-fated attempt to topple the government. They might have had greater success if their mission had not been botched from the very beginning. Two days earlier, they had hijacked a DC-9 in Dar es Salaam. The plane was supposed to make a brief stop in Kilimanjaro before continuing on to Entebbe. However, the inexperienced pilot blew out the plane's tires upon landing, thus making it impossible for the commandos to get off the ground. Despite the setback, Obote and his troops decided to move forward with a coordinated ground assault on Masaka and Mbarara Barracks. Although they expected a fight, the guerrillas were entirely unprepared for the fierce resistance they faced, both by the soldiers and by the general public. After suffering numerous losses, the "liberators" had no choice but to retreat.

Within twenty-four hours of the invasion, Amin retaliated by bombing the Tanzanian towns of Bukoba and Mwanza, killing nine and injuring eleven. He also called in a favor from his new ally Gaddafi, who immediately dispatched four hundred Libyan commandos, as well as five transport planes loaded with arms and equipment. When the planes crossed into Sudanese airspace on September 21, a group of fighter jets intercepted them and forced them to land in Khartoum. Fully cognizant of the danger they posed to regional peace and security, President Nimiery confiscated their weapons and ordered them to return home. Although the empty planes managed to land at Entebbe the following day, they arrived too late to provide any meaningful assistance. Their presence, however, indicated the growing strength of Gaddafi's alliance with Amin.[90]

Escalating conflict seriously undermined regional peace and security. Both Amin and Nyerere realized that it was in their best interests to negotiate a peace settlement sooner rather than later. On October 5, 1972, the foreign ministers of Uganda, Tanzania, and Somalia met in Mogadishu to work out a plan for peace. After ten hours of heated debate, they signed the Mogadishu Agreement, which officially went into effect two days later. The agreement called for a cessation of all military operations, the withdrawal of all military forces to a distance of no less than ten kilometers from the border, and the immediate halting of hostile propaganda. It also prohibited either country from harboring "subversive forces" and required them to release any nationals or property belonging to the other side. Despite the formal peace agreement, both leaders remained fiercely antagonistic toward one another.[91]

The invasion motivated Amin to launch a fresh campaign against "subversives" and "saboteurs" within the country.[92] Benedicto Kiwanuka, the chief justice of Uganda, was the first of many prominent Ugandan citizens to be "disappeared" in the days and months that followed. Security forces forcibly abducted him from his chambers on September 21, 1972. There is strong evidence to suggest that they took him to Makindye Prison and brutally murdered him less than a week later.[93] They also assassinated one of Obote's former ministers, Basil Bataringaya, during this period. In a spectacular display of violence, security forces dragged him away from his home and decapitated him. Then they marched through the streets of Mbarara with his head impaled on a stick.[94] Several other former ministers and high-ranking civil servants likewise disappeared during this time. Although the state staged these murders to intimidate political opponents, they ultimately signified the frailty of the regime. By late 1972, Amin was facing external threats and desperately struggling to maintain his popularity at home. With limited popular support, he had little choice but to rely on the use of terror. In the end, however, it was terror that "devoured his regime from within."[95]

Although many women, like Winnie Mugenyi, initially welcomed Amin's coup, they soon realized the difficulties of life under a military dictatorship. By consolidating power in the hands of military men, the state reinforced a violent form of masculinity, which, as we shall see in the following chapters, had a profound impact on women and their households. Even though the coercive arm of the military state was gendered masculine, most civilian men did not fare any better. Many, in fact, were emasculated by soldiers and security agents, who thought that "real" men had to be fierce, aggressive, and loyal. Those who did not measure up were chastised as "women" and targeted for abuse.

Some were brutally tortured, while others simply disappeared. Under Amin's leadership, militarized versions of masculinity were just as dangerous for men as they were for women.

Throughout this chapter, I have argued that the state's use of violence was not arbitrary or coincidental. On the contrary, agents of the military government administered pain and torture to various "subversives" and "saboteurs" to cultivate a widespread culture of fear, which they believed would stifle opposition and allow them to maintain power. Within the State Research Centre, for instance, security operatives wanted the public to know, or at least to imagine, what was taking place inside. The ominous sign that professed the need for secrecy was likely a prop that agents used to terrify prisoners. After all, if they did not want the outside world to know the type of "research" that was taking place at the center, they would not have released Joshua Wakholi from custody after allowing him to witness such a brutal massacre. This suggests that state violence, like Amin's foreign policy posturing, was a gendered performance. By looking carefully beyond the masquerade of hypermasculinity, the fragility of the military state becomes much more apparent.

3 ⤸ Of Miniskirts and Morality

Femininity in Service of the State

LYDIA BALEMEZI could hardly believe the news. She had heard the elders' grumblings and had been following the fierce debates in the newspaper for quite some time, but she never expected that their complaints would amount to anything. People were always muttering under their breath about some problem or another. Why should this be any different? The announcement seemed so sudden, so dramatic. Surely the president could not be serious. Yet there she was, ensconced in a crowded taxi barreling toward the city center in a miniskirt that had just been declared illegal. Lydia was not alone. The taxi was filled with young women who were making their way to work or to school in smartly pressed dresses that had suddenly become "indecent." Once the taxi reached the main stage, the women quickly entered nearby shops in search of something to wrap around themselves. Lydia was still a secondary school student and had no extra money. Therefore, she had no alternative but to give her student identity card to an understanding shopkeeper who gave her a piece of material on credit.[1]

After leaving the shop, she maneuvered through the crowded taxi park, tightly clutching the fabric she had wrapped around her waist. As she pushed her way forward, she tried to avoid eye contact with all passersby. She wanted to remain invisible, unseen by the prying eyes of the state. Overzealous police officers had already descended on the park and were eagerly rounding up young women for examination. They immediately arrested and jailed those whose dresses were too short—more than three inches above the knee-line. Although Lydia was fortunate to escape the park unharmed, many other women were not as lucky. In the days and months ahead, they experienced significant verbal and physical harassment. Indeed, there is strong evidence to suggest that the ban on miniskirts and other "indecent" attire unleashed a torrent of abuse against young urban women. Instead of helping them "get the respect they deserve," Amin's morality decrees undermined women's authority and exacerbated gender-based violence.[2]

But why was the military ruler so concerned with women's fashion in the first place? On the basis of numerous photographs that show Amin posing with miniskirt-clad women during his first year in power, it might seem strange that he would suddenly profess his moral outrage at young women's fashion choices. Some observers have suggested that Amin banned miniskirts to signify his break with the Western world and to impress his new Libyan and Saudi Arabian benefactors.[3] While this was certainly true to some extent, local politics likely played a more significant role in his decision making. Because Amin came to power through the barrel of a gun, his political legitimacy was much more tenuous than that of other leaders. Unlike both of his East African counterparts, Jomo Kenyatta and Julius Nyerere, Amin had never been involved in nationalist politics. As a soldier, he had learned to follow orders, not to mobilize the masses. If he wanted to earn the respect of the Ugandan people, he needed to demonstrate that he was the "father of the nation," the arbiter of moral authority.[4] This chapter explores Amin's attempts to establish political legitimacy through the regulation of women's dress. I contend that by promoting a particular version of femininity—one that temporarily bolstered the popularity of the regime—he militarized women's bodies while shifting the public's attention away from his own improprieties. Although these decrees provided Amin with a certain degree of performative traction, violence ultimately undermined his legitimacy as a ruler.

REGULATING MORALITY IN A MILITARY STATE

Amin was not the first to express concern about Ugandan women's virtue. When Catholic and Protestant missionaries first arrived in Buganda in the late nineteenth century, they found most women dressed in long, sleeveless gowns of bark-cloth made from the soft, pliable inner bark of wild fig trees. Bark-cloth had been the national dress of Buganda since the late eighteenth century, although there is evidence to suggest that it had been introduced to the region three hundred years

FIGURE 3.1. Amin standing with miniskirt-clad Ugandan women, ca. 1971–72. *Source: Photographic Section, Ministry of Information and Broadcasting, Kampala, Uganda.*

earlier.[5] Missionaries were embarrassed by African women's "scanty" dressing and sought to clothe them in a manner that was "moral" and "disciplined." They designed a long, colorful dress with elbow-length sleeves puffed in the popular Edwardian style, as well as an elaborate sash for tying the garment around the waist. This fashion, known as the *busuti* or *gomesi*, became extremely popular and quickly spread throughout the country.[6]

After Uganda gained independence in 1962, women's dress became an important topic of conversation once again. Fierce debates over national identity raged between proponents of "modernity" and those who supported African "tradition." These were hardly distinct categories but instead "popular idioms through which to contest the nation's future."[7] Women's bodies became the battlegrounds for these struggles. In their now-classic text, *Women-Nation-State*, Floya Anthias and Nira Yuval-Davis argue that women serve as important symbols of the nation, either as modernizing figures or as bearers of cultural authenticity.[8] Men, in contrast, are routinely positioned as the state's chief agents and beneficiaries. This means that the political or cultural objectives of the state often force women to conform to idealistic behaviors. This was certainly the case in Uganda during the late 1960s and early 1970s.

Uganda was by no means the only nation grappling with morality-driven identity politics at this time.[9] In numerous African countries, leaders developed campaigns to promote virtuous living, many of which specifically targeted women. Some, to demonstrate their country's modernity, addressed cultural practices perceived as "primitive" or "backward." Others focused on styles of dress that imitated the West or were seen as antithetical to autonomous cultural development. Still other campaigns were less ideological and more pragmatic. In these cases, immorality served as a useful scapegoat to mask larger political and economic problems. Taken as a whole, these measures reflected a nascent form of what Ali Mazrui calls "political puritanism," a social climate demanding moral rectitude within the public domain.[10]

When Amin seized power in January 1971, miniskirts were at the epicenter of a heated debate linking women's clothing to immorality. Through impassioned letters to the editor, citizens expressed concern over the cultural decay associated with the mini dress. In one such letter, titled "Minis Not for Us," Peace Nyenga voiced her position: "To shame a woman is to shame a nation. . . . [A]ny woman (and girl) who wears a mini-dress puts the whole nation—Uganda—to shame. . . . The Government should realize that the 'mini' girls or daughters have failed their parents and the state of Uganda. . . . Action must be taken to discipline and limit the freedom of mini dressers so that Uganda can unburden *herself* of the mini dress yoke."[11] This letter illuminates important generational concerns about the cultural significance of women's bodies. As symbols of the nation, women were expected to wear clothing that connoted modesty and respectability. By covering women's thighs—a highly sexualized part of the body in many parts of the country—these long dresses theoretically preserved feminine virtue. Elders thought that miniskirts were "dangerous" because they tempted young women to sacrifice their dignity, as well as the nation's traditions, in pursuit of something as fleeting and ephemeral as fashion. Because many Ugandans believed that proper dress was an extension of one's civic duty, they urged the government to establish minimum dress lengths "for the good name of our country and the dignity of those concerned."[12]

Miniskirts were not only about immorality but also about the struggle to maintain African authenticity in the face of rapid social change. Although many men embraced modernity, they expected women to remain the bearers of tradition to preserve culture.[13] Because men saw women as symbols of the nation, they encouraged women to remain "natural" or "authentic." This message came from the highest levels of

Amin's government. Following a state visit to neighboring Zaire in late 1971, for instance, Uganda's foreign minister, Wanume Kibedi, praised Zairian women for their hospitality and their commitment to maintaining culture. "Women in Zaire are well-dressed and the question of minis and micro-minis does not exist," he said. "There is little make-up. This is one of the very few African countries which is proud of natural beauty."[14] His words implied that Ugandan women were not natural or proud of their heritage, a premise undergirding much of the morality rhetoric at this time.

The need to preserve culture was also an important theme in many letters to the editor. In one letter titled "To All Ladies of 35 and Older," N. P. Jolly advised "older" women not to wear short skirts, wigs, or makeup. This would help the younger generation gradually "realize that African culture should be restored."[15] The problem, argued another, was that "African girls mar their beauty by trying to look like Europeans. . . . It is a ridiculous sight to watch a micro-skirted girl with a bleached face wearing an Everest of a wig on her head."[16] To maintain "African culture," the author urged Ugandan women to reject Western styles.

When Amin eventually banned miniskirts on May 27, 1972, he too framed his decision in nationalist terms: "I would like to tell the people of Uganda that they should not be brainwashed by imperialists and be made to think that our women should wear mini-skirts. . . . African women must dress decently so that they can get the respect they deserve."[17] By linking fashion to Western imperialism, he inscribed his nascent foreign policy orientation onto the bodies of Ugandan women while performing his role as "father of the nation." Amin's campaign to promote female respectability translated into the Penal Code Act (Amendment) Decree, otherwise known as "a decree to prohibit the wearing of certain dresses which outrage decency and are injurious to public morals." Officials amended Section 162 of the Penal Code to read as follows: "Every person of or above the apparent age of fourteen years who in any public place wears any dress, garment, skirts, or shorts the hem-line or bottom of which is 7.62 centimetres (3 inches) above the knee-line or wears any dress popularly known as a midi or a maxi having a slit on any part of the circumference of such dress the apex of which is above the knee-line [will be in violation of the decree]."[18] In addition to risqué dresses, the decree also banned short, tight-fitting pants, popularly known as "hot pants." Any person arrested for violating the dress code was deemed "idle and disorderly" and subject to a fine and/or imprisonment. One of the major problems with this decree, however, was that it failed to define the knee-line. No one seemed to know whether it was above, below, or in the middle of the kneecap. Because of mounting confusion over the knee-line, Amin amended the decree in February of the following year, mandating that hemlines extend no more than two inches above the upper edge of the patella, or kneecap.[19]

Other morality-based decrees soon followed. In early 1973, for instance, Amin banned female civil servants from wearing trousers, tights, and snug-fitting dresses. Establishment Notice No. 1 went into effect on January 10 and was based on "the need for female public officers to dress decently while on official duty."[20] In February of the following year, Amin extended the prohibition to all women, not including those persons whose official duties required them to wear pants.[21] He later rescinded the ban in November 1974 after learning that trousers were acceptable attire for women in Islamic cultures.[22] In a face-saving maneuver, he announced that he was lifting the ban to "enable women tourists from various countries such as Asia and the Arab world and Europe where they wear trousers to put on their trousers when they come to Uganda." Because trousers offered protection to tourists on safari, women would be allowed to wear long pants. Nonetheless, he promised to "keep an eye on them to ensure that they [were] disciplined and . . . properly dressed all the time."[23] Although Uganda was not an Islamic state, Amin worked hard to convince his Arab benefactors that he was a good Muslim leader. This was another one of his clever performances, one in which women's bodies figured prominently.

Much of the gendered rhetoric about discipline and morality was explicitly linked to cultural nationalism—how a "good" woman in Ugandan society was supposed to act. Amin expected women's bodies to reflect his evolving cultural and political ideologies. On January 28, 1974, he announced that "with immediate effect, nobody is permitted to wear wigs in Government offices or on official functions. This includes members of the President's family. Any member of the President's family who wears a wig will not be regarded as a member of his family with immediate effect."[24] Amin claimed that various officials within the army had asked him to ban wigs because women looked "artificial" and "some were really stinking because they never have time to clean their artificial hair."[25] Several days later, on February 8, Amin enacted a decree making it illegal for women to wear wigs in any public place.[26] The state newspaper reported the dramatic banning order as follows: "Matters came to a head when President Amin learnt from reliable sources that the wigs craved by unsuspecting Uganda customers were made by the callous imperialists from human hair mainly collected from the unfortunate victims of the miserable Vietnam War, thus turning human tragedy into lucrative commercial enterprise. . . . Seldom cleaned, often neglected and harboring articles injurious to life from lice to lizards, wigs promoted health hazards besides making our women look un-African and artificial."[27] The new decree was not only a blatant rejection of "imperialism" but also a way of preserving "culture" and promoting African "authenticity."

As the country's political stability deteriorated, the ban on wigs took on additional meanings. During an International Women's Year celebration held on May 1, 1975, for instance, Amin made the following statement: "We are all aware that when my Government came to power and during the invasion [of September 1972] some spies and also guerrillas worked through women and such activities caused a lot of harm. . . . Some women were even given pistols, which they kept in their wigs. The wigs had to be banned because they were unnatural, untidy and in some cases were harboring dangerous weapons."[28] Operating under the constant threat of rebellion, Amin convinced the public that certain women collaborated with imperialists or so-called confusing agents. During this performance, however, he never revealed who these women were or how they engaged with the enemy. They were simply scapegoats who took the blame for political insecurity. Men's equally full "Afro" hairstyles remained unregulated, which sent a deliberate message to women that they could not be trusted and had to be controlled.

On May 6, 1975, just five days after accusing the nation's women of subversion, Amin banned makeup and skin lighteners, which he claimed "change the natural beauty of women and make them look like half-castes." He said that "women who use these creams and change the appearance of their faces and skin lose their natural beauty and as a result . . . look like monkeys or gorillas." Others, he said, looked as if they were suffering from leprosy, which was why men chased them from their homes.[29] These spiteful remarks had nothing to do with promoting female respectability. Instead, they belittled women and undermined their authority. What had begun as a fairly innocuous plan to enhance Amin's reputation at home and abroad had clearly morphed into a brutal campaign against young urban women.

THE AFTERMATH

Amin's decision to ban "indecent" clothing was a popular topic in the press, particularly among those who were known as the arbiters of morality and tradition. After the first ban went into effect, the National Parents' Association penned a congratulatory message to the president thanking him for his "timely drastic step to ban the miniskirts and others of the like, which have been increasing prostitution and *kondoism* [armed robbery] in our young generation in Uganda."[30] A group of elders sent a letter expressing a similar sentiment: "The ban will maintain national culture and revive the former decent dressing and discipline among girls and women of our country. Minis, hot pants and v-split maxis were not only embarrassing to the general public, but also were a second *kondoism* in Uganda."[31] These letters illustrate a tension between the young girls who wanted to follow the latest modern trends and the older generation who felt embarrassed by their fashion choices. Many elders perceived "indecent" dressing as a violent assault on societal norms, a veritable theft of cultural values.[32] By taking action to ban provocative styles, Amin endeared himself to such elders.

Other letters of support came from ardent cultural nationalists who appreciated Amin's efforts to restore "African dignity and culture."[33] One letter writer, Y. D. Okot-Omara, expressed his gratitude to the president for banning "disgusting, immoral and unrepresentable minis, hot pants, and maxis." He asked the military ruler to consider banning "imperialist cosmetics" as well, arguing that unless women "regret being born black," they have no need to wear such products.[34] In another letter, John Atwoki thanked Amin for having "the guts" to ban minis, since they were "really degrading our country."[35] Deti Nteeko too expressed appreciation for the ban on "foreign-oriented" clothing, arguing that the move was "very patriotic and moralizing."[36] The authors of these letters seemed to believe that by carefully regulating women's dress, the state protected the nation's dignity.

Despite the tremendous euphoria surrounding the bans, some regarded Amin's measures with apprehension. Young women, for instance, expressed concern that "unruly" people would take the law into their own hands, "molesting women whether dressed in a mini or not."[37] Parents also worried that their daughters would be "victimized by hooligans," a fear that became a reality shortly after Amin announced the ban.[38] Indeed, in the days and months ahead, numerous girls and women in urban centers throughout the country experienced great violence at the hands of soldiers and local vigilantes. Whether the escalation of violence was a direct result of the state's inability to enforce the bans or a reflection of male anxiety about urban women more generally is unclear. What is apparent from police records, however, is that the law enforcement system was unable to stem the tide of dress code violations for several years.

Less than one week after the decree banning miniskirts and hot pants went into effect, police arrested a young woman for "physically conduct[ing] herself in a manner likely to cause a breach of the peace."[39] The new law stipulated that hemlines (and dress slits) rise no more than three inches above the knee-line. The state deemed anyone found in violation of the decree "idle and disorderly" and subjected them to three months imprisonment and/or a fine of two hundred shillings. During the first few months that the ban was in effect, police officers, prosecutors, and magistrates struggled to define the knee-line.[40] Margaret Ndawula, one of the attorneys who drafted the decree, remembered the confusion. She said,

> The law was stating that the dress shouldn't go three inches above the knee but then that was subject to interpretation. Where is the knee? So in that aspect his police officers would just look at you and they suspect you were three inches above the knee and then you were arrested. But what they would do, they would take you to the police and they measure. But also that measuring was subject to interpretation. Where is the knee as far as the law is concerned? So sometimes they would measure from below what would actually be the knee. It was a funny situation.[41]

Ruth Masika, the second woman to qualify as an attorney in Uganda, also participated in the drafting team. "Of course I could not refuse," she explained, "but I tried as much as possible to show the men how ridiculous the whole thing was."[42] No one, it seemed, could figure out what constituted the knee-line. Because officials could not reach a consensus, they initially released most offenders with a warning and/or a nominal fine.[43] As time went by, however, it became apparent that some women (and a few men) were testing the limits of the law, even after Amin amended the penal code to clarify the amorphous knee-line. Frustrated by their blatant disregard for the law, magistrates began issuing more severe penalties, which included higher fines and the confiscation of illicit clothing.[44] Prosecutors even pressed for mandatory jail sentences, though most judges were reluctant to issue the harsh sentence, given the tender age of most offenders.

The war against sartorial indiscipline entered a new phase in early April 1973. Kampala's chief magistrate, Francis Butagira, sentenced a female shopkeeper to one month in prison for violating the dress code; she was the first person to be remanded without the option of paying a fine.[45] In the weeks that followed, the state imprisoned numerous young women for being "idle and disorderly."[46] Despite the hope that jail time would deter indecency, dress code violations continued. Part of the problem was that magistrates did not issue harsh sentences consistently. Of the fifty-eight legal cases that I examined at the Central Police Station in Kampala in 2008, not a single person received mandatory jail time.[47] Instead, the courts continued giving defendants the option of paying a fine. Given that these particular arrests took place between November 1973 and August 1974—the period after Butagira introduced tougher prison sentencing—it is surprising that no one received such a sentence. Again, the issue may have been the age of the defendants. Most of those arrested were young women in their teens and early twenties. In fact, the oldest person to be arrested in the case files that I examined was Maria Kikaziki, a twenty-seven-year-old woman charged with wearing a maxi skirt with a high split. The police released her from jail after she paid a fine of twenty shillings.[48] Because the decree mandated fines of up to two hundred shillings or three months in jail, her sentence amounted to little more than a slap on the wrist.

These arrest reports are significant because they confirm that the police continued to arrest young women for miniskirt violations more than two years after the ban went into effect. This suggests that women were either ignorant of the law or that they were not afraid of the consequences. The police reports clearly reveal the laxity with which most magistrates treated such violations, despite Butagira's move toward tougher sentencing. They are also important because they make it possible to construct a demographic profile of the offenders—most were young women who could reasonably plead ignorance of the law. Only nine of the fifty-eight arrest reports that I examined involved boys or men.[49] This, of course, could also mean that the state did not take men's violations as seriously and that most of the attention was focused on women. In either case, these records indicate that the state constructed young women as the primary culprits of immorality. And finally, these reports demonstrate that although the military reigned supreme, police officers still had a function, albeit one that was severely limited, within the military government. They were responsible for policing morality crimes, petty offenses involving women, which underscores the relative weakness of the force. This is undoubtedly why so many people remembered them as a "force of women."

Various Ugandans confirmed the interesting pattern that I discovered in the arrest reports. Francis Kutosi, a former police prosecutor in Mbale District, agreed that punishments were often light. He explained that although most of the "girls" whom they arrested pled guilty, "courts were sympathetic and hardly any of the ladies went to prison." The magistrates simply cautioned most of them because they were "sympathetic to that kind of law."[50] When I asked why the courts were so sympathetic, the former prosecutor suggested that it was because the crimes were not serious. Because of the law, the police had to arrest the offenders. The magistrates, however, were under no obligation to mete out harsh penalties. Many, in fact, did not. Peter Jermyn Allen, for instance, said that he refused to hear miniskirt cases while he was serving as the chief magistrate of Mbarara because the law was "totally unnecessary but also contrary to the Constitution."[51]

Another part of the problem was making the arrests "stick." Sam Echaku, a retired assistant commissioner of police and former director of the Criminal Investigation Division in the Uganda Police Force, said that enforcing Amin's morality laws was difficult because most of the offenders were "cheeky" young girls.[52] He recalled that many young women would hike up their skirts or roll down their waistbands to make their dresses look like minis. When the police arrested them, they would quickly pull down their skirts "just to annoy." Sometimes the girls would wait until just before they got into court to lengthen their dresses. The officers would then "look foolish and feel ashamed" for making a "false" arrest. Although these subtle acts of resistance were not likely meant as grandiose political statements, they served to further undermine the waning authority of an already emasculated police force.

The inability (or refusal) of the police and the judiciary to halt dress code violations was a source of constant ire for Amin.[53] Here was a powerful military leader—the self-proclaimed Conqueror of the British

Empire—yet he could not prevent young women from flaunting their kneecaps in public. By late 1974, miniskirt violations had become so pervasive that according to Wilson Kityo, then chief magistrate of Kampala, they were "more prevalent than cases of theft."[54] Yet when I asked Ugandans about resistance to the regime, people repeatedly told me that "one wouldn't dare."[55] In that precarious political environment, ignoring the decrees would have been incredibly risky. As Esther Ssengendo, a sixty-five-year-old retired teacher from the Kampala suburb of Kanyanya, suggests, Amin's orders were absolute: "Say Amin said on the radio at nine o'clock that there was no wearing like this, within two hours it would already be finished. Eh! You would see soldiers coming to arrest you and jail you. You had to obey it. And with him, what he says couldn't be questioned. . . . When he alone was the commander, when he said that, it was finished."[56]

Amin used the media "as an infrastructure with which to dictate to Uganda's publics."[57] This framework allowed him to address demographic groups that otherwise fell outside the reaches of government bureaucracy, thus giving him a platform upon which to perform. Through the radio and the newspaper, Amin "addressed, blamed, and exhorted" Ugandans to mend their wicked ways.[58] Derek Peterson and Edgar Taylor argue that there was a "pre-emptory quality to official discourse in Amin's Uganda, a taken-for-granted assumption that directives would be unthinkingly obeyed."[59] Hassifa Namboze, a fifty-two-year-old petty trader from Bwaise, confirmed this pattern. She said that "with Amin, his things had order. He would issue an order at night during the eight o'clock news. By morning, the order would be already in place. He could say that, 'Tomorrow I don't want to see anyone dressed in that dress.' And that is how it used to be."[60]

These statements highlight the performative aspects of military rule. They also reveal the intense levels of fear that permeated everyday life for most Ugandans. People were afraid of those whom they could identify, namely, the heavily armed military personnel on every street corner. But they were also afraid of those they could not—undercover security operatives from the State Research Centre who "disappeared" countless Ugandans. Sarah Adroa, a sixty-one-year-old nursing officer from Arua, explained that "there were so many secret police or secret agencies [that] you wouldn't know who was arresting you for what. It could be a uniformed person or an un-uniformed."[61] She, and many others, lived in a state of perpetual fear. This was another part of Amin's strategy for maintaining power. If the state could keep people wondering whom they could trust, they would not be able to mobilize against him.

Why did so many women like Esther and Hassifa insist that it was impossible to resist Amin's orders when there is significant evidence to suggest that the dress code decrees were in fact being ignored? I suspect that people did not initially take the bans seriously because the repercussions were not that serious. Over time, however, as Amin struggled to maintain internal legitimacy and his anti-imperialist rhetoric became more pronounced, his concerns about women's bodies intensified. Consequently, military soldiers and undercover agents began to assume a more active role in stifling wayward dressers. Their strong-arm strategy was largely successful, and by early 1975, dress code violations had come to an abrupt halt. The newspapers reported very few miniskirt arrests during the latter half of Amin's rule. In addition, none of the Station Diaries that I examined at the Central Police Station in Kampala mentioned dress-related violations during this period. Although this evidence could also suggest a breakdown within the law enforcement system whereby police no longer had the will or the capacity to make arrests — an interpretation that is likely true — my interview data provide strong support for the argument that most women eventually stopped wearing minis because of the risks involved.

Amin ultimately stemmed the tide of mini-clad dressers by promoting, or at the very least ignoring, violence against women. Although the Penal Code Act (Amendment) Decree of 1972 mandated that police officers alone had the power to arrest persons in contravention of the law, countless soldiers and security agents apprehended women and girls for various dress code violations. Indeed, there is significant evidence to suggest that the morality decrees instigated a wave of molestation against women. Military and civilian men interpreted the bans as a license to verbally and physically harass women "whether dressed in a mini or not."[62] In a particularly telling letter to the editor published outside the country by a "Concerned Ugandan Woman," we get a sense of the extent to which the state oppressed women:

> I am one of the oppressed Ugandan women and I feel our government is doing more harm than good to us. Minis were banned, along with wigs and trousers. These ruthless army men have harassed the women. You pass a policeman and he stops you, measures your dress, finds it's the right length, [and] lets

you go. But before you walk two yards, you come across an army man. He stops you and before he has measured the dress he has started beating you, saying your dress is too short and pushing you to the jeep, which takes you to the police station. Nobody can say anything unless she wants to see another world. We have been standing it, but just recently we were shocked and dumb-founded when we heard of the ban on cosmetics. We are tired. Why should we wait for these ruthless nuts to harass us again? Soon they will make it an offence to have Vaseline. Hey women, why don't you wake up and protest?[63]

Perhaps the reason that women did not "wake up and protest" was the futility of resistance. Amin consistently turned a blind eye to the violence and refused to hold the perpetrators accountable. He argued that if men molested women, "the government was not to blame."[64] After an angry crowd assaulted a group of girls and chopped off their hair for not being properly dressed, Amin responded with indifference. He blamed the victims, stating that if the girls had been wearing long dresses, they would not have been assaulted. He then ordered the anti-mini opera-tions to continue.[65]

Many of the women that I interviewed confirmed these accounts of violence, each telling graphic stories about the soldiers' perverse use of knives, bottles, and razors. Nakarema Kyolaba, a sixty-eight-year-old distiller from rural Mukono District, recalled that "they used to cut us using bottles. I remember in Nakifuma there, if someone passed by you with that hair, they would cut her using a razor."[66] The International Commission of Jurists documented similar cases. They learned that in late 1974, agents from the Public Safety Unit arrested more than one hundred girls in Kampala for wearing minis. After bringing the young women to Naguru Barracks, the officers shaved their heads with bro-ken glass and gang-raped one of them. Even though the girls survived the horrific ordeal, they probably never forgot the painful memories of that long night in prison.[67]

In 2005, I had the opportunity to meet Evelyn Nyanzi, a forty-five-year-old teacher from Kampala. She told me how soldiers used to regu-late the length of women's dress. "If they found you in [a] mini, they would cut you with a knife where the cloth reaches," she explained. "If you found him holding a *panga* [machete], he would cut you like this where the dress passes. A *panga!*"[68] Joyce Ondoga, a fifty-six-year-old teacher from Arua, shared a similar story. She remembered that "if you put on a short skirt . . . they had very sharp knives. They would just say, 'Hapana hapo. Va hapo.' That means they would cut you very deep with the knife. It was not easy."[69] This gendered pattern of abuse is particularly disturbing because it demonstrates how soldiers turned ordinary household objects into instruments of torture. So pervasive was this type of violence that people used to call Amin *kijambiya*, or "the machete," because, in the words of one woman, he would "invade you, take you, chop chop you, and murder you."[70]

Young women also risked assault by vigilante mobs policing women's dress. Numerous individuals told me that soldiers used to encourage crowds to strip women naked if they were caught wearing minis.[71] The idea was that if a woman wanted to "walk naked," the community would "let" her do so. Goretti Ssali, a fifty-nine-year-old secretary from Bunamwaya, explained that "if you were moving in the park [and wearing a mini], they would pull you. They were wild and they would strip you."[72] Hassifa Namboze blamed the *bayaye*, or urban street thugs, for much of the violence. She remembered that "whenever they would meet one [woman] wearing a mini they would tear [the dress] and leave you naked."[73]

Frequently these episodes of violence escalated to rape. "If some soldiers found you wearing minis," explained Mary Kyomukama, a forty-nine-year-old secretary from Lusanja, "they would beat you or . . . grab [rape] you forcefully. . . . Even men helped the soldiers to undress the women, beating them."[74] Mary's account is not unique. Nearly everyone that I interviewed discussed similar incidents, which clearly suggests that violence against young urban women was widespread. Fed up with the perpetual harassment, most women eventually abandoned the miniskirt and other forms of "indecent" or "imperialist" fashion. Instead, they began putting on ankle-length dresses known as "*Amin nvaako*," or "Leave me alone Amin!" When a woman wore this dress, she firmly asserted her right to be left alone. In a way then, "*Amin nvaako*" signified women's complex relationship to the military state. On one level, it was a dress that acquiesced to state demands for decency. On another level, however, it sent a powerful message of dissent—a nonverbal yet clearly articulated, "Bugger off! Leave me alone."

⌐

Although Lydia Balemezi managed to avoid arrest or injury after the ban went into effect, many others were not as lucky. Hundreds—if not thousands—of women were harassed, humiliated, beaten, and even raped because of the ways in which they were dressed. It is ironic that a campaign to promote female respectability would be carried out in such a brutal manner. It is also ironic that a military dictator with a disturbing record of violent behavior would be the one to initiate such a movement. And yet, as this chapter clearly illustrates, female-focused laws on morality served an important strategic function. They provided an ideological platform upon which Amin could establish his political legitimacy as "father of the nation," the guardian of moral rectitude who would defend African "culture" and "tradition." The supportive letters to the editor that poured in after the ban on miniskirts went into effect, as well as numerous interviews that I conducted across the country, suggest that this strategy was initially effective. Amin's performance of moral outrage bolstered his popularity among those who believed that young women's dress and behavior had gotten out of hand, particularly within the urban areas. They appreciated his efforts to restore "African dignity and culture" and to "revive the former decent dressing and discipline among girls and women," even if they did not condone the violence that ensued. It was the *idea* of the ban, not necessarily its enforcement strategy, that was most appealing.

As the campaign gained momentum, however, even the military dictator's most ardent supporters had difficulty in looking beyond the violence. Nakarema Kyolaba, for instance, described how the soldiers in Mukono District used to cut women using razors and broken bottles if they found them wearing a wig or a banned hairstyle. The International Commission of Jurists confirmed that security forces of the Public Safety Unit used to shave women's heads using shards of broken glass to punish them for wearing miniskirts. Evelyn Nyanzi and Joyce Ondoga both recounted horrific tales of violence as soldiers used sharp knives and machetes to cut women along the dress line if their skirts were considered too short. Vigilante mobs also participated in the violence, attacking women and stripping them naked on the streets. Sometimes these incidents escalated to rape, a heinous form of punishment for those women who chose to "walk naked." Fed up with the violence, most women eventually stopped wearing miniskirts and banned hairstyles altogether. Nonetheless, as we see in later chapters, this violence—the performance of which was an important strategy for maintaining power—ultimately undermined the legitimacy of Amin's military state.

4 ⌐ An Accidental Liberation
Women on the Front Lines of the Economic War

JOYCE ONDOGA shifted uncomfortably in her chair, nervously thumbing the edges of the small cotton handkerchief that she held in her lap. It had been a long time since she had talked about her late husband, a former officer in Amin's army. She wanted me to know that during their early years of marriage, he had been a kind and loving man. "When he took me to Kampala," she recalled, "things were okay. I never saw a gun from him. He was ever smart in a very good uniform." In late 1972 or early 1973, he helped her procure a wholesale shop on Market Street. Unlike most of the other military wives who had acquired businesses in the wake of the Asian expulsion, Joyce was educated and had a knack for trade. Within a short period of time, she had become highly successful, astutely using her profits to expand her growing business. "I had about five cars, one lorry, a tractor, [and] some farms in Masindi," she explained. "But of course I didn't enjoy that money because I knew it was not the right thing. It was not the right thing, and I knew those things would come to an end." She felt guilty that she had become rich as a result of someone else's loss. "I had no peace of mind," she said. "It was just haunting me. Something you grab from somebody, there's always an end, a bitter end."

The bitter end was closer than she might have imagined. Instead of saving for the future, her husband lived for the moment, spending most of her hard-earned profits on luxury goods and other women. Although she was deeply hurt, Joyce never considered divorce. She loved her husband and was determined to make their marriage work. After the regime collapsed in April 1979, the couple fled into exile, along with their four young children and thousands of other Amin loyalists. Shortly after they arrived in Zaire, her husband began drinking and smoking heavily. "I think it was frustration," said Joyce. "We lost everything. He started drinking after the war. Just they had nothing to do." After the family returned to Uganda in 1986, her husband continued to drink, disappearing across the border for weeks and months at a time. She saw very little of him over the coming years. Finally, in 1993, he died of cirrhosis of the liver, leaving nothing to show for his years of military service. "I regret even why I married a soldier," Joyce whispered as she wiped away her tears. "In the end," she murmured, "I didn't gain any good thing."[1]

Like many other Ugandan women, Joyce had a complex relationship to the military state. During the eight years that Amin was in power, she and her children enjoyed a life of prosperity and privilege. As the wife of a high-ranking military officer, she became one of the chief beneficiaries of the Asian expulsion, gaining access to wealth, power, and lucrative business opportunities. This success, however, came at a steep price. Once the regime began to crumble, she lost her money, her home, and eventually her husband. Instead of bringing liberation as she had expected, the "economic war" brought hardship and pain. Joyce's story clearly illustrates the contradictory effects of the Asian expulsion, not only for the individual beneficiaries but also for the masculine power structure that undergirded military rule.

In what can only be called an "accidental liberation," Amin compelled thousands of poor urban women to step out of the domestic sphere and into the informal sector. By expelling the Asian population in late 1972—a group that had for many years been the nation's primary entrepreneurs—Amin inadvertently opened up a new economic space for Ugandan women. Whether they were forced to engage in petty trade out of necessity or because they received a shop "abandoned" by the departing Asians, numerous women remembered Amin as the one who "taught us how to work." For the first time, many gained access to economic resources and decision-making power. Despite the economic windfall, many women continued to suffer the brutal realities of a harsh military dictatorship. Thus, for most Ugandan women, liberation was partial at best.

THE ANATOMY OF AN EXPULSION

Amin was an unconventional ruler whose style of leadership depended heavily on performance and spectacle. He fed off the energy of crowds and loved to shock them with his bold pronouncements. Many of his most infamous political decisions were based on dreams—either his own or those of his spiritual advisors. His decision to expel the Asian community from Uganda was no different. On the morning of August 5, 1972, Amin stood before a group of army recruits in the eastern town of Tororo and told them about a strange dream he had had the night before. In this dream, Amin discovered that the Asians who had been living in Uganda for many years had "milked the cow" but "did not feed it."[2] He explained to his audience that the dream made him realize that the only way to prevent further economic sabotage was to expel the entire population. Those who did not leave the country within ninety days would be forcibly resettled onto rural labor plantations.[3] Most Ugandans initially ignored the announcement, assuming that it was just another one of the president's off-the-cuff remarks. Within a matter of days, however, they began to realize that this was no joke. On August 9, Amin signed a decree revoking the residence permits of all Asian citizens from India, Pakistan, Bangladesh, and the United Kingdom.[4] Less than one week later, the first group of refugees fled the country on a chartered flight to Britain.[5] Over the next three months, more than 50,000 Asians escaped into exile, including at least 15,000 Ugandan citizens of Asian descent. By the November 9 deadline, fewer than 2,500 Ugandan Asians remained.[6]

Prior to the expulsion, the Asian community had a long labor history in Uganda. In the 1890s, Asian settlers began migrating to the region from the East African coast. Although a significant number of Asians came to the country as indentured laborers—forcibly recruited by the British to build the railroad—many others migrated on their own accord to take advantage of new economic opportunities.[7] Most of the former died in Uganda or returned to their homes after the railroad had been completed in 1901. The people expelled by Amin were therefore descendants of the latter group. Lacking landownership rights and political power, Asians carved out a critical niche as merchants, small business owners, wholesalers, and craftsmen. They introduced a large portion of the population to the cash economy and created invaluable businesses. They also employed numerous Africans in large manufacturing firms, bringing significant economic development and wage employment to the nation.[8] Nonetheless, many Africans resented Asians because of their visible economic success.

When Uganda gained independence in 1962, the new constitution stipulated that Asians would have two years to apply for Ugandan citizenship.[9] Although 26,000 applied, most chose to keep their British passports. This display of so-called political disloyalty angered many Africans. In a 1969 effort to increase his popularity, President Milton Obote enacted a series of socialist reforms to liberate the country economically. In his revolutionary manifesto, *The Common Man's Charter*, he promised to return political and economic power to the masses. The following year, the state assumed 60 percent ownership of all banks, insurance firms, oil companies, and most industries. At the same time, Obote passed the Immigration Act, which required all noncitizens to carry work permits. He also instituted the Trade Licensing Act, preventing noncitizens from various types of trade and from living in certain geographic areas. Many Asians responded by moving their families and their capital abroad.

Because of the economic turmoil created by Obote's socialist reforms, most Asians welcomed Amin's military coup in January 1971. They appreciated his decision to reverse many of Obote's nationalization policies but worried about the increasing hostility of his political rhetoric. In early May 1971, for instance, Amin publicly warned Asians to "stop keeping aloof" and to work hard with Africans to develop the nation.[10] Several months later, he accused them of "economic sabotage" and announced that he would be conducting a formal census of all Asians living in Uganda.[11] In early December 1971, he invited a group of Asian elders to meet with him to discuss nation-building strategies. Instead of focusing on how the African and Asian communities could move forward together, Amin announced that he was canceling all pending citizenship applications, which affected nearly 12,000 Asians.[12] He told them that he was particularly upset by their "refusal to integrate" with the African population:

> It is particularly painful in that about seventy years have elapsed since the first Asians came to Uganda, but, despite the length of time, the Asian community has continued to live in a world of its own to the extent that the Africans in this country have, for example, hardly been able to marry Asian girls. A casual count of African males who are married to Asian females in Uganda shows only about six such couples. And even then, all the six married these women when they were abroad and not here in Uganda. The matter becomes even more serious when attempts by Africans within Uganda to fall in love and marry Asian girls

have in one or two cases even resulted in the Asian girls committing suicide when it was discovered by their parents that they were in love and intended to marry Africans.[13]

It is fascinating that intercultural romantic relationships—or the lack thereof—would figure so prominently in Amin's justification for cancelling Asian citizenship applications. Many people told me that Amin had once proposed to Meena Madhvani, the wife of Uganda's most powerful Asian industrialist. When she rebuffed his advances, he decided to expel the Asian population.[14] Regardless of the veracity of this intriguing rumor, Amin was clearly frustrated that he could not control one of the more intimate aspects of nation building (that is, female sexuality). Yet when he announced his decision to expel the entire population nearly one year later, he did not mention Asian women or their failure to love African men. Instead, he described his economic war in explicitly racial terms:

> In a nutshell it stands for my adherent policy aimed at the total Ugandanization and indigenization of Uganda's economy. This, in simple terms, means placing . . . the economic power in the hands of indigenous citizens of Uganda and our determined effort to support that economic status quo. Secondly, economic war is intended to portray and perpetuate a new economic culture in this country, which . . . is not subject to socialist, capitalist or communist ideological trends and tendencies. It is an independent economic culture which can only be advanced by the indigenous people of this country for the good of this generation and those to come. Thirdly, economic war [is] intended to pave [the] way for the emancipation and liberation of the Black man in general so as to show the world that a Black man, when given peace, security, political independence and economic power, can rule as efficiently if not better than a white man.[15]

Although many Ugandans saw Amin as a hero for returning the economy to the indigenous population, the Asian expulsion did not actually liberate the nation from foreign intervention. Instead, it merely diversified the country's dependence on others. In the years following the expulsion, Amin received arms from the Soviet Union and France, as well as economic assistance from Saudi Arabia, Libya, and other Arab nations.[16] Nonetheless, many Ugandans interpreted the expulsion as an opportunity to become the architects of their own destiny. They believed that they too could become rich by simply transferring existing wealth into African hands. Because most of the beneficiaries were soldiers and not experienced entrepreneurs, the expropriation ultimately failed to promote macroeconomic growth.[17]

THE DEVELOPMENT OF THE *MAFUTA MINGI*

The scramble for booty began immediately after Amin signed the expulsion decree. Soldiers, police officers, and other low-level security operatives confiscated money, jewelry, and various household items from Asian families as they attempted to flee the country.[18] The state, however, orchestrated the worst fleecing operations. On October 24, 1972, Amin passed the Declaration of Assets (Non-citizen Asians) (Amendment) Decree, which established the Abandoned Property Custodian Board to manage property "abandoned" by departing Asians.[19] This board—headed by six prominent cabinet ministers—was responsible for organizing business allocation committees to redistribute appropriated assets and properties.[20] Amin seconded thirty military officers to work closely with the committees to ensure that the interests of the armed forces were well served. When the officers complained that the civilian committee leaders were "too slow," he replaced them with military men.[21] Soon, the new military-led committees began redistributing businesses that had already been allocated. Not surprisingly, most of the businesses they reallocated moved from civilian to military hands. Despite Amin's promise to give indigenous citizens economic power, soldiers and high-ranking military officers were the chief beneficiaries of the expulsion.[22] The state never bothered to compensate Asians for the value of their property.[23]

Uganda then witnessed the birth of a new socioeconomic "class" made up of military men and their female companions. Because of colonial recruitment practices, most members of the armed forces hailed from the northern part of the country.[24] Soldiers from Amin's home region of West Nile became particularly prominent during this period. They were collectively known as Nubians. Although historically linked to urban centers of the north, they did not comprise a distinct ethnic group. Anyone could become Nubian if they learned the language and practiced Islam. Throughout Amin's tenure, this was a particularly lucrative identity to embrace. Once the state began reallocating the property of departed Asians, Nubians (and other select beneficiaries) became known as the *mafuta mingi,* or those who were "dripping in fat."[25] Known for their flashy style and conspicuous consumption, the mafuta mingi enjoyed unsurpassed economic privilege and great political power—at least while they were on top. Once the original beneficiaries fell out of favor with the regime, the state redistributed their properties and a new group of mafuta mingi emerged. Increased rivalry and suspicion led people to begin killing one another for material gain. In local parlance, this was known as *okuliira mu kavuyo,* or "eating in the confusion."[26]

While scholars have analyzed the mafuta mingi on the basis of religion (Islam) and ethnicity (erroneously reduced to Nubian), most have overlooked its gendered dimensions. Nakanyike Musisi is a notable exception. In her work, she describes mafuta mingi as a group of men who victimized innocent women. She writes that "many innocent young women fell victim to these men through whom they had access to luxurious meals and lifestyles."[27] Although countless women undoubtedly did "fall victim" to "these men," it is important to remember that not all mafuta mingi were men and not all women were victims. Some women appropriated the Nubian identity to accumulate wealth and become mafuta mingi themselves. In a 2005 interview, Irene Lubega, a fifty-year-old secretary from Kampala, suggested that a woman might don a veil in order to look Muslim. She explained that "if you had veiled yourself and went to the factory, let us say to get soda . . . it was easy . . . so most businesswomen knew that if you looked like a Muslim, then you were able to succeed."[28] Christine Obbo first identified this interesting pattern in the late 1970s while she was conducting fieldwork for her doctoral dissertation in anthropology. She discovered that many women used "Nubianization" as "a strategy . . . either to acquire respectability by counteracting negative stereotypes and images of urban women, or as a cushion against the rootlessness resulting from separation from the rural home."[29]

Nearly thirty years after Obbo completed her research, I found that women described Nubianization less as a strategy for promoting female respectability than as a means of economic empowerment. Women in Buganda, for instance, regularly dated Nubian men for financial gain. Winnie Mugenyi, a sixty-year-old retired nurse, explained that during the 1970s, women would befriend Nubian men to get money. She remembered that "Amin's soldiers had a lot of money. When they befriended girls they would give them money. Therefore, those girls liked them so much."[30] They were proud to be called mafuta mingi because it signified that they had become rich. Other women utilized their romantic connections with military men to establish businesses. Goretti Ssali, a fifty-nine-year-old teacher, explained how Baganda women in particular manipulated Nubian men's affections to get ahead: "During that time, more especially women from here [Buganda], those men liked them so much. They thought that it was a [matter of] pride to get a Muganda woman. They used to give them money. They gave them money, and women from here were very smart. When they gave them money, they would develop themselves. There are even women here who built houses through these men who were Nubians. . . . So when they gave them money, the women decided to start their own developments. They were smart [*laughter*]."[31]

Goretti's statement confirms Obbo's observation that Ugandan women in the 1970s "used their reproductive abilities to improve their social status."[32] In fact, some women even married mafuta mingi men in order to support their *real* families. Victoria Mwaka, a professor of geography at Makerere University and a former member of Parliament for Luwero District, explained, "The army men couldn't write so what they did was to get the woman who was literate to run the shop and then when these men would die on the front line . . . the woman would remain in the business and many prospered because of that. So that's another way how they succeeded. Others worked and would be sending money to their homes—their mothers, their fathers—building houses and so forth and they pretended to be very good housewives, especially women here from Buganda. They benefited a lot from these army men."[33] Intimate relationships allowed many women to use their sexuality for economic empowerment, particularly within Buganda. They took Nubian lovers (or even husbands) to gain access to businesses, gifts, and/or scarce commodities. Although this strategy benefited some women as individuals, it ultimately reinforced an economic system that exacerbated the labor burden of many other women, which I discuss below. This is why the mafuta mingi windfall did not, in and of itself, "liberate" Ugandan women.

THE ECONOMIC CRISIS AND
WOMEN'S STRUGGLE TO SURVIVE

Despite their privileged economic status, the mafuta mingi were not a social class, because they were incapable of generating wealth and remained outside of the formal economic structure. Few of these new "entrepreneurs" had any relevant managerial skills. Many, in fact, were illiterate and had no idea how to determine the price of stock or reorder merchandise. James Zikusoka, one of Amin's former ministers, told me that if a woman walked into a Ugandan shop in the months following the expulsion, she was likely to find that the "price" of a shirt was actually the size printed on the label. He said that merchants simply assumed that the labels indicated the prices.[34] This lack of business acumen is hardly surprising, given that Asians owned 77 percent of the nation's industries prior to the expulsion.[35] Few Africans had the opportunity to work within these enterprises, save for the lowest entry-level positions. When the Asians departed, Uganda experienced a massive skilled labor crisis.

The shortage of skilled workers had a devastating effect on industries. Between 1972 and 1979, industrial production fell to less than 30 percent of its original level.[36] The loss of production made it difficult for the government to receive foreign exchange, which it desperately needed to purchase spare parts. Once factories were no longer able to operate, the industrial, agricultural, and transportation sectors collapsed. Lower-income groups were the hardest hit because the prices of essential commodities increased at a much faster rate than those of luxury items. Between 1971 and 1977, for instance, the cost of living in Kampala rose by an astronomical 531 percent for low-income workers, 369 percent for medium-income workers, and 234 percent for high-income workers. Many unskilled laborers had little choice but to return to the rural areas.[37]

Essential commodities did not merely become prohibitively expensive but in many cases disappeared altogether. Ugandan women repeatedly told me, "You could be with money but you couldn't get a bar of soap."[38] There was simply nothing to buy. Commodity shortages made life infinitely more difficult, as seventy-year-old Angela Mukasa lamented: "We lacked sugar. We lacked oil. We lacked . . . eh! We used to lack everything. We lived in misery."[39] Many women said that they spent a significant amount of time standing in queues for government rations. Because supplies were limited, they got up early in the morning to line up for whatever item was available. Sometimes they waited outside all day only to find that the commodities were gone by the time they got to the front of the line. Florence Mubiru, an elderly farmer, recalled:

We used to make lines for all. . . . We would wake up early [in the] morning, go there and leave around seven o'clock [p.m.]. You haven't eaten or drunk anything yet they haven't even brought the sugar. Even the next day, you go back. They could say that they're bringing it tomorrow early morning, so you go there. You could easily spend three days but when sugar is nowhere to be seen.[40]

The waste of time and productivity was a source of great frustration for those forced to stand in queues. Mary Kyomukama, a forty-nine-year-old former secretary, remembered the hardship:

After Asians had left, we suffered a lot because just like I told you, if you were going to get sugar at two o'clock or four o'clock you would start lining [up] for sugar right from seven thirty in the morning. And you were there . . . when pregnant. You'd stay there hungry and while you had a baby. You couldn't even get a banana. You feared moving out of the line because they could give you some sugar, a kilo or half. But most used to care most for those with children or if she was pregnant. Those were the ones who would be the first to get [sugar]. But sometimes they could give [it to] ten people and then sugar would get finished.[41]

This distribution system prevented women from engaging in productive labor, while at the same time it exposed them to hunger, dehydration, and heatstroke. Because young children frequently accompanied their mothers, they experienced the same risks. Many women also sent their older children to queue in different lines to maximize their chances of getting commodities. A young Muganda woman named Agnes Kato described this strategy: "You know commodities . . . were very scarce and getting them was so difficult, for example, sugar, salt—those commodities used in daily life. They were difficult to get. . . . That's the time I remember that we used to line up. We were about five children at home and we were all given money to go and line up to buy soap so that we got more soap in the home or if they were giving a quarter kilo of sugar, then you would all go and buy that."[42]

Unfortunately, this important survival strategy deprived many children of education. Economic scarcity compelled young girls to spend entire days lining up for soap or sugar, which meant that they were unable to attend school. But without an education, their chances for future economic empowerment were severely limited. Amin's government also did little to promote education. According to World Bank statistics, government spending on education decreased from 4.1

percent of the federal budget in 1970 to 1.2 percent in 1980.[43] Either out of necessity or in the hopes of "eating in the confusion," many children stopped going to school in the 1970s. Amin's antieducationalist policies have left an enduring legacy that can still be seen today.

Members of the political or military elite did not have to contend with the endless queues. Instead, they benefited from a different type of distribution system that was designed to appease Amin's most important allies. In late 1974, the government created Food and Beverages Limited, a parastatal organization that imported and distributed goods to select customers according to their "status group." Ministers and top army officers were classified as Grade One, while university deans, permanent secretaries, and managing directors were categorized as Grade Two. The government supplied each customer with an identification card. These photo identity cards entitled the bearer to purchase a wide variety of goods at normal prices on specific days.[44] Lydia Balemezi, a former member of Parliament for Mukono District, recalled that lower-level civil servants also received shopping cards: "For me as a worker, a government employee, we had our small shop and that is where every employee in the area would go. But they would assign us days. They'd say, 'The women, you go on such and such a day. Pregnant women, you go on such and such a day.' Yes, because pregnant women couldn't stand. They couldn't manage standing all the day long to wait in the queue."[45]

In addition to the VIP shops, the army battalions also had their own canteens, supplied by Amin's twice-weekly "whisky run" from England's Stansted Airport to Entebbe. One of Amin's former ministers estimated that each flight carried approximately $70,000 worth of goods: sugar, tea, golf clubs, music cassettes, toys, cameras, car accessories, televisions, clothes, shoes, bikes, whisky, brandy, gin, radios, cigarettes, and so forth.[46] The government allowed soldiers to purchase these items for personal consumption or resell them on the black market for a substantial profit.

Given the economic crisis and the resultant lack of foreign exchange, how was Amin able to pay for these "whisky runs"? The answer is coffee. Amin's regime was able to survive for so many years, at least in large part, because of the world coffee boom in the mid-1970s. Ugandan coffee was an extremely valuable commodity, but because of economic sanctions, brokers had to find alternative ways of getting it to market. Highly organized smuggling networks soon emerged, routinely moving vast quantities of coffee across the border into Kenya, where they exchanged it for foreign currency. So lucrative was this enterprise that the Ugandan government established an Anti-smuggling Unit in 1975 to crack down on this illicit trade. Instead of targeting the high-ranking military officers who controlled the bulk of the trade, however, officials arrested low-level smugglers, many of whom were women. Hope Mwesigye, former minister for agriculture, animal industry, and fisheries and a former member of Parliament for Kabale District, recalled, "Commodities started disappearing to the extent that actually people started going to Kenya to buy sugar—a kilo of sugar! And they could [arrest] people. I remember some people were arrested at the border carrying a kilo of sugar, two kilos, calling that smuggling, you know? So things became difficult."[47] Even though women risked arrest to smuggle a small amount of coffee or sugar across the border, they did so to survive. They had no other choice. In fact, when I asked Enid Kisembo, a sixty-two-year-old businesswoman, if she had ever participated in the trade, she laughed and replied, "Why wouldn't I? How could you be in a shop without smuggling?"[48] In other words, smuggling had become a way of life.

In addition to essential commodities, women also smuggled money throughout the countryside. As roadblocks and random household searches became commonplace, women resourcefully hid money in various interesting places. Margaret Mutibwa, a sixty-four-year-old teacher, talked about how she hid money in her "puffed hair."[49] Ritah Lukwago, a seventy-seven-year-old retired farmer, described how she used to sew money into her clothes: "Those double clothes where they joined it, we would sew and it's where we hid our money and it was pushed to one side. . . . You tell him [soldier at roadblock] that there is nothing while you are holding there and you are busy spreading your clothes [*laughter*]. They would check in your hair, in your bra, everywhere. They even checked in our panties!"[50] Security agents did not think twice about strip-searching passersby, nor would they hesitate to humiliate a woman in an attempt to find money. Some women resorted to hiding money in their babies' diapers, a risky endeavor because, according to Ritah, if "they found money in a baby's nappy . . . they shot the baby. . . . They would kill the baby and so many were killed in that way!"[51] Under the Economic Crimes Tribunal Decree of 1975, the state classified smuggling as a capital offense that was punishable by death.[52] Yet despite the inherent risks, smuggling remained an important survival strategy for many Ugandan women.

Those who were unwilling or unable to take these sorts of risks either did without or looked for natural alternatives. For example, some women used papaya leaves in place of soap. Evelyn Nyanzi, a forty-five-year-old teacher, laughed as she remembered, "Soap, we weren't seeing it. . . . [W]e even washed using flowers, papaya. But it was the flower that used to wash the best. Yes, we were young children but [we] used to wash clothes using those things."[53] Another woman said that she did not like to use these types of local products because "the solution caused cotton clothes to get torn very quickly." Instead, she recalled, "I would start filtering fat or any kind of oil, boiling it until a black sediment was left at the bottom of the pot. I would carefully scrape that sediment and compact it in a container to get shape while it cooled. I then used the tablet for washing clothes and bathing."[54] Other women remembered squeezing sugarcane into their tea or simply doing without.[55] The mafuta mingi, of course, were immune to these ravages of poverty, since they were the chief beneficiaries of the expulsion. For these high-ranking military men and women, there were no queues or shortages, only celebrations of conspicuous consumption.

THE ROOTS OF ECONOMIC "EMPOWERMENT"

When I was conducting fieldwork for this project, I asked women to talk about their lives during Amin's rule. One of the most common responses that I received was that "Amin taught us how to work." This struck me as an odd answer, given that Ugandan women have always worked.[56] What I eventually came to realize was that their definition of work was directly linked to economic autonomy. By expelling the Asians, Amin created a space for some women to become successful entrepreneurs.[57] Many of the women who "learned" to work were compelled to do so out of economic necessity. Numerous married women told me that they could no longer rely on their husband's salaries because inflation had so severely devalued their wages. Others claimed that the precarious political situation forced them into the informal sector. Government agents routinely arrested and/or "disappeared" men who posed a threat to the military state. As more of their husbands, fathers, or brothers went into hiding, women had little choice but to look for income-generating activities. Despite the numerous challenges articulated above, the politico-economic crisis proved to be a blessing in disguise. Margaret Mutibwa suggested that "Amin taught people how to work . . . and they started being innovative and creative to widen their minds."[58] Goretti Ssali shared a similar perspective: "During Amin's regime is when women started to work. They started to get engaged in business. They got involved in trade and they started dealing in business. Business boomed so much. . . . I think it was because of the expulsion of Asians. All people got interest. They just lined up in front of the shops and one would be given a shop [*laughter*]. They just lined up."[59] Not every woman who lined up for a shop actually received one. However, the economic climate was conducive to entrepreneurship, and many women began their own businesses. According to Margaret Snyder, founding director of UNIFEM, "a veritable explosion of Ugandan African entrepreneurship was born out of the need to survive amidst chaos."[60] Miria Matembe, former minister of ethics and integrity and a former member of Parliament for Mbarara District, explained,

> Amin's period pushed women from inside homes into [the] public arena because of the hardships that did exist. . . . Every situation comes with an opportunity and a challenge and a disadvantage, so Amin's era actually came in with . . . a disguised opportunity, but it was an opportunity for women to be ushered into public life. . . . When things became so bad and hard— the economic war—women had to come out and [provide] for themselves. Moreover, many women who lost husbands had to come out . . . and see how to [provide] for themselves. Even in their hardship during the economic war, the men's income could not be sufficient, so women had to make ends meet.[61]

Women's extradomestic labor challenged traditional gender norms about "appropriate" feminine behavior. According to Grace Kyomuhendo and Marjorie McIntosh, "good" women did not historically work outside of the home unless they were engaged in service professions (that is, teaching or nursing). Only after the economic crisis began did society grant women the flexibility to earn an income *and* maintain their respectability.[62] One of the women I interviewed explained that because "women started learning jobs that weren't theirs," they gained more power within the household.[63] Winnie Byanyima, former member of Parliament for Mbarara District, expressed a similar sentiment:

> Peasant women came out of their homes to market their food and to look for paid work. In the process, many became permanent

workers or traders in the markets and towns. They learned how to earn money and how to spend it, became decision-makers, developed confidence and authority in their homes. Widows and other female heads of households struggled, some for the first time, to support their families alone. . . . The economic crisis, therefore, enhanced the position of many Ugandan women, especially poor and peasant women, and weakened the basis for men's domination.[64]

By earning their own money, women were better positioned to provide for themselves and their children. Because many were single parents — their husbands having fled into exile or tragically "disappeared" by the state — economic autonomy brought them tremendous relief. They did not have to rely on extended family members for financial support, which gave them a greater sense of independence. And as increasing numbers of women became entrepreneurs, the community no longer stigmatized trade as "male work." This empowered many Ugandan women, as Sylvia Kategaya, a fifty-two-year-old businesswoman, explained: "People were engaged in business and they were happy and they also got money. Before, people didn't know how to engage in business. But they learned during Amin's regime. He introduced business and people left villages and came to town. . . . Women wanted Amin because they were allowed to leave the villages and come to town. They learned how to do business or trade for poverty alleviation."[65]

Some women with access to capital became international traders, traveling to London and Dubai in search of products that would bring a high resale value. Because they usually traveled without a male escort, most of these women were labeled as prostitutes. Nonetheless, they had great financial success. In an interview for Margaret Snyder's *Women in African Economies*, Joy Kwesiga explained, "Women became international traders, taking empty suitcases to London to buy clothes to sell back home. In the 1970s and early 1980s they began going to Dubai. . . . When they returned, they invested in shops to sell their goods, and many of them built houses, established other ventures, and paid school fees."[66] The economic climate pushed a large number of women into business and gave them the courage to travel to distant countries abroad.

Others became entrepreneurs by default, inheriting Asian businesses after the initial beneficiaries parted ways with the regime.[67] Patience Ssekandi, a seventy-four-year-old retired headmistress, remembered when the government allocated a shop to her: "I even got a shop during Amin's regime when he chased [away] the Asians. I got a shop and that was the one that had sewing machines . . . and I was working. I served women. I used to sew nice clothes. I used to sew [for] wives of ambassadors. They would all come and the line was always there. I would sew for them and they were happy. That's what I managed to do."[68] As mentioned above, other women inherited businesses after their husbands "disappeared" or went into exile. By running these shops, they learned many valuable skills. Victoria Sebageleka explained:

> Amin was very frightened by rich men, by educated men, by men who had their own minds and wanted to go with business rather than get into politics. He started picking them up from their businesses and offices, so women started manning [sic] their husbands' businesses. This was the first time Ugandan women tasted running big businesses like dry cleaners, Bata Shoes—big, big enterprises. In my view, the businesses that were most successful in those days were the ones run by women when men were abducted or killed, and women stayed behind.[69]

These recollections confirm that the Asian expulsion was a powerful impetus for change, both pushing and pulling Ugandan women into a variety of new economic activities. By "teaching" women how to work, Amin inadvertently weakened the economic basis for male domination within the household, while at the same time undermining the masculine power structure of the military state.

⤳

Although the economic war brought tremendous hardships, it also presented women with new opportunities to become actively involved in the informal sector. This not only provided them with access to valuable resources but also played a significant role in reshaping gender relations in Uganda. At the highest rungs of the economic ladder, patronage politics ensured that Amin's closest allies received the most significant benefits from the Asian expulsion. Not surprisingly, most of these individuals were fellow soldiers from the north, men like Joyce Ondoga's late husband. While many of them attempted to run their newly acquired shops or businesses on their own, many others decided to turn them over to their wives, girlfriends, sisters, or mothers. As a result of their hard work and determination, many of these women were able to amass great wealth, thereby becoming known as mafuta mingi. Other women became members of this elite social "class" through their romantic liaisons with powerful men, strategically manipulating their lover's affections to get ahead. And still there were other groups of women whose success did not depend on a man's generosity (or folly) but instead was contingent on their ability to work the system, through either "Nubianization" or some other clever strategy. By engaging in these types of activities, mafuta mingi women experienced unprecedented levels of economic empowerment, which in turn helped to produce a new articulation of femininity within the military state.

Nonelite women also challenged gender roles and relations, which often weakened the basis for male domination within the household. Unlike the mafuta mingi described above, such women had little choice but to participate in new types of income-generating activities since most men—the traditional breadwinners—were no longer able to do so, because of the violent political climate. If a woman wanted to put food on the table or a roof over her head, she had to become an entrepreneur. And yet, because the country was immersed in a massive politico-economic crisis, her actions were not stigmatized. Instead, society granted her the flexibility to earn an income and also maintain her respectability. Does this chapter then suggest that women need violence and chaos to carve out an economic space? Or might it suggest that within every political and economic crisis, there is an opportunity to rethink gender norms? The answer depends on one's epistemological orientation, but from my perspective, it is always more productive to contemplate the possibilities of liberation, no matter how partial or accidental they may be.

5 ↦ Neither a Privilege nor a Curse
Women and the Politics of Empowerment

HELEN OYERU probably never expected that she would be standing before the United Nations General Assembly in December 1975, preparing to deliver an official address on behalf of her government. She was not a seasoned diplomat, nor did she have a great deal of international experience. Just six months earlier, she had been working as the district commissioner of Jinja, a respectable position but certainly not one that offered such a prominent political platform. When Amin appointed her as the permanent secretary in the Ministry of Provincial Administration in May of that year, he thrust her into one of the highest-ranking positions within the civil service. Oyeru may have been new to the game, but she quickly distinguished herself as a key player. Amin took notice and asked her to lead the government's official delegation to the International Women's Year Conference in Mexico City the following month.

The young Lugbara woman went to the United Nations on that cold December day to discuss her experiences in Mexico and to reiterate her government's firm commitment to women's empowerment. She told the esteemed body that in 1972, her country had supported the General Assembly resolution that proclaimed 1975 as International Women's Year (IWY).[1] By voting in favor of this resolution, she explained, "we stressed our determination to join the world community to intensify action in order to promote equality of women in the total development of friendly relations and cooperation among states and to strengthen world peace."[2] She described how her government had "meticulously prepared and actively participated in the activities of the international women's year," including sending a "strong delegation" to the global conference in June. "What Uganda stood for in Mexico," she said, "was being implemented at home," a potent symbol of the military state's commitment to equality, development, and peace.

Given the daily realities of life during Amin's rule, what accounts for his attention, at least in public, to issues of equality and women's rights? Most evidence seems to suggest that the beleaguered military dictator used women's issues to consolidate political hegemony and maintain a certain performance of power. He appointed women to important political positions and espoused rhetoric about women's empowerment because it bought him political capital, both at home and abroad. By tapping into global discourses about women's liberation, he was able to demonstrate, at least in theory, that he was a progressive political leader despite his military pedigree. Although Amin was not genuinely interested in empowering women, this does not mean that certain women did not benefit from military rule. Instead, as this chapter clearly demonstrates, the politics of empowerment were complex and resulted in various opportunities and challenges for Ugandan women.

THE PRINCESS AND THE PROMOTION

Elizabeth Bagaya enjoyed a privileged upbringing. As the eldest daughter of the king of Toro and the niece of the king of Buganda, she received a first-class education, both in Uganda and abroad. She was one of the first three African women admitted to Cambridge University, where she graduated with a degree in law in 1962. Three years later, in November 1965, she was admitted to the bar, thus becoming the first female barrister in all of East and Central Africa. Before she had an opportunity to celebrate her tremendous achievement, Bagaya received word that her father had passed away unexpectedly. Her family asked her to return home immediately to help her brother, the future king, with the transfer of power.[3]

Bagaya's homecoming was short-lived, largely because of mounting political tensions within the country. When President Milton Obote abolished the institution of kingship in September 1967, she and many other royals decided to flee. Bagaya's period in exile began in London, where at the invitation of Princess Margaret and Lord Snowdon, she took part in a Commonwealth fashion show. As one of the few black models on the runway, she created quite a buzz with her appearance, and soon she was inundated with modeling offers. Within a short period of time, she began gracing the pages of the world's top fashion magazines, including British and American *Vogue*. With the assistance of Jacqueline Kennedy, she met the editor-in-chief of American *Vogue*, who invited her to visit New York City. Once there, she signed on as a model at the Ford Agency, appearing in *Look, Life,* and *Ebony* magazines. She also began taking acting lessons, ultimately winning the leading role in the film version of Chinua Achebe's classic novel, *Things Fall Apart.*

By the time that Amin seized power in early 1971, Bagaya had become an international superstar. Given her tremendous success and popularity—both in Uganda and abroad—it was no surprise that she was courted for a position in the new government. The minister of planning and economic development, Apollo Kironde, suggested to Amin that Bagaya would make an excellent roving ambassador. Although the two had never met, Amin invited her to return to Uganda, along with several other royal exiles. Without hesitation, she jumped onto a plane and returned home. In the months that followed, Bagaya met with Amin on numerous occasions, discussing the various ways that she might involve herself in the nascent government. The two came to an agreement, and on July 21, 1971, Amin formally appointed her as the country's first roving ambassador.[4] He knew that she would lend respectability to his regime abroad and "soften" his image on the home front, thus making the military dictatorship more palatable to Ugandans.[5] The Uganda Council of Women (UCW) hailed Bagaya's appointment as "one of the biggest steps women in Uganda have attained," a political move that would "show the world that women of Uganda are at the same rank with the men."[6]

Although Bagaya's position required her to promote the regime on the diplomatic front, she spent much of her time at home, mobilizing Ugandan women for national development. She regularly traveled throughout the country, giving speeches to various women's groups about their responsibilities as "mothers of the nation." In an address to the UCW, the national women's organization at the time, she stated that "the role that mothers of the nation can play in terms of culture is more important than that of the leaders of this nation."[7] She said that if they wanted to protect their cultural heritage, they needed to pass on indigenous languages, poetry, proverbs, and songs to their children. The irony is that she herself was not a mother.

Bagaya also encouraged women to embrace modernity. During a speech at a women's leadership seminar held at Makerere University in early 1972, she told participants not to be afraid of losing their femininity if they competed with men. Instead, they should utilize their womanhood to pursue their goals. In other words, it was possible for a woman to be educated and modern, as well as a moral and cultural guardian.[8]

Over the course of Bagaya's first year in office, Amin became increasingly interested in her personal and professional affairs. Although it was standard protocol for the roving ambassador to brief the president after every diplomatic mission, Amin found ways of keeping a close watch on her movements. He required security personnel to accompany her on each of her trips, presumably so that they could report back to him on her behavior. He also issued warnings to various government officials to keep their distance from her. When Bagaya took a short leave of absence in early 1972, Amin ordered security agents to follow her. Once she returned, he confronted her about a series of rumors that had been circulating about the two of them at the highest levels of government. He expressed surprise that onlookers would think that their alleged relationship was a big deal. According to Bagaya's retelling of the story in her memoir, *Elizabeth of Toro: The Odyssey of an African Princess*, Amin reportedly asked the rumormongers the following question: "Am I not a man, and is Bagaya not a woman, what is wrong with that?"[9] Before she had time to respond, Amin invited her to join him on a trip to the Middle East. When she refused, he told her that he no longer needed a roving ambassador. Instead, she should focus her attention on issues closer to home. Bagaya interpreted her new responsibilities as evidence that Amin was taking Ugandan women seriously. However, one could just as easily surmise that the military leader was trying to keep closer tabs on her movements.

Amin then ordered Bagaya to consolidate all women's organizations into one national body, fearing that political opponents would use the various groups to infiltrate the country. One united organization, he believed, would be much easier to control.[10] Bagaya worked closely with Mary Senkatuka Astles, a senior community development officer, and Henry Kyemba, then minister of culture and community development, to organize a national women's conference in late November 1972. Amin opened the conference by asking delegates "to play an effective role in women's organizations and not to limit themselves in pursuit of their own interests." He promised to "leave no stone unturned" in his efforts to develop the nation and therefore wanted them to form one strong organization that would be "working for the interests of all Ugandans regardless of religion, tribe or section of origin."[11]

Bagaya's main responsibility was to encourage delegates to find a way forward. Did they want to dissolve all women's organizations and form one national body? Did they want to retain all organizations but be affiliated under an umbrella organization? Or did they want to dissolve all existing groups and form a new organization with a Department of Religious Affairs with Catholic, Protestant, and Muslim subdepartments? After nearly a week of deliberations, the delegates decided on the third option, since it would cater to important religious differences.[12] After the conference, representatives from ten major women's groups met with Bagaya to draft a constitution for the new national body.[13] Unfortunately, because of opposition from religious leaders and various cabinet ministers, this organization never got off the ground. It was a major setback, although the conference was not a complete failure because it inspired Amin to appoint another woman to a high-ranking political position. In March 1973, Mary Senkatuka Astles became the nation's first female permanent secretary.[14]

After the women's conference, Bagaya resumed her duties as roving ambassador. Even though Amin had reassigned her to other tasks, he continued sending her on various goodwill missions throughout the world. He made sure that top-ranking military and security personnel always accompanied her. Despite his insecurities, Amin needed her diplomatic skills. After briefly flirting with the idea of appointing Bagaya as his ambassador to Egypt in late January 1974, Amin quickly changed his mind. On February 19, the military leader shocked the nation with a bold announcement: Bagaya was to become the new minister of foreign affairs, the first female cabinet member in Ugandan history.[15]

Although there are several theories as to why Amin made such an unprecedented move, the most likely explanation is that he promoted her to publicly humiliate Michael Ondoga, then minister of foreign affairs. This occurred at a time when ethnic tensions riddled the army, as well as the nation more generally. One former minister, Paul Etiang, told me about a cabinet meeting in which Amin chastised the ministers for neglecting their portfolios and for engaging in "tribal activities," petty behaviors that he claimed were typical of women.[16] French filmmaker Barbet Shroeder was shooting footage for his documentary, *General Idi Amin Dada: A Self-Portrait*, and captured the tirade on

FIGURE 5.1. Elizabeth Bagaya is sworn in as minister of foreign affairs, 1974. *Source: New Vision Printing and Publishing Company, Kampala, Uganda.*

film. In a grand performative gesture, Amin told the ministers,

> All of you, you are in very high-ranking governmental posts. Your duty is not to be very weak. You must not be like a woman who is just weak and he [*sic*] can't speak, even talk. . . . You should not be like [the] minister of foreign affairs. . . . This is the weakness of the Ministry of Foreign Affairs. If I see the minister is [a] coward, automatically I kick you out of my office because I know that you have got something wrong with you. I will put another person straight. . . . Whether [or not] you hide, you will be known.[17]

Unfortunately for Ondoga, this warning was no joke. After the meeting ended, Amin ordered the ministers to go to Makerere University for an important announcement. Once there, he asked Bagaya to join him at the podium as his new minister of foreign affairs. According to Etiang, the students did not know how to react. One asked what would happen to Ondoga. Amin assured the student that he would be reassigned. Within twenty-four hours, however, the former minister was dead. It seems likely that Amin promoted Bagaya solely for the purpose of insulting and humiliating an ethnic rival. His actions demonstrated that even a "weak" woman could do a better job.[18]

Although Amin orchestrated this changing of the guards to emasculate Ondoga, it also served to enhance Bagaya's reputation as an unusually strong woman. He wanted a minister who was powerful— not "like a woman who is just weak." Amin confirmed this sentiment when he swore Bagaya into office. He challenged her to be as tough as the women prime ministers in Israel, India, and Sri Lanka, warning that if she failed she would have "let down the country and downgraded [her] womenfolk."[19] In the months that followed, Bagaya demonstrated her fierce loyalty to the regime, garnering significant support for the military government, particularly within the Arab world. One of her crowning achievements as minister came in September 1974, when she delivered a biting indictment of "Western imperialism" before the United Nations General Assembly. Amin was delighted by her speech and awarded her with a prestigious medal, the Order of the Source of the Nile (Second Class).[20] Amin urged her to cut short her diplomatic mission and return to Uganda as soon as possible, worried, perhaps, that she would defect, as many other members of his regime had done.[21]

Bagaya refused to cancel the rest of her trip, although she had no intention of defecting. When she returned home several weeks later, she found that Amin had sent all of his ministers on leave. This was something that he did on occasion to weaken their political control and demonstrate his personal sovereignty. After Bagaya debriefed Amin on her travels, she began her own month-long furlough. Shortly after settling into her new routine, she remembered receiving a phone call from one of Amin's close friends, Roy Innis, the American-born leader of the Congress of Racial Equality (CORE). Innis asked her if he could come by to chat. Bagaya obliged his request and invited him over. When he arrived at her door, he got straight to the point: "If Amin asks you, will you marry him?" Bagaya told him that this was out of the question, since Amin was a married man. Innis responded by saying, "If he asks you, I shouldn't refuse if I were you. It will be very dangerous." And with that, he left.[22]

At the end of the month, Bagaya returned to her work at the ministry. Before she had a chance to settle into her normal work routine, Amin summoned her to his chambers and then relieved her of her duties. A group of police officers escorted her to her official residence and proceeded to search her house. They returned that evening to arrest her. After forcing her to spend the night in jail, they released her on house arrest. According to a declassified report issued by the U.S. Department of State, Bagaya had been tortured while in police custody. A Ugandan informant told the U.S. ambassador to Kenya that she showed signs of "being badly beaten and having her head shaved with broken glass."[23]

Meanwhile, Amin told the press that he had fired her for "the good of the country and the interests of the security of Uganda and Africa as a whole."[24] He alleged that she inappropriately utilized government funds while attending the United Nations General Assembly Meeting in New York. Amin claimed that in addition to spending exorbitant sums on lavish dinners and expensive clothing, she had met with CIA operatives who had succeeded in brainwashing her. He said that on her way back to Uganda, she passed through Orly Airport in Paris and "made love to an unknown European in a toilet." Amin stated that her behavior "ashames [sic] and degrades the standard of women in Uganda." Her actions, he said, were immoral and therefore a threat to national security.

When the police placed Bagaya on house arrest, they ordered her to account for all of the money she had spent during her trip. Because she and her accountant kept detailed receipts, she was able to account for all expenses. French authorities soon issued a formal statement about the airport incident, insisting that it could not have taken place, since she was under diplomatic escort the entire time. Ugandan authorities were unable to charge her with a crime, so they released her from house arrest. Although she did not plan to go into exile, everything changed on January 24, 1975, when the daily newspaper plastered her "nude" photograph across the front page.[25] The newspaper published the photo as "proof" that she had had sex with an unknown man in a Paris bathroom. Several months later, they reprinted the picture to remind readers of her "guilt."[26] At this point, Bagaya felt that she had little choice but to flee. She went into hiding and eventually made her way across the Kenyan border on February 8, 1975. She did not return to Uganda until Amin was overthrown.

INTERNATIONAL WOMEN'S YEAR

Three days before the publication of Bagaya's infamous "nude" photograph, Amin appointed Bernadette Olowo as the ambassador to the Holy See, the first woman in nine hundred years to become an envoy to the pope.[27] Just three months earlier, she had become the first woman in Uganda to lead a diplomatic mission abroad. Although she was not

FIGURE 5.2. Ambassador Bernadette Olowo (*center*) calls on Amin at his Command Post, 1975. *Source: Photographic Section, Ministry of Information and Broadcasting, Kampala, Uganda.*

trained for the position, she happened to be in the right place at the right time. In October 1974, the entire diplomatic team in Bonn defected. The young commercial secretary was the only one to remain behind. Amin was so impressed by her loyalty that he promoted her to the rank of ambassador. She was only twenty-seven years old.[28]

Amin cited Olowo's promotion as evidence of his ongoing commitment to women's empowerment. But this commitment was shallow at best. In actual fact, Amin was involved in a complex game of using women's issues to consolidate political hegemony and maintain a certain performance of power. He wanted people to believe that he cared about such issues because he knew that they would buy him political capital. By tapping into global discourses about women's liberation, he was able to demonstrate his "progressive" politics. Amin's vision for women's empowerment was one that positioned them as "mothers of the nation" who would contribute to the economic and cultural development of Uganda. It is telling that he inaugurated International Women's Year celebrations on May 1, otherwise known as "Worker's Day." In a midnight address to the nation, Amin articulated his position on gender equality: "Men in Uganda have not looked at women as co-associates, or shall I say, co-passengers on the same bandwagon of development. Today we must resolve to refuse to accept that type of thinking. Since the establishment of my Government," he explained, "many ladies have been appointed to hold top and responsible jobs. . . . We in Uganda are happy to report that we have really demonstrated in practice and theory that it is not a privilege to be a woman. Neither is it a curse."[29]

Madina Amin also addressed the crowd on this historic day. As first lady, she served as an important role model for Ugandan women. After her husband divorced his first three wives in March 1974, she willingly took up the mantle as "mother of the nation."[30] Her speech, much of which is reproduced below, confirms the importance of women to society as workers *and* as mothers:

> The importance of women in any society cannot be overemphasized. We know that there is no society or development without the efforts of women and we women in Uganda are very proud to say that we have alongside our men tried to develop this country using the most abundant talents we have. . . . We have been responsible and we shall continue to do so. Come what may, the women of Uganda must prepare to refuse to accept [the] thinking that it is only men who can initiate action. We must at all times show men particularly in our society that we are useful and that we can do things which they can do if not better. . . . Women realize that we are different from men because we know nature has made us different with physical attributes. However, we maintain that we are not inferior to men or that we are superior to men but what we maintain . . . [is that] men and women are equal human beings with a duty to making a contribution to the nation. The women of Uganda have made very many strides in their empowerment to improve the gap between themselves and men. It is very important for me to tell you now that if you look at any great man in Uganda today, living or dead, you will always find that a woman has contributed very much to his being great. My fellow women, this is a very great achievement and I challenge men to come forward to say that this is not true. . . . In our nation today, we have Ugandan women permanent secretaries. We have had Ugandan women ambassadors, district commissioners and other highly placed women officers, not only in the private sector but also in the government structure and in voluntary organizations. Think of Ugandan women in nursing, midwifing, banking, religious institutions and others who have just decided to do social work in voluntary organizations. The numbers are far greater than that of men. . . . *The greatest responsibility we have however in society is that of being mothers. We are either actually mothers or potential ones but the fact remains that we are mothers. We must at any time play the role of mothers to*

*our men but we must also remember that our men must also play
the role of our fathers.* You can easily see the need for interdepen-
dence between the men and women in our bid for economic
and political development. We should therefore not pick favors
from our men but instead demonstrate that we can do any work
that men can do if not better. There has been an allegation by
men that we are shy and lack physical stamina. . . . I say to you
that the women in Uganda are not shy because we are women
and are not physically weak because we are women.[31]

Madina clearly understood the significant contributions that Ugandan
women made to the nation, in terms of both economic and political development. Although these kinds of activities were important, she wanted
them to understand the social and political significance of motherhood.
She urged women to remember that this should be their first priority,
their greatest contribution to the nation. The rhetoric of empowerment
was particularly useful because it gave her and other representatives of
the state a platform upon which to discuss women's citizenship duties.

Six weeks after the inaugural celebration, Amin sent an official
delegation to the World Conference on Women, which took place in
Mexico City from June 19 through July 2, 1975. This conference, organized by the United Nations Economic and Social Council and its
Commission on the Status of Women, focused international attention

FIGURE 5.3. Madina Amin visits Namagunga Primary Boarding School on Parent's
Day, 1975. *Source: Photographic Section, Ministry of Information and Broadcasting,
Kampala, Uganda.*

on the need to develop future-oriented goals, effective strategies, and plans of action for the advancement of women. The conference was a large success with 133 official delegations in attendance, 113 of which women headed. The conference also featured a parallel forum for members of nongovernmental organizations, which attracted an additional four thousand participants.[32]

Amin asked Helen Oyeru to lead the Ugandan delegation, even though she knew very little about women's rights or the status of women. Mary Senkatuka Astles, the permanent secretary in the Ministry of Culture and Community Development, and Marjorie Ddungu, a senior education officer in the same ministry, organized a three-day workshop at Makerere University for the delegates. They invited Joyce Mpanga, a leading women's rights activist, to provide a daily keynote address to participants about the theme of the conference and why it was important to Ugandan women.[33] Shortly before the team left for Mexico, Amin and his wife held a luncheon in honor of the delegates. During this event, the military leader reiterated the delegates' importance as cultural ambassadors. Because their actions were a reflection of the nation, he warned them to "behave" themselves, as they were "mostly women and mothers."[34] He told them that the government would create a national organization to cater to women's affairs, even though there is no evidence to suggest that such an organization was in the works.

FIGURE 5.4. Women delegates to International Women's Year meeting in Mexico, 1975. *Source: Photographic Section, Ministry of Information and Broadcasting, Kampala, Uganda.*

Amin's empty promises did not seem to faze the conference delegates. They proudly defended their government's efforts to promote women's equality, a daunting task considering the negative publicity associated with the regime. When it was her turn at the podium, Helen Oyeru highlighted the various opportunities that the military state had afforded Ugandan women in recent years: "Women in Uganda are encouraged to participate not only in public life but also in policy making. The advancement of women particularly in high-level occupations, has since 1971 been accelerated by the present government which has appointed them to top-level and responsible jobs, denied to them in the past."[35] Oyeru's presence at this important international conference was meant to signify the government's "commitment" to women's equality. It was a grand performance orchestrated by Amin to enhance the legitimacy of the military state. Yet it was not a complete ruse, because some women enjoyed new opportunities and status. Jena Doka and Farida Kateregga, for instance, received appointments as permanent secretaries within the Office of the President shortly after delegates returned from the conference.[36]

In the midst of International Women's Year celebrations, from July 28 until August 2, 1975, Amin hosted the annual conference of the Organization of African Unity (OAU). The decision to hold the international meetings in Kampala was highly controversial, and a few countries boycotted the event. Seretse Khama, the president of Botswana, was the first to announce his decision not to attend the conference. On June 27, he sent the following message to the OAU headquarters in Addis Ababa: "This decision has been taken because the Botswana Government fears for the personal safety of the members of its delegation, if they should attend the meeting in Uganda. The factors which have led to this decision are General Amin's apparent disregard for the sanctity of human life, and his exhortation to the armed forces in Botswana, Tanzania and Zambia to overthrow their elected Governments, because of their participation in recent attempts to find a peaceful settlement of the Rhodesian dispute."[37] The president of Tanzania gave a similar explanation for his decision to boycott the meetings. Nyerere said, "Tanzania cannot accept the responsibility for participating in the mockery of condemning colonialism, apartheid and fascism in the headquarters of a murderer, an oppressor, a black fascist and a self-confessed admirer of fascism. By meeting in Kampala, the Heads of State are giving respectability to one of the most murderous administrations in Africa. For this meeting will be assumed to have thrown the mantle of OAU approval over what has been done, and what is still being done by General Amin and his henchmen against the people of Uganda."[38] Zambia was the only other country to boycott the conference, although many African leaders signaled their dismay by sending low-level delegates to the summit. Out of forty-six member countries, only nineteen were represented by heads of state, fourteen of whom were military leaders themselves.

Amin ignored the controversy, focusing his attention instead on the various preparations that needed to be completed in time for the big event. Using financial donations from the Saudi Arabian government, he imported two hundred Mercedes Benzes, as well as a host of other luxury cars.[39] He also purchased a fleet of white motorcycles for the police to use during the conference. He later redistributed them according to military patronage networks.[40] In the posh hotels and gift shops, conference organizers made sure that scarce commodities made their way onto shelves. Amin carefully "staged" the country to create the appearance of political stability and economic prosperity. The clean streets and orderly markets masked the hidden dirt, the deeper layer of filth that the regime could not reveal to the outside world.[41]

The military dictator wanted his guests to believe that all was well within the "Pearl of Africa." On July 15, less than two weeks before the conference began, the Defense Council promoted Amin to the rank of field marshal in recognition of his "brilliant service to the state and the army."[42] Bedecked in a brilliant sky-blue uniform heavily laden with medals and stars, Amin proudly accepted the honor in front of two thousand loyal soldiers. In an additional display of political theater, Amin ordered all residents of Kampala to wear special costumes during the conference, which featured the military dictator's picture, the OAU symbol, and a map of Africa. Tailors across the city sewed countless shirts and dresses in preparation for the big event. When state officials discovered that some of them had sewn the clothing improperly by putting the map of Africa upside down or cutting the president's image in half, they lashed out, warning tailors to observe professional ethics by showing dignity to Africa and the head of state.[43] Kampala's provincial governor, Abdullah Nasur, suggested that "politically minded" tailors had defaced the outfits on purpose—a serious affront to Amin and the nation.[44]

One of the highlights of the conference was supposed to be the Miss OAU pageant, which organizers had designed "to promote mutual understanding and cooperation among Africans, especially women."[45]

FIGURE 5.5. Amin congratulates Miss OAU, Margaret Nasawuli, at Nile Mansions in Kampala, 1975. *Source: Photographic Section, Ministry of Information and Broadcasting, Kampala, Uganda.*

Instead of fulfilling these goals, the pageant ignited a firestorm of controversy and was a tremendous flop. More than two months before the contest took place, the *Voice of Uganda* published a derogatory cartoon, which features an unattractive woman with a young child in tow, applying to participate in the contest. The man behind the registration desk points to the application requirements: young (eighteen to twenty years old), attractive, single, capable of paying the fifty-shilling fee, and not a sugar mommy (implying that she might try to buy her way in).[46] Several weeks later, the state newspaper featured another disparaging cartoon. This one depicts a group of judges quizzing a Miss OAU contestant. Although they pose easy questions, the contestant gets every answer wrong.[47] Given the negative messages embedded within these cartoons, it is not surprising that organizers had a difficult time convincing women to enter the competition. When the state eventually held the pageant on July 26, there were only sixteen participants—all Ugandan. Margaret Nasawuli, a nineteen-year-old university student from Eastern Province, won the title.[48]

On August 1, the penultimate day of the conference, Amin grabbed headlines once again by marrying his nineteen-year-old girlfriend in an elaborate ceremony attended by visiting heads of state.[49] Amin met Sarah Kyolaba two years earlier when she was working as a singer in the Uganda Army's Suicide Mechanized Jazz Band. He fell deeply in

Cartoon depicting requirements for the Miss OAU Pageant. *Source:* Voice of Uganda, *May 10, 1975.*

The interview round of the Miss OAU Pageant. *Source:* Voice of Uganda, *May 9, 1975.*

The end of International Women's Year. *Source:* Voice of Uganda, *December 1, 1975.*

The return to "normality" after International Women's Year. *Source:* Voice of Uganda, *January 6, 1976.*

The "challenges" of equality. *Source:* Voice of Uganda, *February 19, 1976.*

love with the young Muganda woman, despite the fact that she was already engaged to another man. When Sarah gave birth on Christmas Day in 1974, Amin claimed the child as his own. The next day he sent his wife Madina to visit the new mother and her baby at Mulago Hospital. He made sure that a team of photographers was on hand to capture the "happy" scene so that it could be reproduced in the newspaper for a larger audience.[50] In the months that followed, Amin sent his bodyguards to collect Sarah on numerous occasions. When her fiancé finally protested, he was "disappeared" by security agents and never seen again.[51] Whether out of love or fear, Sarah ultimately agreed to marry Amin. Three days after the wedding, the couple repeated the ceremony due to "popular demand." The press dubbed the new bride "Mrs. Africa" in honor of her husband's role as OAU chair.[52]

The last several months of International Women's Year were relatively quiet, in large part because Amin was preoccupied with his new leadership position. He spent a significant amount of time out of the

FIGURE 5.6. Amin weds Sarah Kyolaba at International Conference Centre in Kampala, 1975. *Source: Photographic Section, Ministry of Information and Broadcasting, Kampala, Uganda.*

FIGURE 5.7. Amin meets with group of female pilot trainees at Cape Town View, 1976.
Source: Photographic Section, Ministry of Information and Broadcasting, Kampala, Uganda.

country engaging in various types of OAU business. This meant that many Ugandans finally had an opportunity to catch their breath, if only for a brief moment. Some women in the Uganda Police Force were not so lucky. In mid-August, Amin decided to create a squadron of female pilots for the Police Air Wing. He claimed that they would be the first such unit in Africa, Asia, or the Arab world. After recruiting thirteen promising young women, he urged them to be "very revolutionary by working very hard and by using their brains properly." He explained that it was up to them to raise the standard of women. If they failed, they would have let down all the women in Uganda.[53]

International Women's Year may have provided women with a variety of new opportunities, but it also placed high (and often unrealistic) expectations on them. Leaders regularly exhorted women to "prove their worth," to "start thinking seriously," and to "be active."[54] In Amin's Uganda, equality was *not* a given—a basic human right—but instead something to be earned. The rhetoric circulating in the press suggested that women's liberation was a limited-time offer, something that would fade into the background once IWY had come to an end. One telling cartoon, published on the first of December, features a woman nagging her husband to buy her a pair of shoes. She says, "You promised to buy me platform [shoes] today. Why hide here in the park?" The man looks up at her and replies, "Stop bullying me Anna. 1975 women's year is coming to an end and I gained nothing from you."[55] Instead of celebrating women and their contributions to development, this cartoon implied that men had done women a favor by "allowing" them to celebrate International Women's Year. They assumed that once the year ended, gender relations would return to normal.

MOVING BEYOND THE YEAR FOR WOMEN

Cartoons are designed to be funny or satirical, but this does not mean that they cannot be read as important historical sources. Often they tell us a great about social norms and expectations. Take the following sketch, which the newspaper published on January 6, 1976, less than one week after IWY celebrations came to an end. This cartoon features a woman beating a man with a frying pan. She says, "Take that, that and . . . You pig, never abuse my equal right[s] again—[you] hear?" The man replies coolly, "Stop riding me Bena. 1976 has dawn[ed]. I'll fight you back for husband right[s] and we make resolution."[56] This cartoon implies that men should reassert their "rights" as household heads. Another cartoon, published the following month, features a young couple and their child walking hand in hand. The child looks up at his father and says, "But dad, why does mom always want to use your money only yet you have agreed to [a] term of equality?"[57] The cartoon implies that women did not understand the true meaning of equality. Instead, they embraced the rhetoric of equal rights to take advantage of their hardworking husbands.

Despite the hostility promoted by the press, the military government honored its professed "commitment" to women's equality. On May 1, 1976, one year after the inauguration of International Women's Year, Uganda began celebrating Women's Day.[58] Amin gave a speech in Mbale to mark the occasion, promising to allocate a building that could be used as a headquarters if women agreed to form a national organization that would have ties to the "grassroots." He did not mention that women leaders had written a constitution for such an organization several years earlier, an initiative that the government ultimately stymied. Instead, he accused them of petty jealousies. "Some women in high posts find it easier to work with men rather than their fellow women," he said. "If you are in a big post you must work together and those below you must be loyal." He concluded his Women's Day speech by warning rumormongers not to gossip, because they were like "women prostitutes," perhaps implying that they were useless to the nation.[59]

The second incarnation of a national women's organization got off the ground one month later. On June 3, the state newspaper announced the formation of the Ugandan Women's National Council, which would serve as the national machinery for women's empowerment.[60] In early September, the government hosted a national conference, which gave participants an opportunity to discuss the structure and function of the nascent organization.[61] Although most wanted to maintain a network of independent women's organizations, Amin urged them to promote unity regardless of religious, tribal, or other differences.[62]

The president's push for unity ultimately undermined the autonomy of women's organizations. Instead of creating an umbrella organization, Amin abolished all independent women's groups when he enacted the National Council of Women Decree on Women's Day in 1978. Contrary to the expectations of those who had drafted the constitution for the new council, the decree stated that "no women's or girls' voluntary organizations shall continue to exist or be formed except in accordance with the provisions of this Decree."[63] This meant that all existing organizations had to apply for membership. If a group's application was rejected, the minister of culture and community development had the right to disband the organization. If the organization failed to comply, then every member would be guilty of an offense and liable to a fine of up to two thousand shillings. The state controlled which organizations would and would not operate. As a result, most women's groups became dormant or operated quietly underground.[64]

In September 1978, the military government formally launched the National Council of Women. During their first annual meeting, members (those brave enough to join) elected Molly Okalebo, the assistant information and education officer with the Uganda Family Planning Association, as chairperson. In her inaugural speech, she said that she would "stick to the wings of the plane and fly with her women-folk," implying that she would be a strong and responsible government ally. After expressing her appreciation to Amin for creating the council, she promised that women in the country would always rally behind the government through "humble ways."[65] It was, after all, the only way to survive the harsh repression of the dictatorship.

～

Helen Oyeru may have firmly believed in the government's commitment to equality, development, and peace, but most evidence seems to suggest that the military dictator's interest in women's issues stemmed from a different set of motivations, namely, to consolidate political hegemony and maintain a certain performance of power. Amin promoted women to high-level political positions for strategic reasons. In the case of Elizabeth Bagaya, he appointed her roving ambassador because he knew that she would lend respectability to his regime abroad and "soften" his image on the home front. This was a very popular move and seemed to make the military dictatorship a bit more palatable to Ugandans. She worked tirelessly on behalf of the state, encouraging women to be productive citizens and responsible "mothers of the nation." When Amin promoted her to minister of foreign affairs, he did so not because of her work with women but instead because it humiliated an ethnic rival. He emasculated Michael Ondoga by replacing him with a "woman who is just weak," and then killed him. Within a short period of time, Amin turned his wrath on Bagaya. When she rebuffed his amorous advances, he fired her and placed her on house arrest. He later added insult to injury by encouraging the newspaper to publish "nude" photographs of her as evidence of her supposed immorality.

After Bagaya fled into exile, Amin made several other high-level promotions, in large part because of International Women's Year. By tapping into global discourses about women's liberation, he attempted to demonstrate that he was a progressive—not repressive—political leader. The rhetoric of women's empowerment was also useful because it gave representatives of the state a platform upon which to discuss women's citizenship duties. Amin's wife Madina played an active role in molding women into "mothers of the nation," much as Bagaya and his first three wives had done during his early years in power. International Women's Year also coincided with Amin's election as chair of the Organization of African Unity, which meant that Uganda hosted the organization's annual conference. This provided yet another opportunity for Amin to perform on a global stage. Once the conference and IWY had come to a close, the state's interest in promoting women's issues lessened considerably. As hostility toward women mounted in the popular press, the government began chipping away at the autonomy of independent women's organizations. This culminated in the creation of the National Council of Women in 1978 as the only recognized national machinery for women's "empowerment." Unfortunately, this was a mechanism to control, not empower, the nation's women. As this chapter clearly demonstrates, the politics of empowerment in Amin's Uganda were certainly complex and oftentimes contradictory.

6 ↫ Widows without Graves

Disappearance and the Politics of Invisibility

CONSTANCE APUNYO sensed that something was terribly wrong when she heard the sound of unfamiliar vehicles pulling into her family's compound in the middle of the night. It was March 31, 1971—just two months after Idi Amin had seized power in a military coup—and insecurity was rife. Before she had time to alert her husband, the police superintendent of Fort Portal District, she heard footsteps moving toward the house. Within an instant, the intruders banged on the door and shouted, "We are police and we want you." Constance was terrified and did not make a sound. When one of them asked whether her husband was at home, she remained silent. The attackers began pounding on the windows, shouting in English and Kiswahili, "Today you will see. Even if you keep quiet, we know you are inside." A gunshot rang out, and the front door burst open. Constance bravely narrated the rest of her traumatic ordeal:

> They entered into one of the rooms but they didn't know which one we were occupying. They broke the door leading to the children's bedroom. They asked the children to tell them where we were sleeping, [*sic*] then the children showed them where we were. They forced us to open the door but we did not, eventually they broke the door. . . . Some people caught me and others caught my husband. . . . Some people were assaulting me and others tried to bring him outside. Then they brought him back in the bedroom. . . . Some people were taking away the property from the house and others were assaulting me and he was then

thrown outside and he was shot twice and I was in the sitting room when I saw him being shot and I heard him say, "I am dead." Some people argued that "why do we leave the woman— let us kill her too" and others said "what will she do with all these many children?" Then they threw me outside, and those who were outside returned me inside. When I returned in the house then one of them ordered me to sit down. He held his gun and shot but he missed me. One of them then picked me up and took me back to the bedroom. He picked up a bottle of beer which was there and he hit me on the head with it.[1]

Constance remembered that the man who hit her kept calling her "Akokoro," which was former president Milton Obote's home region. He was muttering, "You used to boast saying that you were a big man in the police." The group then debated killing her, but in the end they avoided the trouble, saying, "No, let us leave them; this is a bloody woman." They took most of the property from the house, including the car keys. After beating Constance and her children a bit more, they took her husband away. She managed to crawl to the bush naked, where she stayed until morning. When she reported the matter to the regional police commander, he said that there was nothing he could do. She believed that he and the other police officers were too frightened to help her. They even denied her request for transportation, forcing her and her six children to return to their home village in Lira on foot. She never saw her husband again.

During Amin's violent military dictatorship, clandestine security forces of the state "disappeared" countless Ugandans.[2] Most of the abducted were men, largely because they were the ones who posed the greatest threat to the state and therefore "deserved" the most heinous punishments. And yet, as Constance's story clearly illustrates, the violence of disappearance cannot be fully understood without serious consideration of women. They were the ones who were left behind, who were forced to pick up the pieces and carry on despite the tremendous hardships. They were the survivors, the ones who traveled near and far in search of their loved ones. And it was they—the wives, mothers, and daughters of the disappeared—who refused to be silenced, who gave voice to a crime that was supposed to leave no trace.

In an effort to more fully engender the history of disappearance in Uganda, this chapter critically examines the narratives of women who testified before a 1974 commission of inquiry that was investigating a spate of recent disappearances in the country. More than just a tragic litany of devastation and loss, these testimonies reveal important details about the workings of Amin's security apparatus. Most significantly, they confirm that the military regime's use of violence was far more calculated and strategic than has previously been imagined. Disappearance was not simply an unfortunate consequence of military rule but instead a deliberate ruling strategy that was designed to spread fear and stifle opposition. By analyzing disappearance as a performance of hypermasculine military violence, we can better understand the logic of political terror. These narratives also clearly demonstrate that most women's experiences of military rule were very different from those of men and reflected the logic of political survival.

A "MYSTERIOUS" PROBLEM

People started disappearing during the early days of Amin's rule. Some seemed to vanish without a trace, while others were violently "disappeared" in broad daylight. It did not matter whether one was rich or poor, a northerner or a southerner. Anyone had the potential to become a target. Because no one seemed to know who was responsible for the disappearances or even why they were occurring, an "aura of mystery" enveloped the nation. Former U.S. ambassador to Uganda Thomas Melady and his wife, Margaret, suggest that such ambiguity "engendered fear, but at the same time, people did not know who they should fear—the government or the robbers."[3] To stave off criticism, state agents insisted that any reports of violence and killings were "unfounded" and should be written off as the work of "confusing agents."[4] And yet the rumors continued.

In July 1971, people in Kampala began hearing disturbing allegations about a mass murder that had recently taken place in Mbarara at the military barracks of Simba Battalion. More than two hundred Acholi and Langi soldiers—so-called ethnic kin of the former president—were said to have been killed. The rumors prompted Nicolas Stroh, a freelance journalist with the *Philadelphia Evening Bulletin*, and Robert Siedle, a lecturer in sociology at Makerere University, to investigate. The Americans' inquiries must have uncovered some pretty damning evidence, because neither of them was ever seen again. After nine months of pressure from the U.S. government on behalf of the families of the missing men, Amin decided to establish an official judicial commission of inquiry chaired by Justice David Jeffrey Jones.

The commissioners issued their report in July 1972, but only after Jones had resigned from the High Court and fled the country. They found that senior members of the armed forces had in fact murdered Stroh and Siedle on July 9, 1971.[5] Although the government eventually paid compensation to the men's relatives in the United States, no one was ever charged with their murders.

Shortly after the publication of the Jones report, Ugandan women began speaking out against violence and disappearance. In late November 1972, for instance, Amin convened a national women's summit in an effort to connect with the masses. Although the forum was meant to discuss the role of women in nation-building activities, delegates used the opportunity to complain about the recent spate of disappearances.[6] One prominent activist, Thereza Mulindwa, boldly asserted, "We are tired of being widows without graves." She demanded a judicial investigation and implored Amin to intervene.[7] News of the women's complaints reached a broader audience through *Munno,* a leading Catholic daily. Several weeks later, the editor of the newspaper, Father Clement Kiggundu, was murdered, his charred body discovered alongside his burned-out car near the edge of a forest ten miles from Kampala. The autopsy revealed that he had been shot and strangled. According to one of Amin's former ministers, Edward Rugamayo, government agents killed Kiggundu "for daring to report the complaints, moans and groans of women whose husbands were mysteriously 'disappearing' or being publicly tortured and then murdered."[8]

In an effort to avoid further public condemnation, Amin appointed an ad hoc committee to investigate the disappearance of eighty-five prominent Ugandan citizens.[9] The government never revealed the actual members of this committee or their methods of inquiry. What we do know is that when they published their findings on January 9, 1973, blame fell squarely on the shoulders of the exiled president, Milton Obote, and his so-called confusing agents. According to an official government statement, it was Obote who had orchestrated the kidnappings in order to create "discontent and confusion in the country."[10] Obote had, in fact, attempted to topple the government in September 1972 when he launched an invasion from Tanzania. But he could hardly be blamed for disappearances that occurred long after the invaders had been repelled.

Amin recognized that if he was to maintain power, he had to convince the world that he could uphold law and order. In a speech given in early December 1973, he pledged to undertake new investigations to "unearthen [sic] the mysterious stealing and disappearance of people in Uganda."[11] Not surprisingly, this promise did not come to fruition until the International Commission of Jurists forced his hand by releasing a condemnatory report on violations of human rights in Uganda. On June 4, 1974, the same day that they released the report, Amin announced that he would establish his own judicial commission of inquiry to investigate all such allegations.[12] Wanume Kibedi, the exiled minister of foreign affairs, saw right through the smokescreen, sharply criticizing the decision in an open letter to Amin: "If you appointed not one but 10 'judicial commissions' to inquire into the disappearances, they would not be able to exonerate you. Nor would they be able to serve any useful purpose as long as you remain in power since, as all Ugandans know, you are the main culprit."[13] Despite the scathing criticism, Amin announced that he would move forward with the investigation "in the interest of justice, fairness, security and social tranquility."[14]

When Amin inaugurated the commission on June 30, 1974, he directed commissioners to "leave no stone unturned" in their search for evidence.[15] He appointed Justice Mohamed Saied, a British-Asian Muslim, to serve as chair. Other commissioners included Captain Haruna Salim, a military officer and agent for the notorious State Research Centre, and two police superintendents—Stephen M. Kyefulumya and A. Esau. Women were noticeably absent from the panel. Under the terms outlined in Legal Notice No. 2 of 1974, anyone who wanted to give evidence before the commission could do so in person.[16] Amin encouraged Ugandans to come forward to testify "without fear or favor." In an official public statement, he warned that if anyone tried to interfere with the proceedings of the commission or with any witness, such person should be reported to the security forces or to the president on telephone number 2241 Entebbe.[17]

Although the Saied Commission was supposed to begin its work on July 1, 1974, investigations did not get off the ground for another two weeks. Part of the problem was finding people to testify. Despite Amin's reassurances, very few were willing to provide evidence against a sitting military government. Local newspapers and radio stations continued to advertise the importance of the commission, and gradually people began coming forward.[18] By July 15, commissioners were able to commence their inquiry in Kampala. After three months of grueling interviews, the team traveled to the northern town of Lira. Although many signed up to provide evidence, time constraints allowed only ninety-two people to testify. There was also an abundance of witnesses in Kitgum, Gulu, Mbarara, and Fort Portal, which suggests that people believed it was an important and legitimate exercise despite the risks.

After completing nearly one year of work, the commissioners wrapped up their investigations in Kampala. When they delivered the eight-hundred-page document on June 13, 1975, Amin happily concluded that "the report would explain to the entire world that Uganda observed the rule of law, respected human dignity and tried in all ways to protect the lives of the people."[19] The report did no such thing, but that hardly mattered, since few people had the opportunity to read the massive tome. Amin never published the findings, and until recently only one copy of the document was said to exist in Uganda.[20] The point of the exercise was never to get to "the truth" but instead to make everyone believe that he actually cared about the "mysterious" problem that was plaguing the country. As such, it was a fine performance of political theater.

WOMEN'S TESTIMONIES

Amin's enthusiastic reception of the report clearly belied its sobering contents. In no way did it demonstrate that Uganda observed the rule of law, respected human dignity, or tried to protect the lives of the people. Instead, it chronicled a disturbing pattern of violence that had permeated the deepest layers of the nation's social fabric. Many of those who had the courage to speak out against the regime were women—the wives, daughters, or mothers of the disappeared. In fact, they constituted more than 30 percent of the 545 witnesses who testified before the commission. This is an impressive figure because women were not expected to engage in such overt political activities at the time. In painstaking detail, they bravely recounted unimaginable stories of loss and survival. Although they had the option of testifying anonymously or in camera, none chose to do so. They refused to be silenced. And now, because of the recent release of the commission's report by the U.S. Institute of Peace, we have the opportunity to learn what they had to say.[21]

Most of the women who testified before the commission were family members of the disappeared. (This was not necessarily the case for many of the men who testified; the state had summoned many of them to give evidence in an official capacity.) Because these women had experienced close personal losses, their narratives focused on three overlapping themes: (1) the physical and psychological trauma of witnessing the abduction of a loved one, (2) the tremendous challenges of searching for someone who had been disappeared, and (3) the hardships and/or losses that accompanied a disappearance. Their testimonies also reveal that men were not the only ones to be abducted. As we see from a limited number of poignant examples, the state also targeted women. Although it is impossible to describe "women's experience" of disappearance or abduction as if they were a homogenous group, it is possible to discern important similarities among the various case studies. This is an important first step toward engendering a history of disappearance during Amin's rule.

TO WITNESS

Women's testimonies vividly describe the physical and psychological trauma of witnessing the abduction of a loved one. Enforced disappearances were not hidden from view but instead orchestrated by the state as public spectacles that were meant to promote uncertainty and fear. Agulani Ayer, for instance, had to watch as her husband—a corporal in the Uganda army—was brutally beaten and dragged away, never to be seen again. At the time of the assault, the couple had been living in the military barracks at Mbarara, along with their six children. On the afternoon of July 15, 1971—nearly one week after the disappearance of Stroh and Siedle—military officials summoned her husband to attend an important meeting. Not long after he had gone, Agulani learned that he had been detained at the quarter guard. She was given permission to bring him some food and a blanket, although she was not allowed to visit him. When she arrived the next day, the guard returned the blanket and told her not to visit anymore because they were moving him to Kampala. Later that day, she saw a lorry parked near the quarter guard. The officers were beating the prisoners and shuttling them onto the truck. She described the horrific scene to the commissioners: "The first person who was brought out to be taken in the lorry, he was beaten until he died. The second person was brought but that one was taken in the lorry, the 3rd person was also beaten to death and my husband was the 4th one, having seen some of his fellow friends, he started falling down, he was beaten, he kept on falling down but all through this time I was busy trying to rescue my children who were also with me there."[22] Agulani remembered that all of the prisoners had their hands tied behind their backs. She said that her husband was nearly unconscious when the other soldiers threw him onto the lorry "like a bag of cotton." In total, they loaded nearly one hundred Langi and Acholi soldiers onto the trucks that day. Most of them died as a result of their injuries. Once the trucks pulled out of the base, the remaining soldiers taunted the women, saying, "They used to tell us that you Langi . . . were strong and you were boasting with your husbands." The commanding officer had to intervene so that the women could pack their things in peace. One week later, the wives of the missing soldiers received one month's salary and bus warrants to go home. Agulani recalled that about eighty women left the barracks en masse, children and possessions in tow. She was "lucky" in that she was able to collect most of her husband's property—save for a radio and a bed. She was also able to access money in her husband's bank account. Most women, as we shall see, were not as fortunate.

Margaret Acilo had a similar experience. Her husband had been a private in the army and was stationed at Jinja Barracks. She lived there with him and their four children. As she was outside bathing her baby on the evening of July 11, 1971, three loud gunshots rang out. She became frightened and quickly ran inside. Later that night, an armed soldier came to the door looking for her husband. She said that he was asleep, so the soldier went away. Later that night, she heard another knock. This time her husband went to the door. The soldier told him to get dressed and to come with him. He never returned home. The next day, she went to the office to report her husband's arrest. The officers had no information but asked Margaret to be patient. On the following day when she returned to the office again, they told her to pack up her things and go home. As she was leaving the barracks, a group of soldiers stopped her at the quarter guard. Instead of letting her proceed, the soldiers sent her back to her quarters. Shortly thereafter, she remembered hearing the crackling pop of gunfire, followed by a large explosion. Two days later, on July 15, she received a bus warrant and a small sum of money. As she was leaving the barracks with a group of at least fifty other women, she noticed that the quarter guard that housed the prisoners had completely collapsed. She received no word about her husband. He had simply "disappeared."

It is difficult to imagine what it would be like to witness a loved one's demise. Agulani saw her husband severely beaten and loaded onto a truck, essentially left for dead, while Margaret heard—and probably felt—the blast that likely ended her husband's life. Catherine Akoko's experience was slightly different in that she too was violently assaulted when her husband, who was a Kampala police superintendent, was abducted. The couple had been eating dinner in their home at Naguru Barracks on September 19, 1972, when they heard a loud knock at the door. Before they had a chance to answer, eight policemen from the Public Safety Unit burst in. They announced that the minister of internal affairs wanted to speak with the superintendent right away. When her husband picked up the phone to confirm the meeting, one of the policemen said that they had been sent to arrest him. Catherine explained what happened next:

> They started removing the belt, the hat and they started pushing him towards the car while others were trying to push us to go back to the house. But I did not want to [leave him.] They dragged me back to the house. I told them I would rather go with my husband where they were taking him on seeing how they were handling him. Then one of them threatened to shoot me if I did not go back to the house. Of course, we were dragged back to the house by force while they took my husband. But on the way while they were dragging me I could see them opening the boot of a car and put my husband in. Then they went away. I went back to my house.[23]

The following morning, Catherine went to see the assistant commissioner of police. He tried to find out who had ordered the arrest but received no assistance. Later that evening, the driver from the Public Safety Unit brought Catherine a note from her husband. He wanted her to bring the checkbook so that he could sign a check for the children's school fees. The next day she went to Makindye Barracks—a well-known prison and headquarters of the military police—with one of her sons. She was not allowed to see her husband, although she did get a signed check from him. He also sent along a message that he wanted a bank form so that she could withdraw his savings. When she returned with the form several days later, an official told her that they had transferred him to Luzira Prison. Before she had a chance to go there, she received orders to leave the barracks. Because her husband had been a high-ranking police officer, the government provided her with transportation to take her things back home. Later, when she returned to Kampala, she heard a radio announcement stating that her husband had escaped from prison and run away to Tanzania. Catherine knew that it was virtually impossible to escape from a military prison, but according to the state, he had simply disappeared.

TO SEARCH

The women who testified before the commission also discussed the tremendous challenges of searching for someone who had been disappeared. What is most striking about these narratives is the women's perseverance and bravery despite the many obstacles they faced. Instead of resigning themselves to fate, they courageously marched into the unknown, determinedly moving from person to person and place to place in search of answers. Their movements followed a particular social logic—one that reflected an intricate network of personal and political relationships. As the wives, daughters, or mothers of the disappeared, they called upon family, friends, and acquaintances for assistance. In turn, these persons moved the search in different directions depending on their own web of contacts. Most pursuits ultimately ended in Kampala, whether at the offices of a high-ranking government official, at the entrance to a military barracks, or at the edge of a forest or swamp. These were the places where the disappeared often became lost forever.

Lydia Acha's search followed a similar trajectory—at least at first. Her father was a chaplain for the Church of Uganda attached to Simba Battalion in Mbarara. On February 23, 1971, military officials called him to Kampala for a briefing. After three days, Lydia went to the adjutant and asked when her father might return. The adjutant showed her the orders from army headquarters. She pressed him for more information but sensed that he was reluctant to talk. He told her that "he himself may also face the same problem one day."[24] She then asked him for permission to go to army headquarters to see her father. He refused, but she decided to go anyway. When she got to Kampala, Lydia met with several other army officers, including Michael Ondoga, who was the commanding officer of Simba Battalion at the time. He told her that he had no information about her father. After three days, she decided to return to Mbarara. Once she was home, she ran into one of her father's colleagues at the barracks. He told her that he had seen her father at Luzira Prison recovering from severe injuries on his head, hands, and legs. He said that her father could no longer walk and was in a wheelchair. Lydia asked him to take her to the prison, but he refused, saying he would do it only if she became his girlfriend.

She ultimately decided to give up the search because, in her words, "I believe I do not have to offer myself to a man in order to [get him to] help me."[25] In April 1971, she received a bus warrant to return home. She never found her father, although evidence suggests that he was murdered in the "Mutukula massacre" in January 1972.[26] Lydia's testimony, the commissioners suggested, demonstrates the "degradation and moral bankruptcy of some of the soldiers of the Army."[27]

Christine Anywar also had a fierce determination to learn the truth. Her husband had been a police inspector stationed at Moroto. On the night of July 11, 1971, Christine was in the hospital giving birth to her fifth child. That was the same night that an Acholi guard opened fire at the barracks and killed seventeen people, including fourteen recruits and three instructors. Chaos ensued, and the shooter was able to get away. Christine remembered hearing the gunshots while she was in the hospital, but she did not know what was happening. The next day, the police arrested her husband, as well as many other Acholi and Langi police officers. The officer in charge suspected that they were guerrillas who were collaborating with the escaped shooter. When Christine got out of the hospital, she immediately went to see the police commander about her husband. He informed her that the military had detained the arrested men at the army barracks. Several days later, he told her to return to her home in Gulu because they had transferred the prisoners to Kampala.

From August 11 until the end of the year, Christine wrote numerous letters looking for news of her husband. She wrote to the chief justice, who forwarded a copy of her letter to the minister of defense. On September 23, the minister of internal affairs sent her a copy of a letter that he had recently written in response to the minister of defense's queries, explaining that there were no records of police officers in any of the government prisons. The former wanted the assistance of the latter, since the arresting officers had been soldiers from Moroto. Christine wrote another letter to the minister of internal affairs on October 28 asking for additional information and financial assistance. She later went to police headquarters to get permission to see her husband, who was imprisoned at Luzira. They told her that she needed to request a letter from the chief of staff if she wanted to see him. On November 9, she arrived at the prison with the mandatory letter. The guard told her that the chief of staff actually needed to call the prison. When she reported this request to the chief, he told her that there was nothing else he could do. Nearly at her wit's end, Christine wrote a letter to the chief of defense staff on December 13 and copied it to the bishop of the armed forces. In her letter, she said, "Have pity on me, poor wife and mother, and please send back my husband as soon as possible so that I and my children can have amongst us our dear beloved Wilson Anywar."[28] Despite her determined efforts, she never saw her husband again. She eventually lost all of their marital property to her brother-in-law after she refused to marry him (a cultural process known as widow inheritance). And although her husband had money in the bank, the manager refused to release it without a death certificate.

Both women clearly faced many difficult obstacles in their search for answers, ranging from sexual exploitation to bureaucratic hurdles. In the final case study, we get an even greater sense of the tremendous strength and fortitude it must have taken to sustain such a search. On October 4, 1972, Betty Odong received word that two men from Kampala had arrested her husband—the postmaster of Moyo—while he was at work. They claimed that he was wanted by His Excellency. She telephoned the commanding officer of Moyo Barracks, but he denied any knowledge of the arrest. The following day, she went to see the district commissioner, who promised to send his assistant to Kampala to look for her husband. When the assistant district commissioner returned, he said that he had found no evidence of her husband. On October 17, Betty traveled to Makindye Barracks in Kampala. At the main gate, a compassionate soldier from her home region told her, "Sister you go home. Don't waste your time. We are now as dogs. Sometime you may leave your husband in Karuma Falls or in the forest there."[29] (He was referring to popular "dump" sites.) Betty lost all hope. She knew that her husband was dead. Adding further insult to injury, she lost all of her household property and custody of her two children when she refused to marry one of her brothers-in-law.[30]

In these testimonies, we find numerous stories of women traveling far and wide in search of their loved ones. Commenting on the "extraordinary courage" of Ugandan women, one former British colonial official notes, "In the majority of cases it has been the wives, the sisters, the mothers who have tramped from the military police barracks at Makindye, to the Public Safety Unit at Naguru, to the Malire Regiment at the Lubiri, to the Air Force Detention Center at Entebbe, searching for their men." He suggests that it was "marginally safer for the women to make such efforts, but only marginally."[31] Women's narratives seem to support this assertion. Mary Ekit, for example, told commissioners that her brother-in-law had sent her to the police station alone because "women were in a better position" to make such inquiries.[32] The state imagined women as mothers of the nation who were supposedly incapable of subversion or sabotage. Of course, as we see below, this was not always the case.

Women traveled between prisons and barracks in desperate search of answers. They frequently hired professionals to accompany them into the forests and swamps that had become the most popular dump sites for bodies. Because of religious and cultural imperatives to bury the dead, body finding emerged as a lucrative new career, particularly for those with ties to the regime.[33] According to Henry Kyemba, one of Amin's former cabinet ministers,

> Body-finders work in teams. If anyone disappears, relatives immediately contact the team and arrange a fee for the tracing of the body. The teams are in daily contact with the murder squads. Sometimes news will come directly from the murderers, via the body-finders, who offer assistance to the relatives in finding the body. The fee varies depending on the status of the victim. To trace a junior official, the family might be asked for 5,000 shillings (600 dollars); it could take anything from 25,000 shillings (3,000 dollars) upwards to find the body of a senior member of the administration. There are also many bogus-finders who offer their services, take the money and vanish.[34]

At first, Amin's henchmen disposed of bodies by throwing them into rivers, swamps, or water reservoirs. Over time, however, Mother Nature could not keep up with the military government's momentum. As bodies floated to the surface, clogging dams and attracting vultures, soldiers had no choice but to begin throwing human remains into the bush.[35] Thus, the forests of Namanve, Najembe, Nandere, and Mabira will forever be remembered as the final resting place of countless disappeared.

TO LOSE

Another common theme focused on the tremendous losses that accompanied a loved one's disappearance. Betty and Christine, for instance, both faced significant hardships when they refused to marry their brothers-in-law. Local gender politics determined whether a woman was able to maintain her home, her property, and even her children. Military wives (and other loved ones) often had to cope with an added layer of difficulty because officials forced them to move out of the barracks within days of a family member's disappearance. They were given bus warrants and told to return to their home regions. Many lamented that they had not been allowed to take their property from the barracks or that the soldiers stole it as they were leaving.[36] The women who lived off-base faced similar challenges. Many women reported that when they arrived at the barracks to collect their husband's belongings, they were refused entry. Others said that they arrived on base only to find someone else occupying their husband's quarters and all of his property missing.[37]

Nakaliya Akello never received a bus warrant, because she had been attending a funeral in her home village when her husband was disappeared. The military seized power while she was away. By the time she returned to Jinja Barracks, her husband was missing. A soldier told her that he had been arrested, along with other Acholi and Langi soldiers, and taken to Luzira Prison. Not knowing what else to do, Nakaliya returned home. She left all of her property in the barracks, assuming that she would move back as soon as they released her husband. By July 1971, however, there was no change. Nakaliya tried to visit him in prison, but the guards did not allow her through the gates. In fact, she never saw him again, nor was she able to reclaim any of the property left in their quarters at the barracks. Although her husband was insured and had some money in the bank, she did not know how to access it.

The families of high-ranking military officers seemed to fare no better. Grace Atto, for instance, was married to a lieutenant who was stationed at Mubende. Instead of living in the barracks, she remained in Hoima with their two children. Grace received word that her husband and several other soldiers had been arrested and taken to Kampala on February 5, 1971. Ten days later, another officer arrived at their house with three large military trucks. He told her that she needed to vacate the premises, because they had arrested her husband. He informed her that her car would also be taken to Hoima Police Station for safekeeping. She and her father-in-law later went to retrieve the car but were told to wait until things "cooled down." Grace decided to go to Malire Barracks in search of her husband. Once she was there, officials told her that they had transferred all detainees to Luzira Prison. When she reached the prison, she learned that her husband was detained at Makindye Barracks. Once she reached Makindye, a soldier told her to go back home because it was "useless."[38] He said that her husband had already been killed. Before she could learn any additional details, the commanding officer chased her away. She had no choice but to return home. Months later, she tried to collect her car from the police station. She was told, however, that the car was being used by an army officer — the same person who had taken it there for "safekeeping."

Although many of the women testified about their financial hardships, few were aware of their legal rights as dependent relatives of the disappeared. In August 1973, Amin signed the Estates of Missing Persons (Management) Decree, which allowed a relative to apply to the courts to administer the estate of anyone who had not been heard from within six months.[39] (The previous law stipulated that one must wait three years.) It also reduced the length of time that had to lapse before a person who was missing could be presumed dead from seven to three years. In theory, this decree made it easier for women to manage the estates of their missing husbands. In practice, however, few knew about its existence and therefore never benefited from the law.

TO DISAPPEAR

Through women's testimony, the commissioners discovered that men were not the only ones to be disappeared. Although women's disappearances were much less common, agents of the state did also abduct women. Anna Kampi's story is particularly disturbing. According to her friends Mary Akurut and Grace Apio, both of whom testified before the commission, Anna's problems began when she was involved in a traffic accident involving a young child. The arresting officer told her that if she paid him a bribe, he would make the matter go away. Anna refused and reported the officer to the Criminal Investigations Division. They arrested the officer for corruption and then suspended him. One week before her disappearance, Anna met the same officer outside of the courthouse. He asked for her forgiveness. When she told him that she had no intention of dropping the case, he responded, "If I am chased away from my job do you think you will stay here in Kampala?"[40] Anna replied, "It does not matter even if you kill me. I want to go ahead with the case." On the night of August 7, 1973, roughly two weeks after the courthouse encounter, Anna went to see a movie with her husband. He told her friends that after leaving the cinema, six people abducted Anna at a nearby petrol station. When he tried to intervene, the men threatened to throw him in the trunk of the car if he did not leave them alone. Since one of the men had a gun, her husband was forced to run away. On August 9, Anna's body and that of another woman were found in Najembe Forest tied to some trees. Mary identified her friend's remains. She had a wound on her forehead and rope marks on her body. Mary later met the arresting officer and told him that everyone suspected him of the murder. He offered her a small amount of condolence money and asked whether they were going ahead with the case. She told him that it was impossible since the main witness was dead. This case illustrates the violent lawlessness that pervaded the country during Amin's rule. Anyone could become a victim—man or woman. Anna just happened to pose a threat to someone with "connections," and as a result, she was abducted and murdered.

Evasta Ndagano testified about the disappearance of her daughter, Margaret Matama, an assistant inspector of police attached to Interpol. Evasta remembered that her daughter had received a telephone call around lunchtime on August 21, 1973. Shortly thereafter, a car carrying three men pulled into their compound. Margaret went outside to speak to them, and soon they began to quarrel. Evasta watched in horror as the men bundled her daughter into the car and then drove away. Shortly thereafter, a neighbor took her to see Ali Towelli, the director of the Public Safety Unit, who was also her son-in-law. Towelli told her that he knew nothing about the kidnapping but promised to look into it. His investigations proved fruitless. Evasta had no choice but to leave police housing and return to her village home in Toro District. She never saw her daughter again.

The disappearances of Anna Kampi and Margaret Matama clearly demonstrate that men were not the only targets of the regime. The state also abducted women. We know much less about their experiences, however, because the state rarely investigated cases involving women. Out of the 308 disappearances examined by the commission of inquiry, only three involved women (i.e., 1 percent). If the realities in Uganda were anything like those in Argentina during the infamous "Dirty War," women likely accounted for at least 30 percent of the disappeared.[41] Because the state never investigated most of their cases, the disappearance of women apparently was never taken seriously by the state.

OUTCOME AND ANALYSIS OF THE COMMISSION

The final report of the Commission of Inquiry into the Disappearances of People in Uganda since January 25, 1971, is a fascinating read. By carefully documenting hundreds of disappearances—some in more detail than others—the report clearly demonstrates the culpability of the state in destroying the lives of countless Ugandans. Yet this is not how the commissioners interpreted much of their evidence. Far from condemning the violence described by 545 witnesses, they attributed much of it to the "logical and natural events of the military take-over of the Government in January, 1971."[42] This violence, they concluded, was a result of "mopping up" operations that were meant to deal with "dissenting elements."[43] However, for the women who testified before the commission, their loved ones' disappearances were far from logical or natural.

The commissioners blamed the rest of the violence on the security forces, namely the Military Police, the Public Safety Unit, and the State Research Centre. Part of the problem was the Armed Forces (Powers of Arrest) Decree, which gave soldiers and prison officers the power to arrest, search, and detain.[44] The commissioners found that the security forces had not been complying with the decree in the spirit in which it had been promoted. Instead, they used it as a license to arrest with impunity and settle old grudges. "Such soldiers," they declared, "became pinchback [sic] dictators in their own right where they abused those powers and obligations."[45]

In an effort to rein in the security forces, Amin repealed the decree in late August 1973 and replaced it with the Military Police (Powers of Arrest) Decree.[46] According to the state newspaper, Amin extended the powers of arrest to military police officers because "the strength of the Police Force as it is at the present with the facilities available to them, are not sufficient to deal with organized crime in the country."[47] Although the new decree limited powers of arrest to civilian police officers and military police officers in uniform, the reality was quite different. All security agents continued to apprehend people at will. The commissioners found that those who were charged with enforcing the law were among "the worst offenders."[48]

That the poor behavior of soldiers had an adverse effect on the police force is hardly surprising. It had become common practice for soldiers to randomly arrest persons and then drop them at the local police station for processing. After the police officer finished logging in a prisoner, the soldier would return to collect the individual. This person was usually never seen again. Since the only remaining link to the disappeared was through the police, they received the blame. The police officers had no power to stand up to the heavily armed soldiers and as a result became known as a "force of women."[49] The emasculation of the force led to a "systematic degeneration of the police morale," which resulted in a "complete break-down of the law and order."[50] Despite the blatant lack of professionalism within the security forces, the commission did not find Amin responsible for their conduct. The commissioners argued that "there was no evidence where there was even the remotest suggestion that your Excellency had directed the disappearance of any person or the annihilation of any ethnic group of persons."[51] This was perhaps their most astounding conclusion.

The commissioners recommended a series of structural reforms that would restore police morale (read: masculinity). To reinvigorate the force, the activities of the Public Safety Unit and the Military Police would need to be circumscribed. The commissioners believed that the former should focus exclusively on violent crime, while the latter should deal solely with military offenses (that is, those that should be tried before a military tribunal). They also suggested that intelligence officers—members of both the State Research Centre and Military Intelligence—be split into new teams and moved around the country every twenty-four months. This would prevent individuals from amassing too much power in any given place. They also mentioned the need to review Decree 8 of 1972, which offered government agents immunity for protecting national security.[52] Because the decree absolved the government of any misdeeds committed on its behalf, the commissioners thought it should be amended.

In addition to various security sector reforms, the commissioners also thought that educating women about their legal rights was important. Most wives, for instance, had never heard of the Estates of Missing Persons (Management) Decree, which gave them the right to apply to administer the estates of their missing husbands.[53] They also wanted women to know that they were entitled to their husband's pensions if their husbands had served as loyal soldiers. However, because many of the women's husbands had died or disappeared trying to resist the coup, their actions automatically forfeited their widows' rights to compensation. Unfortunately, they had been loyal to the wrong regime.

Despite the (mostly) thoughtful recommendations of the commission, there was very little change in Amin's Uganda. None of their recommendations for restructuring the security forces was ever implemented, nor was there any sustained effort to educate women about their rights. Although a military tribunal eventually tried a few senior police and security officers, all received acquittals. The problem, it seemed, was that no one wanted to testify against them.[54] Shortly after the inquiry concluded, Amin appointed Justice Saied as chief justice. Saied apparently tried to resign in June 1977, but Amin refused to accept his resignation. Not wanting to flee into exile, Saied carried on as chief justice until the end of the regime.[55] The army representative to the commission also continued serving Amin as the provincial governor of Busoga. The police superintendents, in contrast, abruptly left the government. One (Esau) was arrested for murder and sentenced to ten years in prison, while the other (Kyefulumya) was forced to flee the country.

In what was perhaps the most ironic twist of fate, Uganda was elected to the United Nations Commission on Human Rights in May 1976.[56] Commenting on the highly contested election, Amin said that it was "not unexpected, but still we have enjoyed the pride of standing clean before the eyes of the world to disprove all shit that was smeared over our face to mar us and defame our true picture."[57] Given the content of the testimonies cited above, it is difficult to imagine how this might have occurred. According to the International Commission of Jurists (ICJ), Amin sent a copy of the Saied Commission's final report to the United Nations. This measure likely precluded them from launching their own investigation, even though the ICJ had been pushing for an inquiry since 1974. One month after Uganda was elected to the UN Commission, the ICJ submitted a second report about violations of human rights. The Working Group on Communications of the UN Sub-Commission on the Prevention of Discrimination and Protection of Minorities considered the report and then referred the case to the Commission on Human Rights in August 1976. By the time the commission met in February 1977 to consider whether they should investigate the case, Uganda had already begun its term as a member of the thirty-nation elected committee.[58]

Although few could have predicted this shocking turn of events, the outcome aligned perfectly with one of Amin's larger political goals, namely, to be taken seriously on the world stage. As ridiculous (and oftentimes deadly) as Amin's antics were known to be, we must not forget that he also managed to get elected as chair of the Organization of African Unity in 1975. Clearly, this was a man who was far more politically savvy than most have assumed. In fact, I maintain that the commission of inquiry was little more than a political ruse—another one of Amin's attempts to hoodwink the public into believing that he was a compassionate and caring leader who had their best interests at heart.[59] By establishing an official investigation into disappearances, Amin demonstrated that he had "heard" the desperate pleas of the nation's wives, sisters, and mothers and was taking their concerns "seriously." His actions, of course, were nothing more than a display of political theater.[60] Amin must have known that the truth would be devastating to him and his regime, but he went forward with the charade because it bought him social capital. It allowed him to perform the role of the embattled patriarch, a concerned leader who would stop at nothing to liberate his people from tyranny. It was a clever performance, indeed, but did the people buy it?

Many Ugandans thought that the commission of inquiry was a sham and refused to testify before it. Others, however, must have believed in its legitimacy, assuming that testifying in front of a sitting military government would somehow make a difference. Perhaps they thought it would lead to answers. Perhaps they thought it would result in compensation. Perhaps they thought it would usher in a more peaceful social order. Or perhaps they feared the consequences of not speaking out, either in terms of retribution by government officials for not participating in the exercise or the larger political consequences of maintaining silence. In the end, it does not really matter *why* so many women (and men) chose to testify. What matters is that they spoke out against the dictatorship, powerfully utilizing their voices to counter the deafening silence of disappearance, indelibly recording a crime that was supposed to leave no trace.

⤴

Women's testimonies did not seem to make any difference to the commission's outcome, since the entire exercise was ultimately a sham. Nonetheless, they are significant because they clearly demonstrate that disappearance was a calculated ruling strategy and not simply an unfortunate consequence of military rule. Their testimonies confirm that the regime's use of violence was far more calculated and strategic than most scholars have previously imagined. There was a particular logic to this political terror, which is reflected in the narratives analyzed in this chapter. Agulani Ayer, for instance, watched as her husband was brutally beaten and then thrown onto the back of a lorry "like a bag of cotton." The soldiers administering the abuse knew that she and the other men's wives were watching and taunted them for "boasting" about their husbands' so-called strength. They used extreme violence to emasculate the men while creating a spectacle that would terrorize the rest of the population.

We also see the logic of political survival woven throughout the testimonies of Ugandan women. Through the narratives of Lydia Acha and Christine Anywar, among others, we can map out the social networks that would have come into play when a woman began searching for information about a loved one. We can discern the types of people she would have contacted, as well as the various places she would have visited. We can also get a sense of the tremendous challenges she would have encountered along the way. Through the narratives of women like Grace Atto, the wife of a high-ranking military officer who was disappeared shortly after the coup, we can better understand the ways in which women coped with loss—not only that of their family members but also that of their personal possessions. Sometimes, as Grace and her father-in-law learned, survival necessitated the acceptance of defeat. And finally, through the narratives of Mary Akurut, Grace Apio, and Evasta Ndagano, we can clearly see that men were not the only targets of disappearance and that one's survival depended on more than simply sex. Taken as a whole, these testimonies present a much more nuanced picture of disappearance as a gendered strategy of rule that influenced men and women's lives (and deaths) in very different ways.

7 ✍ Violence in the Shadows
Gender and the Collapse of the Military State

MARIAM OGWAL awoke to the shrill cry of the early morning whistle, which meant that her husband, as well as all of the other police officers who were stationed at the barracks in Fort Portal, had to scramble out of bed and report for duty immediately. It was February 1977, and given the recent spate of mutinies, defections, and attempts on the president's life, the officers knew that they could be summoned at any time of the day or night. Miriam peered through her window as the men assembled in front of the main office. She watched in despair as her husband and many other Langi and Acholi officers were forced to the ground and tied up with ropes. Heavily armed men loaded the police officers onto a bus and then drove them away. When her husband did not return, Mariam set off on foot in search of answers. She did not get far before she was arrested by Abdulla Hassan, an agent of the State Research Centre (SRC), who resented the fact that she was asking so many questions. He started beating her and calling her a "fool" for chasing after the people who had arrested her husband. He then arrested her and took her to jail. When agents released her the following day, they told her to return to her home in Lira so that she could take care of her five children. They gave her a bus warrant and sent her on her way.

Several months later, Mariam was arrested once again by Abdulla and another security agent. She said that she had been detained because, as she recalled, "I kept on bothering them about my husband [saying] that they should go and show me where my husband is."[1]

When they arrived at the police station, Abdulla pulled out a knife, cut off her ear, and then forced her to eat it. While the blood streamed down her face, he shoved her into a car and drove her to the SRC head-quarters at Nakasero, nearly 165 miles away. Along the way, he stopped at Karuma Bridge—a notorious dump site for bodies during Amin's rule—and threatened to throw her into the river. Fortunately, a col-league objected and her life was spared. Mariam spent the next month locked in a cramped cell with twelve other women. "We were kept in a very small room," she said. "You lie down and then a certain metal object is put on your chest [as a method of torture], you cannot raise up your head, or you cannot sit."[2] She said that the women received daily beatings and were compelled to drink their own urine to survive. One of her cellmates even died as a result of the harsh conditions. Agents removed the woman's body at night, likely dumping it in one of the forests or swamps nearby. Mariam probably would have died in custody if one of her husband's friends, another agent of the SRC, had not intervened on her behalf. But her nightmare did not end once she was released. The day after she returned home, Abdulla arrested her again and took her to the military barracks in Lira. She endured three additional weeks of violence and deprivation, after which the soldiers released her from detention. The officer in charge of the prison warned her to "go deep in the village" where Abdulla would not be able to find her again. She took his advice and quickly fled, seeking refuge in the shadows until the regime eventually collapsed.

Mariam's story illustrates the extreme levels of violence that ordi-nary women endured at the hands of the state's security forces during the latter years of Amin's rule. It also confirms that the commission of inquiry did not signal an end to disappearances in Uganda but instead ushered in an era of even greater violence and instability. As the mili-tary state collapsed, soldiers lashed out in violent displays of hypermas-culinity to demonstrate that they were still strong and powerful even though resistance to the regime was clearly mounting. They continued disappearing "enemy" men at an alarming rate, which brought tremen-dous pain and hardship to the families that were left behind. They also began targeting women for rape and physical assault on a level that was unprecedented. These gendered acts of violence were about humili-ating the men, who were unable to protect "their women," as much as they were about demonstrating male dominance and punishing women for their perceived "indiscretions." As a result of this brutality, those women who had once supported Amin, who had considered him the "father of the nation," began referring to him as *kijambiya*, or the machete. This chapter maps the gendered terrain of violence and harassment that accompanied, indeed precipitated, state collapse, thus setting the stage for the liberation war that would ultimately oust Amin from power.

ENFORCED DISAPPEARANCES

The enforced disappearances that marked the latter half of Amin's rule were different from those of the first primarily in terms of their frequency. As threats to the military state grew increasingly commonplace, security agents ramped up their attacks on "subversives" and "saboteurs," both within and outside of the barracks. The Entebbe air raid exposed the tremendous vulnerabilities of the regime and therefore can be seen as an important turning point, signaling the beginning of the end of the military dictatorship. On June 27, 1976, a group of Palestinian and East German extremists hijacked a French Airbus traveling from Tel Aviv to Paris and rerouted the plane to Uganda. Amin welcomed the hijackers on "humanitarian grounds" and allowed them to create an operational base at Entebbe Airport. For close to a week, Ugandan soldiers stood guard over the frightened hostages while Amin played the mediator. In true performative style, he feigned concern about the situation in front of the cameras, delighting in the spectacle that had thrust him back onto the world stage. However, before he could heroically mediate the crisis, a group of Israeli pilots successfully executed a predawn raid on Entebbe Airport. The team rescued the hostages and killed all of the hijackers, as well as twenty Ugandan air force pilots. Deeply humiliated, Amin expressed outrage that Ugandans had been killed instead of thanked for their hospitality. "In Kampala and the surrounding areas," noted Ugandan historian A. B. K. Kasozi, "anyone who talked about the raid or seemed to belittle the weakness of the Ugandan armed forces was killed."[3]

The Entebbe air raid shook Amin to the core. He and his henchmen repeatedly warned Ugandans to avoid "rumor-mongering" and "malicious letter writing" because such activities, they alleged, spread fear and panic.[4] They wanted everyone to believe that they were firmly in control, even though the circulation of rumors and anonymous letters signaled the public's mounting discontent with the military regime. Those in exile recognized the frailty of Amin's government and intensified efforts to overthrow him. Amin suspected ousted president Obote of orchestrating much of the violence and retaliated by sending "death squads" into the Acholi and Langi regions of the country. From mid-1976 until late 1977, state security agents massacred, or disappeared, approximately ten thousand people, many of whom were soldiers or police officers.[5] Because most of the violence was carried out by heavily armed military men to demonstrate their absolute power over other "weaker" men (namely, civilians and ethnic rivals), it can be read not only as a deliberate ruling strategy but also as a gendered manifestation of state collapse.

Betty Engur's husband was publicly disappeared during this period of retaliatory strikes. Although he was an ethnic Langi and a cousin of the deposed president, he served as minister of culture and community development in Amin's first cabinet. In late 1972, he (along with three others) was relieved of his ministerial duties because he purportedly could not "cope with the speed" of the new government.[6] He returned to his rural home in Lira, where he resumed farming. In 1975, security agents arrested him and took him to Luzira Prison in Kampala, where he was held without charge for an entire year. Once released, he returned to Lira. On the morning of February 6, 1977, a white unmarked van pulled into the couple's compound. Several men dressed in army fatigues jumped out of the vehicle and said that they were looking for a man named Engur. Betty's husband raised his hands and stepped forward. "The two gun men then escorted my husband and when I tried to follow my husband one of them turned round and then pointed the gun at me," she explained. "He was then pushed into the vehicle. He was thrown down, those who had run and hidden behind the house came and then sat on the body of my husband. They turned the vehicle and drove off at very fast speed."[7]

The following day, Betty went to the local police station to inquire about her husband's whereabouts. The police were unable to provide her with answers because "the situation was very bad, arrests were very many," so she decided to go to Kampala.[8] Once there, she contacted a friend from the region—an army man. He told her that it would be hard to trace her husband; rumors indicated that he had been taken to the State Research Centre. Betty said that she was too afraid to look for him there because "those people were really very cruel, they could not entertain any person going there."[9] She decided to return to Lira. Shortly thereafter, an agent from the SRC came to her home and appropriated two of her vehicles—a lorry and a car. When she tried to intervene to stop him, he became "wild," so there was nothing she could do. Betty never saw the vehicles or her husband again. In the years that followed, she provided for her eight children by engaging in small business activities. Most of her children, however, were unable to complete their education because of financial hardship. Betty resented Amin and thought that he had "the intention of finishing the whole of Langi" because they posed a threat to the military state.[10]

Mitolesi Arach also lost her husband, a county chief in Apac, around the same time. He, too, was a Langi and therefore represented a potential threat to the military establishment. On the morning of February 27, 1977, a group of armed men arrived at the county's administrative headquarters looking for the chief. One of the clerks informed the soldiers that he had left for a meeting but pointed them in the direction he had taken. A while later, the *askari* who had escorted the chief to the meeting went to Mitolesi's home to report that her husband had been arrested and taken to Lira. The soldiers provided no explanation as to why they had arrested the chief. The following day, Mitolesi and her brother-in-law went to Lira Barracks looking for her husband. The man who was in charge of the barracks told her that her husband was there, but she was not allowed to see him. When she attempted to visit her husband on another occasion, she was told that he had been taken to Kampala. She eventually learned from a fellow captive that he had been taken to the State Research Centre. Although she was desperate to see her husband, she did not go there because "if you tried to follow you would also just go."[11] In other words, she was afraid that she might also disappear. Mitolesi knew that it would be safer for her to return to her natal village along with the sixteen children in her care. She never saw her husband again. He had simply "disappeared."

Disappearances in the barracks were particularly terrifying because they were so public. Soldiers brutally attacked their fellow soldiers in ritual displays of gendered power to spread fear and stifle opposition. Violence was a performance in which women were forced to watch helplessly as their husbands were beaten, stabbed, and then hauled away to face certain death. Some of these women were killed, but many others were kept alive, witnesses to the violence that was Amin's Uganda.[12] One thing was certain: Amin and his henchmen were not going down without a fight. Joy Odong clearly remembered the March day in 1977 when her husband, a Langi soldier who was stationed at

Mubende Barracks, was viciously assaulted and then disappeared. A fire alarm sounded early one morning, signaling that all soldiers should report to the main parade grounds. The soldiers were then divided into two groups—the Acholi and Langi versus everyone else. Joy's house was near the edge of the field, so she had a clear view from her window. "What I saw very well was the cutting of somebody in the field," she explained; "his knees were cut."[13] Many others were also "cut." The officers used machetes and bayonets to carry out the attack, after which they ordered the remaining soldiers to load the wounded men onto the back of a truck, as well as into an empty bus. Joy remembered that the vehicles hauled away three loads of bodies each. The officers then forced the women to leave the barracks. They were not allowed to pack up their belongings but instead were ordered to report to the bus park immediately so that they could be transported back to their rural homes. "The bus in which we traveled had a lot of blood stains but we just sat like that," Joy explained as she painfully recalled the difficult journey back to Apac with her six children.[14] Neither she nor her traveling companions ever saw their husbands again.

These three women's stories of disappearance are in many ways similar to those examined in the previous chapter. They are important to briefly mention here, however, because they confirm that disappearances were not halted by the investigations of the commission of inquiry. Instead, they increased in frequency because the state had grown ever more unstable. Military men targeted "weaker" men to demonstrate that they were still powerful and strong, despite evidence to the contrary. Because most victims were Langi or Acholi, we can ascertain that ethnicity also strongly underpinned much of the latter violence. Security forces perceived the Langi and Acholi as the most likely enemies of the state. And finally, these three stories reveal that women seemed more afraid of being "disappeared" than they had been in earlier years, hence their reluctance to trace their abducted husbands.

RAPE AND SEXUAL ASSAULT

Many Ugandan women experienced the violence of state collapse through rape. Agents of the hypermasculine military state used sexual violence to demonstrate their power over women and punish them for supporting "subversives" and "saboteurs." In addition, they violated women's bodies to emasculate, or humiliate, those men who were unable to protect them. By the mid to late 1970s, violence against women had reached an unprecedented level. According to Winnie Byanyima, a former member of Parliament for Mbarara District, "rape by soldiers became so common that a raped woman was often told she had only herself to blame for getting caught—soldiers were rapists and women were expected to know how to avoid them."[15] However, as the military state unraveled and lawlessness reigned supreme, most women found "avoiding" such men to be increasingly difficult. At Makerere University, for instance, female students were not able to escape the sexual harassment and demeaning remarks made by soldiers and military officers who routinely patrolled the campus in search of "confusing agents." The political climate at the university had always been tense, in large part because Amin and his military henchmen were not highly educated and therefore felt threatened by intellectuals, but things worsened when the students began to vocalize their discontent more forcefully.

On January 22, 1976, Amin announced that all university students would be required to participate in festivities commemorating the fifth anniversary of the military coup. He sent one of his army captains to the campus to teach the students how to march in formation. During the course of the training, the officer insulted the students by suggesting that the university trained "idiots." He also made the incendiary claim that he had had sex with "every female student" on campus and that they all had gonorrhea.[16] The following day, the student body wrote an angry letter of protest to the minister of education and threatened to withdraw from the celebrations. The minister apologized for the captain's behavior and eventually persuaded them to march. When Amin learned of the incident, he complimented the captain for having been "very brave." Instead of reprimanding the officer for acting in a manner that contravened the principles of gender equality that Amin had so ardently espoused during International Women's Year, Amin promoted him to major.[17] Such actions confirm, once again, that women's liberation had never been a genuine priority for Idi Amin.

Sexual harassment on campus escalated to widespread sexual violence shortly after the Entebbe air raid. On August 3, 1976, the students staged a large antigovernment demonstration on campus. Amin's military forces, still licking their wounds from the humiliation they had suffered at the hands of the Israelis, were in no mood to tolerate dissent, especially from members of the educated elite, and lashed out using gendered forms of violence to terrorize the student body. According to eyewitness testimony gathered by the International Commission of Jurists, "Some students were shot on the spot, others were made to lie down and beaten, some women students were raped and those resisting had their breasts slashed off, and up to a thousand students were rounded up and taken to prisons at Makindye, Bugulobi and Naguru. There many were tortured and beaten and some killed."[18] Other observers claim that although no one was actually killed during the notorious "massacre," sexual violence was widespread.[19]

Another mass rape occurred in January 1977 when agents from the State Research Centre commandeered a bus that was transporting a group of hospital nurses home from a university dance. After ordering the vehicle to pull off to the side of the road, several gun-toting agents entered the bus and demanded proof of authorization to travel at night. When the driver failed to produce the required documents, one of the operatives got behind the wheel and drove directly to the SRC headquarters. Once at Nakasero, the agents ordered the nurses, as well as their male student escorts, to take off their shoes and go inside. The agents led the women into one room, while they took the men into another—within earshot but unable to intervene. Henry Kyemba, who served as the minister of health and later investigated the matter, described what happened next: "The women were told to undress, to stand up holding their clothes and to march around to be viewed. They were then raped. There was not enough room for them all to be raped in the room, so several were raped in the cars, in the bus, and in small, temporary office cabins. The men kept calling their friends to come and help themselves to the nurses. Many of the State Research patrols were returning after the night's operations, so anyone who wanted, joined in."[20] After the brutal assault was over, the agents bundled the women into various SRC vehicles and drove them back to the nurses' dormitory at Mulago Hospital. They also "roughed up" the male students before releasing them. The nurses were fortunate to get out of Nakasero alive: they could have easily been imprisoned, mutilated, or disappeared like countless others. George Ivan Smith, an Australian diplomat who explored the dungeons of the State Research Centre shortly after the fall of Amin, described what he found there: "The cells and rooms on the fourth floor, in which women captives were kept, were also larders, doors ajar so that captors could, when lust came, take out a woman in whom to satisfy that lust. There in the corridor I saw the torn ribbons of what once had been a woman's clothes.

A girl of fifteen had been raped to death in that place just a few weeks earlier."[21] These rapes should be interpreted not as the product of lust, as Smith has suggested, but instead as an expression of hypermasculine military power. As threats to the military state intensified, gender-based violence became increasingly common.

Unlike the early years of military rule, older women had become just as likely as younger women to experience violent sexual assault. Florence Wanaswa, a young civil servant from eastern Uganda, witnessed one such brutal attack when she and her brother were traveling by train from Bunyole to Kampala in 1978. She explained why traveling by rail at that time was dangerous: "Usually there were soldiers moving from one barracks to another or just boarding the train to harass passengers on the train, [to] steal and to do all sorts of things."[22] However, given that it was the cheapest way to travel, she and many others had little choice but to accept the risks. She recalled that on that particular day, a group of soldiers had embarked at Mukono to check the train for bandits and guns. All of the passengers were worried because they knew that "anything could happen." One of the soldiers stopped in front of Florence and told her to sit down. An elderly woman who was seated nearby warned her not to move, because soldiers were "not human beings now." Another soldier, who was high on drugs, pointed at Florence and said that he had to have her. Her brother begged the soldier to leave her alone, explaining that she was his "wife" and that she was traveling to the hospital to treat a "very strange disease." The soldier must have decided that she was not worth the risk, so he turned his attention toward the old woman who was sitting next to them. Florence explained what happened next: "The soldier pushed the old woman down and put a knife across her neck promising to cut her throat if she made any negative move. He ordered us to put our legs up since he had to put the woman between the two sitting rows. All of us just covered our heads in shame. He went ahead, as if he was in the privacy of his room or whatever, and raped the woman. When he completed his mission, he laughed excitedly, as if we had all been sharing in his actions, and walked off."[23] The old woman reached into her purse and pulled out a small tin of Vicks VapoRub. She begged Florence to help her smear it over her private parts because the attack had been so painful. When Florence hesitated, the woman told her that since everyone had witnessed the assault, she had no reason to feel ashamed. This rape, she insisted, had been a collective experience. When the soldiers got off the train at Namanve station—another notorious dump site for bodies—everyone breathed a deep sigh of relief. Florence later learned from other passengers that the same thing had taken place in the other compartments. No one had been killed because, according to the soldiers as they exited the train, "people had shown sense and enabled them to carry out a peaceful mission."[24]

These three stories provide a glimpse into the world of sexual violence that was pervasive in Amin's Uganda, particularly during his final years in power. Soldiers and security agents raped greater numbers of women to demonstrate that they were still strong and powerful, even though antigovernment attacks clearly suggested otherwise. Like disappearance, rape was a deliberate strategy of military rule in that it reinforced the masculinity of the perpetrators. It was also a precipitant of state failure, since sexual violence ultimately undermined the military dictator's final vestiges of support.

BECOMING *KIJAMBIYA*

By the late 1970s, violence had become so pervasive, so commonplace, that agents of the military state imagined everyone as a potential enemy. The petty trader who was once considered "safe" was now a suspect. She could no longer assume that she would find security in the village. Gone were the days when ordinary women could fade into the shadows, quietly minding their own business until a new government came to power. The state had eyes and ears everywhere, and this meant that no one was safe. "It's not necessarily the top people who are being killed or beaten now," suggested one person who was interviewed by investigators for the International Commission of Jurists. "It's small people, anybody, for any reason—property, wife, money, new car, or just indiscipline. The most important thing is that there is no law in Uganda. Anybody, soldiers in the army, can take anything from anyplace. He can take your wife, daughter, money or your life. He just kills you. Finish."[25] As a result of the violence and fear, women who had once been Amin's most ardent supporters gradually turned against him.

Like many of the women whom I interviewed for this book, Hassifa Namboze initially had great respect for Amin because he opened women's eyes to business and restored morality to the younger generation. "Now, when he was there approaching seven years, things started getting spoiled," explained the fifty-two-year-old petty trader from Bwaise. She said that Amin's soldiers began arresting and killing people for no apparent reason. "People would arrest someone, put him in the boot [car trunk], bring him in, and start beating him. If you are easy [offer little resistance], you can die. If you don't die, you can get damaged." Hassifa maintained, "If they see you not dying and you have spent long [in custody], they release you. Very many people died. They could get one man to chop off the other's head. Okay, they were murderers." She insisted that although the first five or six years of Amin's rule were good, he eventually "became mad."[26]

Irene Lubega, a fifty-year-old secretary from Bulemezi, attributed Amin's behavioral changes not to madness but instead to his fears or suspicions regarding educated people. "They first liked him," she said. "We all first liked him, expecting a lot from him. But slowly by slowly, what most made us furious is that he didn't want the literate. To say that you are educated or are at Makerere, you work or you wear spectacles—they knew that those who put on glasses were the elite. They would not like them at all. They didn't like the literate." Over time, people began wondering whether he was capable of leading the nation. "And we also got to know that this man wasn't going to like those who were educated," she said, "because prominent people started disappearing. You got to hear that the other one was taken. They put him in the trunk. You don't see him again. Kidnapping of people changed people's attitudes a lot, and they started disliking him."[27]

But prominent people were not the only ones to disappear. By the end of Amin's rule, everyone was a potential target. "People were being kidnapped and taken in the trunk," explained Evelyn Nyanzi, a forty-five-year-old teacher from Kampala. "People were being chopped, murdered. You could hear that they had slaughtered six people. . . . That was common, that bodies were there. So people started to hate him, and by the time he left, I think there was nobody who still liked him. People hated him, but it was all because of his rule. It had changed from the things he said when he was starting. He was now ruling badly."[28] Betty Mayiga, a fifty-nine-year-old seamstress from Kampala, agreed with this assessment. When I asked her why people's attitudes toward Amin changed over time, she said, "Mostly it was due to killing and they got fed up. He made a lot of killings. It's killing that he had on his mind. Killing, killing."[29] Rebekah Matua, a sixty-year-old retired teacher from Arua, explained the violence in this way: "Of course, as I told you, soldiers at that time became supernatural, almost supernatural. That's why things went into a mess. I mean, if they were not supernatural, how could you cut someone's neck into pieces? It would not happen."[30] Violence had become so extreme, so over-the-top, that she could process it only as something that had supernatural origins.

Amin's regime eventually became so violent that women began calling him *kijambiya*, or the machete. Catherine Asiimwe, a sixty-year-old petty trader from Kitende, claimed that although his government was good at the beginning, "people were so much murdered. Don't you hear? That's why he was called *kijambiya*. Whoever does something against him they would only murder him. You know it was a military rule . . . He really ruled us in a military way."[31] Jane Walusimbi confirmed that people's hostility stemmed from the widespread killing. "The reason why they started hating him," said the forty-nine-year-old peasant farmer from Kitende, "was because he started killing people and started being Mr. Machete."[32] Ritah Lukwago, a seventy-five-year-old peasant farmer from the same region, agreed with this assessment. She said, "That killing of people changed people's minds, and they said that this Amin is now Mr. Panga. They called him that name, *panga*, because he killed people."[33] It is important to remember that those women who referred to Amin as *kijambiya* were not members of the political or economic elite (that is, potential enemies of the state). They were ordinary women who had supported Amin during his early years in power. The fact that they had begun calling him "the machete" was a testament to the military dictator's mounting lack of popularity.

᷍

Although violence—and gendered performances of violence—had been defining features of the military state since the early days of Amin's rule, brutality had reached unprecedented levels by the mid to late 1970s. After suffering tremendous public humiliation in the wake of the Entebbe air raid, Amin and his military henchmen lashed out in increasingly violent displays of hypermasculinity to prove that they were still strong and powerful (read: manly). As we have seen from the case studies examined within this chapter, these gendered acts of violence targeted men and women in very different ways. Men continued to be the primary targets of enforced disappearance, while women were the ones left behind to pick up the shattered pieces. Ugandan women's narratives confirm that abductions continued unabated even after the commission of inquiry completed its work. As threats to the military state intensified, security forces disappeared increasing numbers of men, most of whom were Langi or Acholi. This suggests that the "enemy" had become more ethnically circumscribed than ever before. The fact that women had become too afraid to trace the whereabouts of their abducted loved ones also suggests that they were no longer above suspicion or reproach. Given Miriam Ogwal's repeated arrests and brutal assaults, it is no surprise that women like Betty Engur and Mitolesi Arach were so reluctant to search for answers.

Many other women experienced the violence of state collapse through rape and sexual assaults. As previously mentioned, these gendered acts of violence were about humiliating the men who were unable to protect "their women" as much as they were about demonstrating male dominance and punishing women for alleged "misdeeds." Like disappearance, rape had become an increasingly important ruling strategy because it bolstered the (wounded) masculinity of the perpetrators. By participating in mass rapes, security forces engaged in ritual performances of gendered power that belied political realities on the ground. In the end, however, sexual violence was a precipitant of state failure, because it eventually undermined the military dictator's last remaining vestiges of support. Those women who had initially appreciated Amin, who had once considered him the "father of the nation," began thinking of him as *kijambiya*, or the machete. By failing to rein in his security forces, Amin lost one of his largest bases of support, thus setting the stage for the liberation war that would ultimately oust him from power.

8 ⟋ Militant Motherhood
Women on the Front Lines of the Liberation War

ESTHER SSENGENDO paced nervously back and forth beside her daughter's hospital bed, desperately trying to ignore the thundering clap of gunshots in the distance. If her youngest child had not been so seriously ill, she would not have remained in the city. Nearly everyone that she knew had already fled their homes in hopes of finding refuge in the countryside. It was now too late to flee. The *bakombozi*, or Tanzanian liberators, had already reached the outskirts of Kampala and were preparing for their final offensive. Esther had known that Amin's days were numbered. Only two weeks before, when she had first left the hospital in search of medical supplies, she had noticed a caravan of vehicles "very, very packed with luggage," heading toward Bombo Road. Most of Amin's soldiers had begun their exodus north, leaving behind a small contingent to repel the invading forces. This would ultimately prove to be too little, too late.

As the fighting grew near, Esther made the difficult decision to leave. She understood that because of her daughter's medical condition she was taking a tremendous risk. Nonetheless, she knew that if they did not get out of the hospital at once, they would both be killed. Hastily removing the feeding tube from her young daughter's nose, Esther picked up her child and ran. When she reached the outside of the building, she was immediately confronted by the putrid stench of decay. The mortuary had been without electricity for weeks, and the bodies in storage had rapidly decomposed. Adding to the macabre spectacle were the hundreds of bodies that littered the streets, unfortunate victims of Amin's last stand. After several terrifying hours, Esther and her daughter safely reached their home in Kanyanya, where they remained for the duration of the siege.[1]

Like many of the other women whom I interviewed for this book, Esther had memories of the war that were reflected through the lens of motherhood. She remembered the fall of Amin as a protracted struggle to protect her family from harm's way. Other women found themselves in a similar position, having lost their husbands to the violence of militarism. Like Esther, they experienced the war as mothers who were desperately trying to protect their children from a similar fate. These women's stories provide important details about the liberation war, yet they are curiously absent from the historical record.[2] This chapter seeks to more fully engender the history of the struggle by highlighting women's voices and experiences. I suggest that Ugandan women were not simply victims of a violent conflict but instead dynamic historical actors who engaged in complex decision-making processes to protect their families throughout the war. This chapter also confirms the centrality of gender to the larger war effort by revealing how Amin invoked and deployed masculinity and femininity throughout the conflict. By feminizing the enemy through various performative gestures, he attempted to bolster his own masculinity, thus confirming, at least in theory, that the military state remained powerful.

THE PRELUDE TO WAR

The roots of the war can be traced back to a series of interlocking conflicts that became increasingly acute during Amin's final years in power. By the end of 1977, the price of coffee on the global market had decreased by 40 percent, thus causing the Ugandan economy to plummet. Without ready access to foreign exchange, Amin was no longer able to import the military hardware and luxury goods that were necessary to ensure the loyalty of his troops. This resulted in a fierce wave of discontent among the rank and file. Those who were fed up with Amin's leadership rallied behind his second-in-command, General Mustafa Adrisi, who had promised to purge non-Ugandans from the army and the government.[3] Many soldiers thought that Adrisi would be a better leader than Amin, but in April 1978, he was critically injured in a mysterious car accident and then airlifted to Cairo for medical treatment. No sooner had he left the country than Amin stripped him of his ministerial portfolio and took control over the Ministries of Defense and Internal Affairs.[4]

Amin then proceeded to arrest several high-ranking prison and police officers, including the former head of the Public Safety Unit, Ali Towelli. He also fired Lieutenant Colonel Juma Oris and took over his ministerial portfolios as well (foreign affairs and information). Other targets of the president's wrath included the minister of finance (Brigadier Moses Ali), the army chief of staff (Major General Isaac Lumago), the chief of police (Kasim Obura), and the commander of the Revolutionary Suicide Mechanized Regiment in Masaka (Lieutenant Colonel Nasur Ezega). Many of the followers of these men were also arrested or killed as "subversives." Following the dramatic purge within his inner circle, Amin's movements became more secretive and erratic. According to Tony Avirgan and Martha Honey, veteran journalists who were embedded with the Tanzanian army during the liberation war, "He darted unpredictably from one heavily guarded residence or hotel to another, frequently changing cars and making few public appearances."[5] This behavior simply increased uncertainty and discontent among the soldiers.

In the months to come, disgruntled soldiers mutinied in nearly every military barracks across the country.[6] Amin recognized that if he wanted to maintain power, he needed to find a way to restore order among the troops. He did so by inventing (or reinventing) a collective enemy—the Tanzanians. In May 1978, he asserted that Tanzanian soldiers were engaged in troop movements within three miles of the border, a direct violation of the Mogadishu Agreement. This, of course, was complete nonsense, but it temporarily diverted public attention away from domestic turmoil. It also provided Ugandan soldiers with an excuse to begin moving troops and military equipment closer to the border. Tanzanian military officers kept a close watch on the situation but were not forced into action until mid-September, when Ugandan planes began flying into Tanzanian air space. The local battalion commander made frantic pleas for reinforcements, but none were forthcoming. This provided Ugandan troops with the perfect opportunity to strike.[7]

THE OFFENSIVE

On the ninth of October, Ugandan soldiers set the war in motion by crossing the border into Tanzania and torching two houses in the small village of Kakunyu. When Lieutenant Colonel Morris Singano received word of the attack, he ordered the military to open fire, killing two of Amin's soldiers and destroying several armored vehicles. The

Ugandan press falsely claimed that a Tanzanian battalion had crossed the border into East Ankole District and was burning houses, destroying property, and killing people. Amin prepared for battle by warning local residents that violence could spread to other areas.[8] Less than one week later, he changed his tune, announcing that Ugandan troops would not be crossing the border because they were observing 1978 as a year of "peace, love, unity, and reconciliation." Drawing upon familial rhetoric, Amin claimed that the people of Tanzania were "his children" and that he would not betray "mother Africa" by conquering them.[9] By doing so, he tried to position himself as a father figure who still enjoyed legitimate political authority.

However, Amin's paternal promises of peace and love were short-lived. On October 25, more than two thousand Ugandan troops poured across the border at Mutukula, rapidly overtaking the small Tanzanian contingent that was standing guard. Singano forced the invaders back across the border by gathering reinforcements and mounting a counterattack. Two days later, the conflict escalated when three Ugandan fighter jets bombed the Tanzanian town of Bukoba. Although the bombs caused very little structural damage, the incident resulted in widespread panic among residents. By the afternoon, most had fled to the rural countryside, where they established a network of makeshift camps. After several days, most of the displaced men returned to their urban homes, leaving their wives and children to fend for themselves in the bush.[10] Singano appealed for troop reinforcements, but none came, so large swathes of the border remained unguarded. This provided a perfect opportunity for Amin's troops to strike again.

On the morning of October 30, thousands of Ugandan soldiers invaded the Kagera Salient, an eighteen-hundred-square-kilometer stretch of land that extends southward from the border toward the Kagera River. The invading army met very little resistance, save for the valiant efforts of a few dozen members of a civilian militia. Although Singano knew about the invasion, the Tanzanian commander could not launch a counteroffensive, because of fleeing civilians. He watched in horror as they led their families and their cattle into minefields that his troops had laid to repel Amin's soldiers. As the deafening explosions launched bits of human and animal flesh into the air, throngs of frightened civilians desperately tried to make their way across the river. Instead of allowing them safe passage as mandated by international law, Amin's troops "shot at anything that moved, regardless of age or sex."[11]

A former soldier in the Ugandan army described the scene for *Drum* magazine in April 1979, shortly before the collapse of the regime:

> After taking positions on Tanzanian land, we were ordered to give strong resistance and to loot anything we found valuable and hand these to the government. Government experts were brought from Kakira Sugar Works to dismantle a whole sugar factory, the same thing happened to a sawmill. We found a number of bull-dozers which were in good condition. . . . We got thousands of cattle, goats, chickens, sheep, iron sheets, vehicles, women and house-servants for our soldiers. Most of the captured Tanzanians are now working at Kinyala Sugar Works with no pay except food and housing. Lots of private property was also looted.[12]

Notice how he casually lumps women together with animals, iron sheets, and vehicles. This tells us that Amin's forces saw women as war booty, as "things" to be collected and redistributed to the soldiers. His testimony is confirmed by other similar accounts. In *Cross to the Gun*, for instance, Colonel Bernard Rwehururu candidly describes the violence associated with the invasion. He said that after the Ugandan army blew up the bridge that separated the Salient from the rest of Tanzania, they launched into a series of "wild celebrations," which were followed by "[g]ang rape, murder and the looting of all manner of goods and house-hold property."[13] Amin's soldiers raped, murdered, and looted to express their power and domination over the Tanzanians. They used gendered acts of violence to terrorize (read: feminize) the enemy, which in turn reinforced the hypermasculinity of the military state. Avirgan and Honey confirm that the invasion unleashed "an orgy of looting, raping and kill-ing."[14] They suggest that during the Ugandan army's two-week occupa-tion, Amin's soldiers raped and murdered hundreds, if not thousands, of Tanzanian civilians. They took many others hostage and held them in a forced labor camp in southeastern Uganda. Most were never seen again.

The gravity of the situation seemed lost on Amin. Instead of mak-ing an effort to mediate the conflict through traditional diplomatic channels, he challenged the Tanzanian president to a boxing match. Amin offered to fight Nyerere with one arm tied behind his back and weights on his legs to give his opponent a "sporting chance." He said that he wanted to "fight it out" in the boxing ring "rather than have soldiers lose their lives on the battlefield."[15] This preposterous state-ment was just another one of Amin's attempts to bolster his masculinity in the face of mounting opposition. He needed to demonstrate that he remained a strong and powerful leader. By taking these types of utterances seriously and not writing them off as further evidence of Amin's "insanity," we can clearly see the performative aspects of his leadership style, as well as the centrality of gender to military rule.

Not surprisingly, Nyerere refused to acknowledge Amin's grandstanding, since he was more concerned with expelling Ugandan soldiers once and for all. Although his military commanders required several days to gather reinforcements from various parts of the country, they eventually launched a powerful artillery barrage against Amin's soldiers on the north bank. On the night of November 14, several days after arriving at the front, a reconnaissance team of Tanzanian soldiers crossed the river using a few small boats. Amin's troops did not resist, and they returned without incident.[16] Less than one week later, the Tanzanian soldiers assembled a floating bridge, which allowed them to transport most of their troops and weaponry across the river. Once the soldiers began moving out on their patrols, they discovered the magnitude of the destruction. According to Avirgan and Honey, "Each step into the bush revealed more horrors as decapitated and mutilated bodies were found rotting and covered with flies. The Kagera Salient was an eerie world of destruction and the silence of death."[17] As more Tanzanian soldiers made their way across the river, thousands of civilians began to emerge from the forests in which they had been hiding. The soldiers assembled the frightened masses and transported them to safety on the other side of the river. Shortly thereafter, the Tanzanians repaired the damaged bridge, which allowed them to move the rest of their tanks and heavy artillery into position. There they remained for the next two months, patrolling the region and engaging in minor scuffles along the border.

THE COUNTEROFFENSIVE

During the early morning hours of January 21, 1979, Tanzanian forces crossed the border en masse in preparation for a dawn raid on Mutukula, a small town located just inside the Ugandan border. At first light, a battalion of soldiers started marching down the main road toward the town, doing everything they could to call attention to themselves. Amin's forces immediately began defending their position. Because they were so focused on the enemy in front of them, they completely ignored their rear and side flanks. This gave the Tanzanians a perfect opportunity to attack from behind. Avirgan and Honey suggest that the Ugandans were so startled that they began running away in fear, leaving behind a host of weapons and ammunition. The invading army wasted no time in leveling the town. The embedded journalists noted, "Everything was destroyed and every living thing was killed."[18] In revenge for the massacre in the Kagera Salient, the Tanzanians shot those who were too old to flee.

After their victory in Mutukula, the Tanzanian soldiers began making their way northward toward the towns of Masaka and Mbarara, two major strongholds in the southern part of the country. Several units of the Ugandan exile group, Kikosi Maalum ("special battalion" in Kiswahili), joined them. The combined forces fought battles in nearly every town along the way, which sent most of the civilian population into hiding. On the night of February 24, the Tanzanian military began pummeling Masaka with heavy shelling. At dawn's first light, they launched a brutal ground assault that destroyed the town. They used explosives to level those buildings that had not been devastated by artillery fire. The following day, Tanzanian soldiers and Ugandan exiles captured the town of Mbarara, destroying everything in their wake. Even though the Tanzanians never planned to move deeper into Uganda—largely because of the potential diplomatic fallout—President Nyerere ultimately ordered them to press ahead. He knew that if he ordered his troops to withdraw, he would be leaving the population of southern Uganda at the mercy of Amin.[19]

In response to these devastating losses, Amin issued a public appeal to his allies in "Africa, Arab, the third world, socialist countries and the Palestinian Liberation Organization to come to the rescue of the people of Uganda before the situation gets from bad to worse."[20] He also began quietly moving members of his family out of the country, airlifting eighty of his closest relatives to safety in Libya.[21] In addition to offering refuge to Amin's family, Muammar Gaddafi sent in two thousand troops to assist the embattled leader. The Palestinians also sent reinforcements to the front, although they refused to acknowledge their involvement, suggesting that their fighters were simply participating in a "training mission." In the end, neither group proved to be very useful, since they were poorly trained and lacked combat experience. Many, in fact, lost their lives during the war.[22]

Amin's youngest wife, Sarah, did not flee to Libya with the other family members. The state-run media claimed that she had led a women's striking force to the front lines, successfully "rescuing elderly women and orphans" without her husband's knowledge.[23] Radio Uganda announced that "Suicide Sarah" had been in "the thick of the battle leading a battalion against Tanzanian invaders" and that she was the "bravest woman fighter in Uganda."[24] Avirgan and Honey, however, assert that there were no women on the front lines—neither Tanzanian nor Ugandan.[25] This means either that the reporters did not notice the female combatants or that Amin fabricated the story in another clever performance of political theater. Because there is no evidence to suggest that a women's striking force ever existed, I am reluctant to believe Amin's statements, particularly those which he made during his final weeks in power. This claim is likely to have been a further attempt to feminize the enemy. In other words, Tanzanian soldiers were so weak, so poorly organized, that *even* a team of women could outsmart them. This supposition is not meant to suggest that women were not active participants in Amin's regime but instead to question his use of women in this particular context.[26]

It is also important to note that as Sarah and her female troops were allegedly in "the thick of battle," many of Amin's *male* soldiers were on the run. Instead of losing their lives in combat, they attempted to escape while they still had the chance. Robert McGowan, a reporter for the British media, interviewed refugees as they fled across the border into Kenya. One woman told him that she blamed Ugandan soldiers for most of the violence. "They are panic-stricken, hungry and desperate," she said. "I have witnessed open theft and abduction. I've been told of brutality and rape. I believe it." Another person explained that "if you have a pretty wife or daughter, soldiers or the officials of the government just take them and use them. To protest would mean they could kill you and the woman."[27] When I was conducting interviews for this book, I heard many similar accounts of sexual violence. Sylvia Kategaya, a fifty-two-year-old businesswoman from Kampala, told me that during the war "soldiers of Amin used to come to homes and they raped women and their children. They raped their wives and then later they killed them."[28] This resulted in widespread fear and panic, thus providing the retreating army with ample opportunity to escape across the Sudanese or Zairian borders. In other words, rape was not an unfortunate consequence of war but instead a deliberate strategy of engagement.

Amin's soldiers also sought revenge against civilian populations who supported—or were perceived to support—the liberation war.[29] In the northern town of Lira, for instance, rogue forces terrorized the community simply because residents were former president Obote's ethnic kin. In the late 1980s and early 1990s, numerous women testified before the Commission of Inquiry to Investigate Violations of Human Rights within Uganda. Philda Rose Ayao was one such person. She was just twenty-two years old and pregnant when she became a war widow. On March 11, 1979, a group of Amin's soldiers abducted her husband, a local pastor in Lira, from his church. Philda said that as he was preaching, a government soldier walked up to the pulpit and directed him outside. The soldier then forced him into a truck and drove away. She never saw him again. After the abduction of her husband, Philda returned to the church to pray. She noticed that many other soldiers had surrounded the building, preventing the parishioners from leaving. Although she knew that her husband was not guilty of any crime, she did not report the matter to the authorities because, in her mind, everyone already knew about it. She made a strategic decision *not* to tell. Two years after her husband's disappearance, Philda was "inherited" by her brother-in-law. He died several years later, leaving her twice-widowed by the age of thirty.[30]

Margaret Etenu Ebesu became a widow at the age of twenty-nine. Her husband had been the town clerk in Lira. On March 18, she received word that a group of soldiers had arrested her husband from his office, accusing him of supporting the liberation war. The following day, Margaret and her co-wife went into town to investigate. They went straight to the local barracks to see whether they could find their husband. After a guard turned them away, they went to see the district commissioner. There, they learned that the governor—Captain Gala—had ordered their husband's arrest because he wanted to appropriate the town clerk's car. Margaret and her co-wife decided to visit the governor in Gulu, the provincial capital. Despite running into numerous difficulties along the way, they finally managed to reach the governor's office. After receiving assurances that their husband would be released the following day, the women returned home to Lira. Shortly thereafter, they learned that soldiers had killed their husband. When the governor traveled to Lira several days later, he announced that the military had arrested several people for helping the rebels, including their husband. Even though Margaret and her co-wife were supposed to get money from a widows' fund for their children's school fees, they never did.[31] Both women suffered tremendous loss as a result of their husband's death, but they were not simply victims. On the contrary, they were resilient survivors who made calculated decisions on behalf of their family during wartime.

Less than two weeks after the abduction of Margaret's husband, Catherine Boyi witnessed the murder of her brother-in-law and seventeen other people in a village outside of Lira. On the afternoon of March 29, she had gone to her sister-in-law's house to borrow some tea leaves. Moments after her arrival, she heard the unmistakable clamor of gunfire and quickly ran into the kitchen to hide. She described what happened next:

> When we heard the gun shots, we then again escaped into one of the stores in the main house. While we were there, we heard the daughter of Mr. Ogwal who had just come from Kampala seriously crying. . . . [Catherine's sister-in-law] tried to get up [to see why her daughter was crying] but I was trying to stop her not to stand up but she managed to pick up herself. When the woman went to see what was happening, she did not come back to me. She proceeded to another kitchen store [room]. While the gun shots were still continuing, I hid myself just under the elephant grass which was inside the house. When the gun shots stopped, I heard people saying "gasia kwisha" (rubbish finished).[32]

Catherine continued hiding for a long time. When she thought it was finally safe to emerge, she exited the house through the back door. Because "all the dead bodies were on the front side of the main house," she decided to run in the opposite direction. Instead of returning to her home, she spent the night in the bush. It was there that her husband later found her. "Always when there is any problem or change in the government and people are not very sure," she explained, "normally they run [to] the other side of the swamp so it is automatic that you can meet your relatives." She said that to stay alive, "we come during the day time and do the cooking and when night comes then we go away."[33] For three long days, the bodies remained where they had fallen. No one wanted to tend to them, because they were afraid that the killers would come back and attack again. Community members eventually collected the bodies and then buried them in a nearby public cemetery.

Although the police never arrested anyone for the murders, there is strong evidence linking Amin's soldiers to the crime. At the time of the massacre, the government had been holding a large rally in Lira, approximately one and a half miles away. Because Catherine's brother-in-law was a soldier in the Uganda army, his attendance would have been mandatory. Amin's henchmen must have read his absence as evidence that he and his family members were supporters of the liberation war (that is, "legitimate" enemies of the state). To some extent, this was true. Catherine admitted that "people were happy with the situation which was in Kampala because Amin's people were killing people anyhow."[34] In other words, her family was fed up with the government and welcomed its collapse.

THE FINAL DAYS OF THE REGIME

While Amin's forces pillaged the countryside, the liberators pushed onward toward the capital. Meanwhile, in preparation for the inevitable political transition, President Nyerere held a planning conference in the Tanzanian town of Moshi. Representatives of more than two dozen exile groups attended this historic meeting, held March 24–26, 1979. The delegates formed the Uganda National Liberation Front (UNLF), a consortium that comprised three distinct organs. The National Consultative Council (NCC) was the supreme governing body and consisted of thirty representatives, one from each of the exile groups, plus other appointed members. They also created an eleven-person National Executive Committee (NEC), or cabinet, which was responsible for organizing elections within the next two years. And finally, they established a Military Commission, which served as the Front's military arm. The delegates elected Edward Rugamayo as chair of the NCC, Yusuf Lule as chair of the NEC, and Paulo Muwanga as chair of the Military Commission.

While members of the nascent UNLF hammered out the details of their new coalition, Amin's Defense Council issued a dusk-to-dawn curfew and ordered a blackout in Kampala and the surrounding areas.[35] Within twenty-four hours, the beleaguered military ruler reported that Entebbe—home to the country's only international airport—had been cut off from the capital. Despite this major setback, Amin claimed that he was "not very worried" and urged everyone to resume their normal activities. He said that his morale was "very very very high" because he still had tanks to use.[36] The following day, he reassured the public that the situation in Kampala was "normal" and that they did not need to worry about safety. Wives in Uganda, he claimed, were happy because their husbands were coming home early in the evening and now had plenty of time to spend with their families.[37] If there was anyone who could put a positive spin on a state of emergency, it was Amin. Performance, after all, was a crucial mode of governmentality in Amin's Uganda.

Ugandan women, however, told a very different story. Instead of focusing on the curfew as a positive development, many of the women that I interviewed remembered it in a negative light. Lydia Balemezi, the young woman who found herself in a public taxi when Amin banned miniskirts in 1972, was then heavily pregnant with her second child. Her husband, a chief engineer for Nile Breweries, had recently fled into exile to avoid "disappearance." Not wanting to arouse suspicion, Lydia continued working as a tax assessor and waiting for her baby's arrival. Because she was unable to care for a large home, she downsized and began renting a small house behind Makindye Barracks. Shortly after moving into her new home, she went into labor. Although the military government had imposed a strict curfew, she knew that she would need help with the delivery. After leaving her one-year-old child in the care of her "house girl," she began walking toward the hospital.

When she was less than a mile into her journey, Lydia's contractions worsened, and she had to sit down along the roadside. While she was resting, a small car slowed to a stop beside her. Much to her chagrin, the driver and his companion were soldiers. "During those days," she said, "if they saw any pregnant woman, they would open the stomach and say that you are hiding guns and whatever, all the ammunition." Fearing that the soldiers would slice open her womb, Lydia began to cry. The driver got out of the car and started calling her *wadui*, or "enemy" in Kiswahili. She was terrified and began pleading with him in Luganda. "Sir, you are going to kill me for nothing," she said. "I'm in labor pains. I just want to deliver and I was walking to go to Nsambya Hospital." The soldier doubted her story and told her that if she was *really* pregnant, he would take her to the hospital to deliver her baby. Lydia was terrified, but she got into the car.

When they reached the hospital entrance, they found the main gate locked. The watchman on duty refused to open the gate because it was past curfew. Only when the soldier threatened to kill him did the *askari* change his mind and allow them to pass. Once they reached the labor ward, the soldier summoned the midwives and told them to deliver the baby right away. He told them that he would be returning the following morning. Lydia explained what happened next:

Now the midwives started abusing me. "You soldiers' wives, you come here. Now why did you tell your husband that this is where we are to deliver you? Now you want to bring problems to us? Now the man has said that this woman must deliver tonight." So they were telling me, "You go on the bed there. Start pushing because if you don't push, we shall just cut [you] open because your husband has said that you have to deliver today." And somehow I never said that that was not my husband. Because maybe because of the pain . . . because I always wonder as to why I never told those people that that man was not my husband. Anyway, fortunately the contractions came. I delivered. But they refused to administer any medicine to me, so you can imagine.[38]

After giving birth without painkillers, Lydia asked for a glass of water. The nurses told her, "We don't have any boiled water for you. You are a soldier's wife. Why didn't you bring water?" Lydia had no choice but to drink untreated water from the sink. When she asked to be moved to the maternity ward, the nurses refused to take her there because they did not want to disturb the other women. Lydia pleaded with them, and they eventually let her go. Instead of taking her to the ward in a wheelchair as was protocol, however, the nurses forced her to walk. "After all, you soldiers' wives, you are very strong," said one of the nurses. "Walk. Carry your baby and walk." So she had to carry her baby and walk, even though the distance was very far. When she reached the ward, she collapsed onto a mattress on the floor. She was still bleeding, and as she later recalled, "the whole mattress was red." No one seemed to notice.

When Lydia failed to return home, her house girl became worried and decided to seek help. Although it was the middle of the night, she walked to Lydia's sister's home in the Kampala suburb of Kololo. She told her employer's sister, "Mummy went away last night, but she never came back." She thought that her employer had gone to the hospital to give birth but did not know whether she had arrived safely. In the morning, Lydia's sister and mother rented a car and went to Nsambya Hospital. When they got to the labor ward, the midwives told them that a soldier's wife had given birth the night before. The women insisted on seeing the woman and discovered that it was Lydia. They found her "full of blood." Lydia had nothing with which to cover herself because, as she recalled, "even the dress I was putting on was all soiled." They removed some clothes from her sister's baby and prepared to leave. Lydia knew that the soldier would be coming back and wanted to get away as quickly as possible. With her family's assistance, she managed to leave the hospital undetected. When she returned the following month to get her baby's first immunizations, she ran into the midwives who had delivered her baby. They told her that the soldier had returned later that day and was furious to learn that she had left the hospital. The nurses said that he wanted to kill them for letting "his wife" leave without his permission. Lydia told them that although she was not his wife, she could not tell them the truth or they would not have helped her. "I benefited from being a soldier's wife much as I suffered the consequences—the revenge [of] the midwives," she said with a laugh.

It is difficult to imagine the horrors described by Lydia, yet her experiences were not uncommon, at least not for women living near Kampala. Sylvia Kategaya, for instance, told me that as the war intensified, Amin's soldiers tortured and killed many people. "Even those who were young were killed," she said. "Those who were pregnant, their wombs were opened. Yes, here at Rubaga Road there were people who were cut. The babies were killed. Pregnancies were cut out like that. . . . You know now they used to torture people."[39] Chance Kawuma, a fifty-year-old market vendor, agreed that there was "a lot of bloodshed." Because so many people died in the fighting, "the war was bad—very, very bad."[40] Another market trader, Fatima Musisi, described the war as "terrible and strong." She said that people got tired because of the bloodshed. "People were killed and there was heavy fighting," she explained. "People started running again. Everything was spoiled. When you leave a place, you come back when they had stolen everything. The war was very bad."[41]

Many of the women that I interviewed also remembered the Katyusha rocket launchers used by the liberators. Enid Musenyi, a sixty-eight-year-old retired birth attendant, said that "when those men came, the Tanzanians, they came with a gun. That gun was called *Saba Saba*. They could shoot it from here and the missile would land in Kyebando. If it fell there, it would dig a hole, a deep one." Fear drove Enid and her family into hiding. "And during that war we ran," she said. "We ran. People ran. When Saba Saba had started, it is the one that most scared people. They ran to go and hide."[42] Theresa Mukiibi, now a massage therapist, was still a young girl during Amin's rule. Despite her tender age, she vividly remembered running away during the war. This, she said, was when they suffered the most: "We used to move on foot running away from Saba Saba, because they used that gun.

You would never see where it was coming from, so it would just hit. So people ran away. Some would die. You would pass someone who had fallen and was dead. . . . Those days were very difficult."[43]

Most of the women that I interviewed in central Uganda also shared stories of flight and displacement. Throughout the war they made strategic decisions about how best to protect their families during the military onslaught. For instance, Patience Ssekandi, a seventy-five-year-old woman from Bunamwaya, had been working as a teacher when the war broke out. She remembered packing up her house and hiding most of her belongings from the soldiers. She said that she always left her door unlocked because "when they found a house locked and big, they thought that there were a lot of things in it. And they would move around and enter and take what they wanted whether during the day or at night." If the owners left the house open, the soldiers had no excuse to break down the door, a costly repair. Patience and her neighbors grew accustomed to spending the night outside. "You would just go anywhere and sleep nights in trees and also in coffee plantations," she said. "As it would get dark, we thought that they would kill us at night so we left our doors open and we would go into banana plantations and sleep there."[44] Because the war compelled people to sleep outside without mosquito nets, many suffered from malaria. Rose Birungi, an elderly retired nurse, remembered, "People were very badly off during that time of war. They would just run the way they were and you would just sleep there [with] mosquitoes biting you. Even war is like that. Some die when in pain. Some die due to diseases, others due to lack of food. So there's nothing like going for treatment. You are just running."[45]

Many women expressed harrowing tales of near-death experiences as they tried to find safety. Miria Matembe, now one of the country's most prominent politicians, fled the city with her three-month-old baby when she was just twenty-six years old. Shortly before the fall of Kampala, she had been staying with her brother-in-law on the campus of Makerere University. Once the fighting intensified, they decided to move to her home in Port Bell, because they thought it would be safer. As they were making their way down Kampala Road, they reached a roadblock at the main post office. A group of Amin's soldiers summoned them to stop. Although it was dangerous to ignore their commands, she knew that it was even more dangerous to obey them. She kept walking. "I'm telling you," said Miria, "that was the longest distance I have ever walked in my life." But then the soldiers cocked their guns. They had no choice but to stop, at which point the soldiers began beating them and threatening to shoot them. Miria knelt down and began praying to God. "They kicked me and I fell down and they kicked my brother-in-law," she said. After they got up, they slowly walked away. Although she fully expected "a bullet to go through the head," she managed to escape without further incident. "They never killed us," she said, "because God saved us."[46]

While Miria and her family fled the university in search of safety, others, such as Namuli Kasozi, sought refuge there. According to the sixty-year-old market vendor from Wandegeya, Amin's soldiers would "invade a place [and] search in the house. They would kill or rape women. We could leave the place and come to sleep at Makerere. We ran up to the hill. We only went back to cook our food. And during the day, they would not attack people. They would start around evening hours, about 6:00 o'clock, and then we would run away and come to . . . Makerere. That's where we used to spend our nights for most of the days up until the war ended. . . . We were sleeping in the students' halls."[47] By this point the campus was largely deserted, since many students had returned to their homes. Only those who were unable to flee remained in the dormitories.

The late Ugandan historian Benoni Turyahikayo-Rugyema was one such student. He remembered that those who remained on campus celebrated the shelling of Kampala because it signaled their liberation from Amin's tyranny. To keep up their morale, the besieged students referred to the Tanzanian rocket launchers, or Saba Saba, as "Paul." Whenever the rockets pummeled the city at night, the students would cry out, "Paul, Paul, where have you been all this time? Please liberate us." He claimed that the female students were particularly enamored with "Paul." Whenever they heard the telltale roar, they would run to their dormitory windows and shout, "Saba Saba me! Long range me!"[48] These exclamations were not only sexually provocative but also suggested a deeper meaning, namely, that they wanted Amin out of power even if it signaled their own demise. By shouting "Saba Saba me," they were announcing their readiness to fight. In other words, "bring it on."

As the security situation in the capital continued to deteriorate, the liberators prepared for their final offensive. On April 1, the Tanzanians launched an artillery assault on the nearby town of Entebbe, forcing Amin to flee State House for Kampala. Several days later, he broadcast an announcement from Jinja stating that he was "in a relaxed and jovial mood." Assuming a posture of masculine bravado, he dismissed all reports that he had gone into hiding and then assured listeners that he was "prepared to die in the defense of his motherland."[49] Shelling intensified during the night of April 6 and reached a crescendo the following morning. Tanzanian forces blew up a Libyan C-130 cargo plane as it attempted to rescue thirty Libyan soldiers. As the attack continued, hundreds of Libyan soldiers tried desperately to find their way to Kampala. Instead of offering them safe passage, the Ugandan civilians turned them over to the liberators or killed them outright. Jane Walusimbi, a farmer who lived alongside Entebbe Road, described how they defeated the Libyans:

> They were all over, and they didn't know where they were going. They didn't know where Kampala was . . . so they just ran anyhow. When they found you they could ask, "Where is Kampala?" and whichever place you pointed to is where they ran to, thinking that it was the direction where Kampala was. Even if you told him, "In the forest," he would run towards the forest. And they were killed. People would find them . . . and then they would shout that "they are here" and they would at times close them in the house and kill them. And they were buried in mass graves. And up there, many were killed and buried there. . . . When they came across them they just killed them and he could maybe come and ask for water and they would tell him to enter and when he entered, they would lock him in.[50]

Women like Jane participated in the capture and murder of numerous Libyan soldiers. During this phase of the war, the liberators and their Ugandan allies killed at least three hundred Libyans and took more than forty as prisoners.[51] This violence added to the mass hysteria sweeping through the nation. As the Tanzanians slowly made their way from Entebbe to Kampala, the rest of Amin's forces fled the capital, violently looting everything in their wake. By the time that the first group of liberators had reached the outskirts of the capital on the afternoon of April 10, 1979, the war-weary population could hardly contain their excitement. According to Avirgan and Honey,

> For the first time that day, people began appearing at the roadsides, at first in clusters of five or ten and then in groups of hundreds and finally, as Kampala came nearer, in tens of thousands.

The civilians were waving branches, beating drums and cheering wildly, running alongside and among the advancing Tanzanian troops. They, too, knew that up to now the Tanzanian and UNLF soldiers could have turned back and left the Ugandans to their fate. That was a very real fear among the Baganda of the area, for Amin had promised retribution. But once Kampala was taken there could be no turning back. Amin was finished and the crowds on the Entebbe Road knew it.[52]

The following morning, on April 11, Colonel David Oyite-Ojok announced the collapse of the regime on Radio Uganda. He said that Kampala was in the hands of the UNLF and that residents should remain calm. He warned Amin's soldiers to surrender immediately. Later that evening, Yusuf Lule broadcast his own speech to the nation. He said that as the chair of the National Executive Committee, he would serve as interim president until elections could be organized. Amin also took to the airwaves the following day, denouncing all claims that his regime had been overthrown. No one believed him, however, since it was apparent that the Tanzanians and the UNLF were firmly in control. Amin and his loyal supporters had no choice but to flee.[53]

THE RETREAT

The looting of Kampala began shortly after Colonel Oyite-Ojok announced the liberation. Wasting no time, throngs of Ugandan men, women, and children took to the streets, grabbing virtually everything that they could seize. By late afternoon, the city streets were so crowded with looters that cars and military vehicles were unable to move. In an effort to maintain the public's goodwill, the Tanzanian soldiers helped the civilians break into warehouses that contained a variety of essential commodities. Instead of appeasing the population, their actions sparked a new wave of hysteria. By the following morning, the looting was completely out of control. Avirgan and Honey suggest, "Mobs were stripping bare not only abandoned homes, but also occupied ones where owners were too meek to protect their property. Every shop, warehouse, office and house was stripped bare. The plate glass windows of car showrooms were shattered and the vehicles minus only keys and gasoline were pushed out through the windows and down the streets. It was as though swarms of locusts in human form had descended to devour the flesh and fat of the Ugandan capital, leaving only the bare bones of brick and mortar."[54] Meanwhile, the last vestiges of Amin's army were frantically trying to get out of town with as much loot as they could possibly carry. The easiest way to escape was in civilian dress, so the soldiers roamed the residential areas in search of clothing, food, and cars. Those hapless victims who were unwilling to part with their belongings were immediately gunned down, their bodies left bloated and rotting along the tree-lined streets. Amin's fleeing soldiers murdered so many civilians that by the end of the week, "scores of corpses were scattered throughout the city's plush residential areas."[55]

Despite the chaos, Yusuf Lule was sworn in as president on the afternoon of April 13, thus marking the end of more than eight years of military rule. Given that all government offices had been looted, the entire cabinet moved into Nile Mansions, an annex of the International Conference Center that Amin had had constructed for the OAU Conference in 1975. The ministers were unable to leave the luxurious hotel because of the ongoing violence. Lule was even further removed from the action. After taking his oath of office, he moved to State House in Entebbe, where he remained a virtual prisoner until his former comrades ousted him from power sixty-eight days later.

Meanwhile, the civilian population began seeking revenge on "Amin's people." Ondoga ori Amaza had been studying medicine at Makerere University at the time. Although he was an ethnic Madi from West Nile, he had no connections to the military and therefore did not expect that he would need to flee. Unfortunately, he seriously underestimated the extent to which Amin's behavior had been "West-Nilized." "For no sooner was Amin overthrown than everybody from West Nile became not only Amin's agent but even a foreigner," he recalled. "We were variously labeled Sudanese, Nubians or Anyanya. People from West Nile, the Kakwa, Lugbara and Madi in particular, found themselves being singled out as those responsible for Amin's misdeeds." Life became so precarious that if a northerner was stopped at a roadblock and forced to reveal his or her name, this person would be treated as an enemy.[56]

The security situation was no better in other parts of the country. In Bushenyi District, for instance, Yudaaya Nakakande witnessed the murder of her husband and two sons in a brutal revenge killing. One morning in mid-April 1979, as she was working in her banana plantation, an angry group of neighbors marched into her compound carrying machetes. They announced that they were looking for Muslims and wanted to "cut them to pieces and see to it that they follow their fellow moslem [sic] Amin." She immediately hid her younger children in the plantation, but it was too late for those at home. "They found my husband in the compound and they did not ask anything except to start cutting him to pieces," she said. "Then they ran after my brother-in-law whom they arrested [or captured] and also brought him back at home in the compound and they started also slashing him." After killing one of her older sons in the attack, they grabbed another one and dragged him toward the river. Yudaaya explained, "They took him alive and, when they reached the river, they killed him and threw him in the river where he decomposed." Although Yudaaya managed to escape, her neighbors warned her never to come back. It took her more than two months to convince the police to escort her to her home so that she could bury her loved ones. When they arrived at the compound on June 26, she found their bodies exactly as they had fallen. The police helped her move the bodies but were unable to offer any additional assistance. Even though she was able to identify the persons who murdered her family, the police never made an arrest.[57]

Kasifa Banyagwine lost her husband and her brother-in-law in the same massacre when she was thirty years old. Her description of the attack was very similar to the one provided by Yudaaya and illustrates the complex decision-making processes that women employed to protect their children:

> We saw people coming armed with pangas. I saw Kyarubale, Buturuna, Ndyaba, Wakasheija, their mother Kyamoima who was making *"enduuru"* (alarm). Karubale first came to us as if he was greeting us and when he reached a certain hill, then we saw many people coming. I ran away and hid in a nearby plantation. The people had stones, spears, pangas. I hid there with children, leaving my husband behind. They had already arrested him and were going to kill him—they were the people I mentioned earlier. They were all Christians. They said that your leader Amin has been removed. I heard this said as I was going to hide. Amin was leader of everybody, but it was said that we had been proud because Amin was a moslem [sic].

After the attackers left, Kasifa crawled out of her hiding place and slowly made her way back to the compound. She found her husband "still alive but kicking about before he died." He was alone. She recalled that he had been speared in the abdomen and that his intestines were falling out. His skull was also fractured and "his brains came out." She and her children ran away to her natal village, where they stayed for nearly three months. She eventually returned to the scene of the massacre with Yudaaya so that they could bury the bodies. Once they completed the burial, Kasifa "organized a few iron sheets and built a house in which [she] still live[s] up to now." She did not understand why the attackers had murdered her husband and his brother. "I did not know of any quarrels between them and us," she said. "We lived our lives peacefully." Because of the massacre, however, she did not think that Christians and Muslims could live together again.[58]

These types of revenge killings continued for several more years, leaving the entire nation angry, wounded, and afraid. Contrary to many people's expectations, the liberation of Kampala did not signal the end of the war. Instead, it represented a changing of the guard—the replacement of one violent military regime with another, albeit one that was cloaked in civilian dress. As the UNLF government struggled to restore order, the Tanzanian military chased the rest of Amin's defunct army out of the country. Although those stationed along the western front engaged in heavy resistance, most eventually fled into exile in Sudan or Zaire, where they remained for many years to come. By the time the liberators reached the northwestern border on June 3, 1979, they found the region largely deserted. Nearly everyone from West Nile had run away.

↬

When Esther Ssengendo fled Mulago Hospital with her youngest child during the final siege on Kampala, she had no idea whether they would make it home alive. The once magnificent city of seven hills had become a war zone, a place where anyone could be killed at any time. It was dangerous to run, but it was even more dangerous to stay behind. Esther, like so many others, took a calculated risk to protect her daughter. Her story demonstrates that Ugandan women were not simply victims of a violent conflict but instead historical actors who engaged in complex decision-making processes throughout the war. Philda Rose Ayao was equally strategic. She made the decision not to inform the authorities after her husband was abducted in broad daylight, because the culprits were likely security agents of the state. She knew that because he was Langi, a member of the former president's ethnic group, the government saw him as an enemy and had targeted him for revenge. Patience Ssekandi, a Muganda from the central region of Uganda, had a different experience of the war. She kept her family alive by moving them outdoors at night so that they could sleep in the banana plantation. She left the doors of her house open so that soldiers would think that there was nothing of value inside. Miria Matembe, in contrast, bravely walked away from soldiers at a roadblock in Kampala with her three-month-old baby because she knew that it would be more dangerous to stay. Although Amin's thugs beat her and her brother-in-law for disobeying their orders, she made the decision that ultimately saved their lives. Yudaaya Nakakande of Bushenyi was not as lucky, although she too displayed tremendous courage. After witnessing the brutal murder of her husband and two sons in revenge killings because they were considered "Amin's people," she hid her younger children in the banana plantation so that they would survive. These stories illustrate the difficult choices that women made throughout the war to protect their families, as well as the tremendous courage, strength, and foresight that each of them possessed.

This chapter also confirms the centrality of gender to the larger war effort by revealing the ways in which Amin invoked and deployed masculinity and femininity throughout the conflict. In the days leading up to the commencement of the war, he positioned himself as a father figure who would protect "his children," even if they happened to live across the border. His soldiers, however, used gender in a very different way. During the offensive, they raped Tanzanian women to demonstrate their dominance. As a deliberate feminizing act, these rapes reinforced the hypermasculinity of the military state. Amin also utilized feminizing tactics as an assertion of his power. When he challenged President Nyerere to a boxing match, for instance, he was attempting to demonstrate his strength and virility. And when he celebrated his wife Sarah's military prowess, it was not because she was the "bravest woman fighter in Uganda" but because it demonstrated the "weakness" of Tanzanian soldiers. He wanted the nation to believe that the enemy was so weak, so poorly organized, that even a team of women could outsmart them. Through these kinds of strategic gender performances, Amin crafted a world of military power and strength that profoundly belied the realities on the ground.

CONCLUSION
Gendered Legacies of Amin's Militarism

"It was terrible, terrible, worse than even what Amin did," whispered Prossi Asumi as she nervously straightened the folds of her long pleated skirt. We were sitting outside a repurposed cargo container that she had converted into a small sundries shop in Arua, discussing her life after the liberation war. "You know, with Amin, he used to pick people who have made a mistake. He'd pick one person. He brings. But with these people, they were taking everybody. So it was terrible, terrible."[1] By "these people," Prossi was referring to the string of rulers who attempted to govern the country after Amin's ouster. *Attempt* is the operative word, since there were four different leaders in power between April 1979 and December 1980, none of whom was able to quell the violence and discontent ravaging the nation. Most of the women I interviewed believed that Milton Obote was the worst of the lot, having come back into power after a widely disputed presidential election in late 1980. His henchmen reportedly "picked," or disappeared, many more people than had Amin and his military thugs.

Goretti Ssali, a fifty-nine-year-old teacher from central Uganda, had a similar perspective. She told me that Amin "didn't kill families like Obote did during his rule."[2] When I asked her to elaborate, she said, "Obote's soldiers would find you as we are here and they would kill all of us. But for Amin, he only came and would say that I want that one. He's the one he would take, and kill [only] him." Goretti believed that Amin's rule was better because his soldiers killed "only" their intended targets, not entire families. These women's stories confirm that despite the brutality of Amin's military dictatorship, what came later was much worse. Many others would agree. For example, as Holger Bernt Hansen and Michael Twaddle suggest, "The material devastation and sheer scale of atrocities perpetrated by the second Obote government (1980–1985) and its short-lived successor in late 1985 are now widely considered by Ugandans to have matched anything suffered under Amin's earlier murderous regime."[3] This does not mean that we should ignore or downplay the violence of Amin's rule; instead, we must also pay attention to the legacies of violence that his militarism produced.

Militarism is alive and well in Uganda today. In fact, if you were to walk down the main thoroughfare in Kampala and glance up toward the High Court Building, you would likely be confronted by an imposing barrage of heavily armed military vehicles, as well as an assortment of military and paramilitary forces standing guard nearby, submachine guns slung across their shoulders, nightsticks at their waists. The fact that there is such a pronounced military presence in a country that is no longer at war or governed by military rule says a great deal about the pervasiveness of militarism in contemporary Uganda. More than thirty years after the collapse of Amin's dictatorship, military values continue to define and shape the nation as a whole, much to the detriment of women, children, and civilian men. These values have been normalized to such an extent that most citizens cannot imagine anything different. This deeply embedded culture of militarism is undoubtedly Amin's most enduring legacy.

One of the ways in which this militarism has been carried into the present is through armed conflict and civil unrest. After the liberation war, soldiers of the Uganda National Liberation Army—the armed wing of the Uganda National Liberation Front—began carrying out revenge attacks on "Amin's people," those who were associated with the ousted military ruler because of their ethnicity, their religion, and/or their relationship to the former regime. These attacks took place throughout the country and resulted in tremendous loss of life, as well as massive displacement and hardship for the affected populations. This is the type of violence that Prossi and Goretti referenced when they talked about life in Uganda after the fall of Amin. Military rule created a pattern of governance that encouraged those in power to use extrajudicial forms of violence to punish "subversives" and "saboteurs." Those so targeted also used violence to destabilize the existing government, thus setting in motion a relentless cycle of bloodshed and terror that continues to this day. In fact, the U.S. National Intelligence Council recently named Uganda as one of fourteen countries at high risk of becoming a failed state because of weak governance and active rebellions.[4]

Since Amin's ouster in April 1979, there have been no fewer than thirteen armed rebel groups operating within various parts of Uganda.[5] The first organized antigovernment resistance efforts began shortly after Obote returned from exile in May 1980 and announced that he would be competing in the presidential elections. In an effort to thwart his candidacy and bring stability to West Nile, two distinct rebel groups emerged, both of which were composed of Amin's former soldiers—the Uganda National Rescue Front and the Former Uganda National Army. Although the former had much more staying power than the latter, both groups posed a major security threat to the state and were therefore met with fierce counterinsurgency measures. At the same time, in the central and western regions of Uganda, two former anti-Amin resistance groups merged to take on the mounting threat posed by the government. Yoweri Museveni's Popular Resistance Army joined forces with Yusuf Lule's Uganda Freedom Fighters to form the National Resistance Army. Shortly after Obote "won" the disputed presidential elections, this motley band of guerrilla fighters declared war on the government, a protracted struggle that lasted more than four years and resulted in the death and displacement of countless civilians, particularly within the Luwero Triangle. In late July 1985, a group of high-ranking military officers staged a successful coup and ousted Obote from power for the second time. Six months later, Museveni and his National Resistance Army toppled the military government, promising to restore peace and democracy to the nation. Within a short period of time, however, several new rebel groups had emerged, thus perpetuating the cycle of violence and instability that had begun during Amin's rule.

Not surprisingly, this incessant conflict has had significant effects on Ugandan women and gender relations. It has resulted in the displacement of hundreds of thousands of people. In northern and eastern Uganda alone, upward of two million people were forced to flee their homes over a twenty-year period because of incursions by the Lord's Resistance Army, as well as the government's counterinsurgency operations. Most women found it difficult to provide food for their families within internal displacement camps, since agricultural land was extremely limited. Many also experienced rape and mutilation at the hands of both government soldiers and the rebels. Those who survived had to deal with severe psychological trauma, physical injuries, and long-term health consequences, such as HIV/AIDS and vaginal fistulas. As if that were not enough, many women have also witnessed the brutal abduction and/or murder of family members, similar to what occurred in the days of Amin's military rule.[6] These violent disruptions have compelled women to assume new roles and responsibilities within the household. While this has proven a source of empowerment for some, for others it has resulted in an increase in sexual and gender-based violence by men who have felt emasculated by their loss of power and control.

The legacy of Amin's militarism is also reflected in the current government's pattern of heavy military spending. According to the Stockholm International Peace Research Institute, the government of Uganda spent US $578 million on military expenditures in 2011, or 3.2 percent of the country's gross domestic product.[7] Angola and South Sudan were the only other countries in sub-Saharan Africa with higher levels of spending (in terms of dollars spent and percentage of gross domestic product), and both of those countries are heavily invested in oil production. While oil development is certainly near on Uganda's horizon, this cannot explain the country's long history of exorbitant military spending. Most of it has been justified on the basis of national security—the need to protect the nation from various internal and external threats. In theory, the security of the state is supposed to result in the security of the individual. In actual fact, however, this has rarely been the case. Amina Mama and Margo Okazawa-Rey maintain, "Militarised notions of security promise protection yet rely on institutionalising fear and violence at all levels of society, thus creating and sustaining profound insecurity, especially among women."[8] The militarism of the contemporary state, much like that of Amin's era, has not offered adequate protection for Ugandan women. In many ways, it has fomented even greater violence and insecurity.[9] As the state's military forces become increasingly involved in external conflicts, either as belligerents or as peacekeepers, one can only expect that "security" will become even more tenuous. Furthermore, there will be less money available in the national coffers to pay for health, education, and other social services that can provide genuine security for the masses.

Although Ugandan women have struggled with the violent legacies of militarism, they have also played an important role in promoting military norms and values. During Amin's rule, they supported the military establishment as the wives, daughters, sisters, and aunties of enlisted men. They also served the military state through their involvement in the police and security sectors. Today they have become even more militarized, bravely serving their country as soldiers and officers in their own right. Unlike Amin, who wanted the armed forces to remain a bastion of hypermasculinity, Museveni has chosen to fully integrate women into the military. This decision has allowed him to expand the ranks, while at the same time providing new career opportunities for women. However, as of 2012, there were only 1,828 women serving in the state's military forces (out of an estimated total of 46,800 troops).[10] The vast majority of them, some 63 percent, lacked decision-making power and were clustered at the lowest rank of "private." One must therefore wonder what types of "opportunities" are really available to women who are serving in a hypermasculine military institution, especially given that their numbers are proportionally low. Perhaps more to the point, has military service empowered even these women, given the context of rape and sexual harassment that military life in Uganda (as in the United States and elsewhere) entails? Whether a part of the military machine or ground under its heel, women who continue to live in the shadows of gendered violence and militarism still have much to teach us.

APPENDIX

Methods and Sources

ALTHOUGH THERE are numerous challenges in writing a book about gender and militarism, none have proven more vexing than those related to sources. First, there is a serious lack of documentation about the regime's inner workings. Amin often prohibited nonmembers from attending meetings of the Defense Council, so there is no record of their proceedings. While he allowed secretaries to attend meetings of the cabinet, these minutes were destroyed during the siege on Kampala in April 1979 when looters pilfered the contents of the Parliamentary Library and the Cabinet Record Office.[1] Similar looting took place at the headquarters of the State Research Centre, but somehow a handful of documents managed to survive. These reports provide important clues about the organizational structure of Amin's most notorious "security" unit.

One of the most important sources for this project was the *Report of the Commission of Inquiry into Disappearances of People in Uganda since 25 January, 1971*. Beginning in July 1974, 545 individuals testified before a government panel about the "disappearance" of their loved ones. At least 30 percent of the witnesses were women, all of whom provided damning evidence about the regime's culpability in the campaign of terror. When the commissioners briefed Amin on the contents of the final report, he refused to publish the findings. Until very recently, there was only one known copy of the report in the entire country.[2] In mid-2009, the U.S. Institute of Peace tracked down the eight-hundred-page document and uploaded it to the Internet as part of a larger initiative to develop a Truth Commission Digital Collection. Though this crucial document is now widely available online, nearly one-third of the report is illegible, which leaves important gaps in the historical record.

Closely related to the problem of "missing" sources is the issue of access, namely, how to locate materials that are said to exist "somewhere." Nothing is more frustrating than knowing that an important body of evidence is nearby but somehow just out of reach. When I was attempting to locate arrest reports at the Central Police Station in Kampala, for instance, I was told that the files had been moved to the Quarter Guard in another part of town. When I arrived at the Quarter Guard, I was told that they had been moved to the police post on Buganda Road. And when I arrived at the police post, I was told that the files had been destroyed and that I needed to talk to the inspector general of police (IGP). After several days of trying to make an appointment, I was finally allowed to meet the IGP, who told me that the records did in fact exist but that I would need to obtain "clearance" before I could access them. Several days later, once I had gotten the necessary authorizations, I returned to the Central Police Station in search of the elusive documents. Not surprisingly, the man with the key to the storeroom was nowhere to be found. After securing an appointment and "bouncing" several more times, I finally had the opportunity to examine the files. The problem, as I soon discovered, was that the files were not organized in any particular order. Floor to ceiling, the room was crammed with assorted folders containing tattered case files that covered the past forty-some years. Files from 1968 were mixed in with files from the previous year, as were random saucepans, blankets, and police batons. That I was eventually able to locate nearly fifty cases of women whom the police arrested in the 1970s for miniskirt violations was no small miracle. I have no doubt that a mountain of valuable evidence remains buried in this and other storerooms across the country.[3]

So how does one conduct this type of research when much of the evidence is missing or otherwise inaccessible? I found that one of the best ways to learn about women's experiences of militarism (as well as the gender of militarism more generally) was through oral interviews. I conducted in-depth interviews with more than one hundred Ugandans from all walks of life, including farmers, market traders, activists, and government officials. The youngest were in their mid-forties— teenagers at the time of Amin's rule—while the oldest were in their late eighties. The vast majority came from the following eight districts: Kampala, Luwero, Wakiso, Nakasongola, Koboko, Yumbe, Maracha, and Arua. To get a better understanding of Amin and his ideas on gender, I also met with six of his former cabinet ministers, as well as several other close associates. Except for public figures and/or those who spoke to me in an official capacity, I assigned them a pseudonym to protect their privacy. A complete list of interview names, dates, and locations can be found in the bibliography.

Oral interviews were an invaluable source of information, but they also presented many challenges. One major concern centered on the issue of trust. How could I convince the people whom I wanted to interview that I was trustworthy, that they should feel comfortable opening up about their most intimate secrets? Although Amin had been out of power for more than twenty-five years when I began my fieldwork in 2004, the subject matter remained politically sensitive. I mediated some of these difficulties through snowball sampling, starting with the Wandegeya market women whom I had known for many years. These women trusted me, for I had spent hundreds of hours hanging out in the market when I was a graduate student at Makerere University in the late 1990s. They answered my questions and then brought me to their homes, and then to their friends' homes, until I had developed an expansive network of contacts. When I returned to Uganda in 2008 to conduct additional interviews, I used a similar strategy to make contacts with individuals from the northern part of the country. Fortunately, I worked with an excellent team of research assistants who also served as important cultural liaisons. They introduced me to individuals in their home communities, who in turn introduced me to others. Their local contacts allowed me to interview a wide variety of people from many different social, political, and religious backgrounds. Although I took the lead on the interviews with public figures, my assistants facilitated those that were done in local languages. While I am fairly conversant in Luganda and Kiswahili, I did not feel comfortable conducting the interviews alone.

Another major concern had to do with the reliability of oral sources, in terms of not only how well people remembered the past but also how they interpreted it. Most of my interviews were conducted twenty-five to thirty years after Amin's fall from power, thus making it difficult for individuals to remember certain points. Although numerous interviewees could not remember many details of their lives during Amin's rule, many others could. I was always surprised by the amount of information that they were able to recall. Fortunately, there were enough similarities across the narratives that I was able to identify key historical patterns, as well as interesting anomalies.

The problem of forgetting was not nearly as pressing as the problem of remembering, more specifically, how the present informed people's understandings of the past. Many Ugandans have grown weary of the current president, Yoweri Kaguta Museveni, and are looking back at Amin's rule with some degree of nostalgia.[4] Many of the women I interviewed remembered the economic opportunities that arose after the Asian expulsion in 1972, opportunities that seem to be sorely lacking in today's global marketplace. They also remembered that Amin restored "morality" to young urban women by banning miniskirts and other forms of "indecent" dress. This undoubtedly stemmed from their frustration over the "loose values" of today's youth. One woman even claimed that if Amin had been president today, there would not be an AIDS crisis in Uganda. She believed that he would have stopped the spread of HIV, just as he had tried to do with venereal disease in 1977.[5] Women's interpretations of Amin were clearly influenced by current political realities but also by the legacies of violence that have enveloped the country for nearly fifty years. Compared to the horrors that emerged in later years, Amin's rule did not seem *that bad* to many women.

To ensure that these types of memories were grounded in historical truths, I compared them with a variety of other types of archival evidence. At the Africana Collection at Makerere University Library, I analyzed local, regional, and religious newspapers. The main government newspaper, *Uganda Argus* (renamed *Voice of Uganda* in late 1972), was published in English six days per week. I scoured the entire series, examining nearly 2,500 print editions. I also frequently read the *East African Standard,* an English daily newspaper covering Kenya, Tanzania, and Uganda, and *Munno,* a Luganda newspaper published regularly by the Catholic Church. These publications allowed me to analyze how gender ideologies were circulated for public consumption in the 1970s. For information on post-Amin's Uganda, I consulted the state-run *Uganda Times.*

At the Photographic Section in what was then the Ministry of Information and Broadcasting, I was able to examine numerous boxes of relevant photographs and negatives. These were particularly useful in helping me to track the movements of Amin's wives. Official photographers carefully documented all of their public appearances, although few of these images ever made it into the actual newspaper. It was there that I also discovered an audio recording of a speech given by Madina Amin on Women's Day in 1975 (analyzed in detail in chapter 5). The archivist told me that although there had once been numerous recordings of all of his wives' public addresses, all but this one had been accidentally destroyed because of rain damage.

The Parliamentary Library was another important repository of evidence. There, I was able to obtain copies of all of Amin's presidential decrees. These documents helped me to verify which of his proclamations had been codified and which had been ignored (or forgotten). This did not, however, help me to determine which of the decrees were actually enforced. For that, I had to rely on arrest records from the Central Police Station and, to a lesser extent, those reported in the daily newspapers.

Another crucial source of information was the fifteen-volume report of the Commission of Inquiry into Violations of Human Rights, which examines violations that occurred from the time of independence until the current government took power in 1986. Over the course of nearly seven years, the commissioners interviewed 608 witnesses about a wide variety of incidents, many of which took place during Amin's rule.[6] Their testimonies provide important clues about the state's security regime, particularly in terms of the effect it had on women's lives. The complete report, which includes verbatim testimony from all witnesses, is housed at the Uganda Human Rights Commission.

In addition to the aforementioned sources, I also discovered a wealth of information in the archives of the Uganda People's Congress. Although the materials were not catalogued at the time, the archivist provided me with copies of numerous unpublished reports and documents. At the Buganda Parliament in Mengo, I met with Medi Nsereko, who is a local broadcaster with CBS Radio Uganda. He shared an audio recording of an interview that he had conducted with Madina Amin in 2005. This interview helped me to better understand the marital relationship between Amin and his fourth official wife.

Some of the most interesting information for the book came from Bob Astles, a British expatriate who was in charge of the Anti-smuggling Unit that was established in 1975. In August 2009, I contacted him via e-mail, asking whether he would be willing to tell me about his Ugandan wife, Mary Senkatuka Astles, who served as a minister in Amin's government. He responded enthusiastically to my request, and we began corresponding regularly over the next eighteen months. In January 2011, he invited me to visit him at his home outside of London. I accepted his offer, bought a plane ticket, and then spent five days as his houseguest. In between our conversations, his companion, Betty, brought me stacks of documents and newspaper clippings that she had collected over the years. Getting to know one of Amin's closest friends was an incredible opportunity, providing me with a wealth of information, only some of which made it into this book. As with any source, I had to pick and choose what made the most sense in light of the story that I was trying to tell. Bob's perspective was not always one that I shared, but I am grateful for the opportunity to have met him. Sadly, he passed away in January 2013 before I had completed this book.

Notes

INTRODUCTION: IN SEARCH OF AMIN'S WOMEN

1. George Ivan Smith, *Ghosts of Kampala* (New York: St. Martin's Press, 1980), 103, 110.

2. Quoted in Joseph Kamau [pseud.] and Andrew Cameron [pseud.], *Lust to Kill: The Rise and Fall of Idi Amin* (London: Transworld Publishers, 1979), 119. For additional information on Amin's "diagnosis," see Loyal N. Gould and James Leo Garrett Jr., "Amin's Uganda: Troubled Land of Religious Persecution," *Journal of Church and State* 19, no. 3 (1977): 434.

3. M. S. M. Semakula Kiwanuka, *Amin and the Tragedy of Uganda* (Munich: Weltforum, 1979), 7.

4. Smith, *Ghosts of Kampala*, 110.

5. David Gwyn [pseud.], *Idi Amin: Death-Light of Africa* (Boston: Little, Brown, 1977), 5; Henry Kyemba, *A State of Blood: The Inside Story of Idi Amin* (New York: Paddington Press, 1977), 111. See also Godfrey Lule, "Life Has No Value for the Butcher," *Daily Mirror* (London), July 4, 1977.

6. For an interesting discussion of Amin as an icon of evil in contemporary Euro-American society, see Mark Leopold, "Sex, Violence and History in the Lives of Idi Amin: Postcolonial Masculinity as Masquerade," *Journal of Postcolonial Writing* 45, no. 3 (September 2009): 321–30.

7. Kamau and Cameron, *Lust to Kill*, 30.

8. Gould and Garrett, "Amin's Uganda," 435.

9. Smith, *Ghosts of Kampala*, 17.

10. Ali Mazrui, "The Resurrection of the Warrior Tradition in African Political Culture," *Journal of Modern African Studies* 13, no. 1 (1975): 67.

11. Ali Mazrui, *Soldiers and Kinsmen in Uganda: The Making of a Military Ethnocracy* (Beverly Hills, CA: Sage, 1975), 149.

12. Other scholars have found Mazrui's analysis problematic for different reasons. Aidan Southall, for example, argues that the celebration of an essential warrior tradition is dangerous because it reinforces racist stereotypes about the "savagery" of Africans. Southall, "Social Disorganization in Uganda Before, During, and After Amin," *Journal of Modern African Studies* 18, no. 4 (1980): 627–56. Timothy Parsons, in contrast, rejects the idea of an African martial tradition altogether. He argues that officers of the King's African Rifles invented martial traditions among particular ethnic groups to bolster recruitment. In other instances, the colonial government militarized cultural

practices. Parsons suggests that ethnic groups in this part of Africa did not possess innate warrior qualities but instead enlisted large numbers of soldiers because of economic underdevelopment. Parsons, *The African Rank-and-File: Social Implications of Colonial Military Service in the King's African Rifles, 1902–1964* (Portsmouth, NH: Heinemann, 1999).

13. Joan Wallach Scott, introduction to *Gender and the Politics of History* (New York: Columbia University Press, 1999), 2.

14. Oyèrónkẹ́ Oyěwùmí argues that gender did not exist in precolonial Yorubaland. Social organization was based on seniority, a relational category, and not on gendered bodies. It did not follow a "bio-logic," or biological logic, as one finds in the West. Oyěwùmí, *The Invention of Women: Making an African Sense of Western Gender Discourses* (Minneapolis: University of Minnesota Press, 1997).

15. Ifi Amadiume, *Male Daughters, Female Husbands: Gender and Sex in an African Society* (London: Zed Books, 1987).

16. Nwando Achebe, "'And She Became a Man': King Ahebi Ugbabe in the History of Enugu-Ezike, Northern Igboland, 1880–1948," in *Men and Masculinities in Modern Africa*, ed. Lisa A. Lindsay and Stephan F. Miescher (Portsmouth, NH: Heinemann, 2003), 52–68.

17. Stephan F. Miescher and Lisa A. Lindsay, "Introduction: Men and Masculinities in Modern African History," in *Men and Masculinities in Modern Africa*, ed. Lisa A. Lindsay and Stephan F. Miescher (Portsmouth, NH: Heinemann, 2003), 4.

18. Butler suggests that gender is "an identity tenuously constituted in time—an identity instituted through a *stylized repetition of acts*" (emphasis in the original). Judith Butler, "Performative Acts and Gender Constitution: An Essay in Phenomenology and Feminist Theory," *Theater Journal* 40, no. 4 (December 1988): 519.

19. Jacklyn Cock, introduction to *Society at War: The Militarization of South Africa*, ed. Jacklyn Cock and Laurie Nathan (New York: St. Martin's Press, 1989), 2. For a general introduction to militarism in Africa, see Yash Tandon, *Militarism and Peace Education in Africa: A Guide and Manual for Peace Education and Action in Africa* (Nairobi: African Association for Literacy and Adult Education, 1989); Robin Luckham, "The Military, Militarization, and Democratization in Africa: A Survey of Literature and Issues," *African Studies Review* 37, no. 2 (1994): 13–75; and Eboe Hutchful and Abdoulaye Bathily, eds., *The Military and Militarism in Africa* (Dakar: CODESRIA, 1998).

20. Amii Omara-Otunnu, "The Currency of Militarism in Uganda," in *The Military and Militarism in Africa*, ed. Eboe Hutchful and Abdoulaye Bathily (Dakar: CODESRIA, 1998), 402.

21. Ibid., 404.

22. Amina Mama and Margo Okazawa-Rey, "Militarism, Conflict and Women's Activism in the Global Era: Challenges and Prospects for Women in Three West African Contexts," *Feminist Review* 101 (2012): 99. See also Amina

Mama and Margo Okazawa-Rey, "Militarism, Conflict, and Women's Activism," *Feminist Africa* 10 (2008): 1–8.

23. Nonetheless, there is a relative dearth of scholarly literature examining gender and militarism in Africa. Various scholars have made this point, including Amina Mama, "Khaki in the Family: Gender Discourses and Militarism in Nigeria," *African Studies Review* 41, no. 2 (1998): 2; Luckham, "Military, Militarization, and Democratization," 23; and Mama and Okazawa-Rey, "Militarism, Conflict, and Women's Activism," 2. See also Patricia McFadden, who writes, "It is exceptionally difficult to find historical narratives on the experiences of African women with militarism or the colonial army, although many anecdotes and allusions exist which attest to black women's experiences with rape and sexual violation generally in all the societies that where [*sic*] colonized and settled by white males of various nationalities." McFadden, "Plunder as Statecraft: Militarism and Resistance in Neocolonial Africa," in *Security Disarmed: Critical Perspectives on Gender, Race, and Militarization,* ed. Barbara Sutton, Sandra Morgen, and Julie Novkov (New Brunswick, NJ: Rutgers University Press, 2008), 153n4.

24. Jacklyn Cock, "Keeping the Fires Burning: Militarization and the Politics of Gender in South Africa," *Review of African Political Economy* 45/46 (1989): 50–64. See also Cock, *Women and War in South Africa* (Cleveland, OH: Pilgrim Press, 1993) and Cock, "Women in the Military: Implications for Demilitarization in the 1990s in South Africa," *Gender and Society* 8, no. 2 (June 1994): 152–69. For additional examples from other parts of the world, see Cynthia Enloe, *Does Khaki Become You? The Militarization of Women's Lives* (Boston: South End Press, 1983) and Enloe, *Maneuvers: The International Politics of Militarizing Women's Lives* (Berkeley: University of California Press, 2000); and Lynne Segal, "Gender, War and Militarism: Making and Questioning the Links," *Feminist Review* 88 (2008): 21–35.

25. Cock, "Women in the Military."

26. Nina Mba, "Kaba and Khaki: Women and the Militarized State in Nigeria," in *Women and the State in Africa,* ed. Jane L. Parpart and Kathleen Staudt (Boulder, CO: Lynne Rienner Publishers, 1989), 69–90.

27. Mama, "Khaki in the Family," 4.

28. Ibid., 6. For an interesting discussion of "state feminism" under military rule, see Amina Mama, "Feminism or Femocracy? State Feminism and Democratization in Nigeria," *Africa Development* 20, no. 1 (1995): 37–58.

29. Yaliwe Clark, "Security Sector Reform in Africa: A Lost Opportunity to Deconstruct Militarized Masculinities?" *Feminist Africa* 10 (2008): 49–66.

30. McFadden, "Plunder as Statecraft," 152.

31. Ibid., 149. For a discussion of the linkages between rape and militarism, see Amina Mama, interview by Preeti Shekar, *KPFA Women's Magazine,* October 11, 2010; and Margo Okazawa-Rey, "Warring on Women: Understanding Complex Inequalities of Gender, Race, Class, and Nation," *Affilia* 17 (2002): 371–83. Paul Kirby and Marsha Henry remind us to look at the historically situated ways that masculinity and violence intersect, instead of assuming that

men are inherently violent. Kirby and Henry, "Rethinking Masculinity and Practices of Violence in Conflict Settings," *International Journal of Feminist Politics* 14, no. 4 (2012): 445–49.

32. Ali Mazrui, "The Lumpen Proletariat and the Lumpen Militariat: African Soldiers as a New Political Class," *Political Studies* 21, no. 1 (1973): 1–12.

33. Mama and Okazawa-Rey, "Militarism, Conflict and Women's Activism in the Global Era," 116–17.

34. A. B. K. Kasozi, *The Social Origins of Violence in Uganda* (Kampala: Fountain Publishers, 1994), 96.

35. Martin Jamison, *Idi Amin and Uganda: An Annotated Bibliography* (Westport, CT: Greenwood Press, 1992); Harold Kleinschmidt, *Amin Collection: Bibliographical Catalogue of Materials Relevant to the History of Uganda under the Military Government of Idi Amin Dada* (Heidelberg: Kivouvou, 1983).

CHAPTER 1: VIOLENCE, MILITARISM, AND MASCULINITY

1. Malyam Amin, "My Idi . . . the Ideal Husband Who Became Amin the Monster," *Daily Mirror* (London), July 30, 1979.

2. Malyam Amin, "The Naked Stranger in Our Bed," *Daily Mirror* (London), July 31, 1979.

3. Jaffar Amin and Margaret Akulia, *Idi Amin: Hero or Villain? His Son Jaffar Amin and Other People Speak* (Charleston, SC: Millennium Global Publishers, 2010), 150.

4. Henry Kyemba, *A State of Blood: The Inside Story of Idi Amin* (New York: Paddington Press, 1977), 146.

5. Malyam Amin, "The Naked Stranger in Our Bed," *Daily Mirror* (London), July 31, 1979. Reports of Amin's violence toward his wives were commonplace. See, for instance, Kyemba, *State of Blood*, 159; and Joseph Kamau [pseud.] and Andrew Cameron [pseud.], *Lust to Kill: The Rise and Fall of Idi Amin* (London: Transworld Publishers, 1979), 192.

6. Norah came from President Milton Obote's home region of Lango. Henry Kyemba, one of Amin's former cabinet ministers, suggests that the marriage was one of political expedience—Amin wanted to demonstrate his loyalty to the president by marrying into his clan. See Kyemba, *State of Blood*, 147. Amin's son, however, said that she was a "gift" from Obote, a reward for loyal service. See Amin and Akulia, *Idi Amin*, 127.

7. John Middleton, "Some Effects of Colonial Rule among the Lugbara," in *Colonialism in Africa, 1870–1960*, ed. Victor Turner (Cambridge: Cambridge University Press, 1971), 12–13.

8. Sampson Geria (1973), quoted in Mark Leopold, *Inside West Nile: Violence, History and Representation on an African Frontier* (Oxford: James Currey, 2005), 126–27.

9. Emin Pasha was born in Austria and moved to the Sudan in search of adventure. While in Khartoum, he converted to Islam and changed his name to Emin. Pasha is an honorific title meaning "governor."

10. Barri A. Wanji (1971) suggests that this three-year period of isolation (1885–88) was decisive in the formation of Nubian collective identity. Holger Bernt Hansen, "Pre-Colonial Immigrants and Colonial Servants: The Nubians in Uganda Revisited," *African Affairs* 90 (1991): 563.

11. The Albert Nile refers to the upper Nile River in what is today northwestern Uganda. It emerges from the north end of Lake Albert and flows for 130 miles toward the South Sudanese border, where it becomes known as the Mountain Nile. It is part of the White Nile River that originates in Lake Victoria and flows north into Egypt. For an excellent account of Emin Pasha's rescue, see Daniel Liebowitz and Charles Pearson, *The Last Expedition: Stanley's Mad Journey through the Congo* (New York: W. W. Norton, 2006).

12. Mark Leopold, "Legacies of Slavery in North-West Uganda: The Story of the 'One-Elevens,'" *Africa* 76, no. 2 (2006): 186.

13. Between 1888 and 1892, Buganda was embroiled in a series of political conflicts that were closely linked to religion. For information on these "religious wars," see Michael Twaddle, "The Emergence of Politico-Religious Groupings in Late Nineteenth-Century Buganda," *Journal of African History* 29 (1988): 81–92. For interesting parallels with the Amin era, see Ali Mazrui, "Religious Strangers in Uganda: From Emin Pasha to Amin Dada," *African Affairs* 76, no. 302 (January 1977): 21–38; and John Rowe, "Islam under Idi Amin: A Case of Déjà Vu?" in *Uganda Now: Between Decay and Development*, ed. Holger Bernt Hansen and Michael Twaddle (London: James Currey, 1988), 267–79.

14. Lt. Col. Hubert Moyse-Bartlett, *King's African Rifles: A Study in the Military History of East and Central Africa, 1890–1945* (Aldershot, UK: Gale and Polden, 1956), 51.

15. Leopold, *Inside West Nile*, 117.

16. Leopold, "Legacies of Slavery," 187.

17. Leopold, *Inside West Nile*, 109–11.

18. West Nile was a district until 1973, when Amin relabeled it as a province. Today, it is known as the West Nile subregion, which consists of seven distinct districts. Amin's ancestral home is located in Pakago Village, Godia Parish, Midia Sub-County, Koboko County, Koboko District.

19. Amin and Akulia, *Idi Amin*, 39–40.

20. Ibid., 42. See also Omari Kokole, "The 'Nubians' of East Africa: Muslim Club or African 'Tribe'? The View from Within," *Journal of the Institute of Muslim Minority Affairs* 6, no. 2 (1985): 437.

21. Amin and Akulia, *Idi Amin*, 57.

22. Ibid., 59.

23. Amin and Akulia, *Idi Amin*, 54–55. See also Manzoor Moghal, *Idi Amin: Lion of Africa* (Central Milton Keynes, UK: Author House, 2010), 8.

24. Amin and Akulia, *Idi Amin*, 57.

25. M. S. M. Semakula Kiwanuka, *Amin and the Tragedy of Uganda* (Munich: Weltforum, 1979), 13.

26. Amin and Akulia, *Idi Amin*, 66. Other sources suggest that the couple divorced just after Amin was born. See David Martin, *General Amin* (London:

Faber and Faber, 1974), 14; George Ivan Smith, *Ghosts of Kampala* (New York: St. Martin's Press, 1980), 42; and Thomas Melady and Margaret Melady, *Idi Amin Dada: Hitler in Africa* (Kansas City, KS: Sheed Andrews and McMeel, 1977), 108.

27. Various sources have suggested that Amin worked as a goat herder and as a laborer on nearby sugar plantations. See Amin and Akulia, *Idi Amin*, 72; and Moghal, *Idi Amin*, 9.

28. Martin, *General Amin*, 15–16.

29. Moghal, *Idi Amin*, 9. Jaffar Amin says that his father attended Islamic school earlier and was in World War II during 1940–44. This is not likely. He said that Amin had a job in the kitchen mess of KAR aboard a navy ship, the SS *Yoma*. His conscription number was N-14610. See Amin and Akulia, *Idi Amin*, 76–79.

30. Moghal, *Idi Amin*, 9; Peter Woodward, "Ambiguous Amin," *African Affairs* 77, no. 307 (April 1978): 155. Iain Grahame claims that Amin joined the army in 1948. See Grahame, *Amin and Uganda: A Personal Memoir* (London: Granada, 1980), 20.

31. Martin, *General Amin*, 15; David Gwyn [pseud.], *Idi Amin: Death-Light of Africa* (Boston: Little, Brown, 1977), 25; Peter Jermyn Allen, *Interesting Times: Uganda Diaries, 1955–1986* (Sussex, UK: Book Guild, 2000), 286; and Smith, *Ghosts of Kampala*, 46.

32. Fred Guweddeko, "Rejected Then Taken in By Dad: A Timeline," *The Monitor* (Kampala), August 18, 2003.

33. Grahame, *Amin and Uganda*, 33.

34. Ibid., 34.

35. Ibid., 40. In 1942, British officers in the KAR created the rank of warrant officer platoon commander to accommodate Africans with leadership potential. Timothy Parsons, *The African Rank-and-File: Social Implications of Colonial Military Service in the King's African Rifles, 1902–1964* (Portsmouth, NH: Heinemann, 1999), 108.

36. Grahame, *Amin and Uganda*, 40.

37. After World War II, British officers reintroduced the rank of native officer, or effendi, for select African noncommissioned officers and warrant officer platoon commanders. Although British officers could command anyone, effendis could command only African troops. Effendis received their commissions from the colonial governor, while the British got theirs from the queen. Parsons, *African Rank-and-File*, 109–10.

38. Judith Listowel, *Amin* (Dublin: IUP Press, 1973), 26. For additional information on Amin's promotion to effendi, see Amin and Akulia, *Idi Amin*, 103; Grahame, *Amin and Uganda*, 42; Kamau and Cameron, *Lust to Kill*, 38; and Smith, *Ghosts of Kampala*, 49.

39. Amii Omara-Otunnu, *Politics and the Military in Uganda, 1890–1985* (Basingstoke, UK: Macmillan, 1987), 45.

40. Listowel, *Amin*, 27.

41. Gwyn, *Idi Amin*, 28–29.

42. Quoted in Martin, *General Amin*, 19.

43. Quoted in ibid., 20. See also Allen, *Interesting Times*, 224–25.

44. Moyse-Bartlett, *King's African Rifles*, 51.

45. Omara-Otunnu, *Politics and the Military*, 12.

46. Ibid., 22.

47. Ibid., 23. See also Parsons, *African Rank-and-File*, 15.

48. Omara-Otunnu, *Politics and the Military*, 25–26.

49. The Baganda also had an impressive military history. For information on precolonial warfare in Buganda, see Richard Reid, *Political Power in Pre-Colonial Buganda* (Oxford: James Currey, 2002) and Reid, *War in Pre-Colonial Eastern Africa* (Oxford: James Currey, 2007).

50. D. A. Low, "The Making and Implementation of the Uganda Agreement of 1900," in *Buganda and British Overrule, 1900–1955: Two Studies*, ed. D. A. Low and R. Cranford Pratt (London: Oxford University Press, 1960), 49. See also C. W. Hattersley, *The Baganda at Home* (London: Frank Cass, 1908), 38; and Audrey Richards, *East African Chiefs: A Study of Political Development in Some Uganda and Tanganyika Tribes* (London: Faber and Faber, 1959), 41.

51. Parsons, *African Rank-and-File*, 5.

52. Quoted in Parsons, *African Rank-and-File*, 54.

53. Grahame, *Amin and Uganda*, 39.

54. Tarsis Kabwegyere (1974), cited in Ali Mazrui, "Soldiers as Traditionalizers: Military Rule and the Re-Africanization of Africa," *Journal of Asian and African Studies* 12, no. 1–4 (1977): 247.

55. Thomas P. Ofcansky, *Uganda: Tarnished Pearl of Africa* (Boulder, CO: Westview Press, 1996), 25–26. For more information on the participation of Ugandans in World War II, see Major E. F. Whitehead, "A Short History of Uganda Military Units Formed during World War II," *Uganda Journal* 14, no. 1 (March 1950): 1–14; and J. C. Worker, "With the 4th (Uganda) K.A.R. in Abyssinia and Burma," *Uganda Journal* 12, no. 1 (March 1948): 52–56.

56. Peter Jermyn Allen, *Days of Judgment: A Judge in Idi Amin's Uganda* (London: William Kimber, 1987), 35–36.

57. Gwyn, *Idi Amin*, 25.

58. Omara-Otunnu, *Politics and the Military*, 50.

59. For information on Amin's promotion to captain, see Grahame, *Amin and Uganda*, 68; Ali Mazrui, "The Social Origins of Ugandan Presidents: From King to Peasant Warrior," *Canadian Journal of African Studies* 8, no. 1 (1974): 6; Amin and Akulia, *Idi Amin*, 113; and Omara-Otunnu, *Politics and the Military*, 50.

60. For a detailed account of the mutiny, see Timothy Parsons, *The 1964 Army Mutinies and the Making of Modern East Africa* (Westport, CT: Praeger, 2003). See also Omara-Otunnu, *Politics and the Military*, 58–64.

61. Omara-Otunnu, *Politics and the Military*, 59.

62. Ibid., 62.

63. This controversy dated back to the late nineteenth century, when the Baganda collaborated with the British government to force the king of Bunyoro into exile. The British had given the Baganda a portion of Bunyoro's territory as a reward for their service. This land became known as the "lost counties." Because this land was home to 40 percent of the Banyoro people and the site of many royal graves, the "lost counties" were highly contested.

64. Aidan Southall, "General Amin and the Coup: Great Man or Historical Inevitability?" *Journal of Modern African Studies* 13, no. 1 (1975): 96–98; Gwyn, *Idi Amin*, 36–38; Kyemba, *State of Blood*, 23–25; and Moghal, *Idi Amin*, 18–20.

65. He wanted to keep the mission a secret and did not trust Opolot, his army commander, because Opolot had recently married into the Baganda royal family.

66. Omara-Otunnu, *Politics and the Military*, 71.

67. Bernard Rwehururu, *Cross to the Gun: Idi Amin and the Fall of the Uganda Army* (Kampala: Monitor Publications, 2002), 24.

68. Republic of Uganda, *Report of the Commission of Inquiry Appointed to Inquire into Certain Allegations Made in Parliament on 4th February, 1966* (Entebbe: Government Printer, 1966), 2.

69. Opolot was dismissed in October 1966 and then jailed.

70. The king died three years later in exile in the United Kingdom.

71. A. B. K. Kasozi, *The Social Origins of Violence in Uganda* (Kampala: Fountain Publishers, 1994), 86.

72. Allen, *Days of Judgment*, 31.

73. Omara-Otunnu, *Politics and the Military*, 83.

74. Kyemba, *State of Blood*, 27.

75. Republic of Uganda, *Report of the Commission of Inquiry into Violations of Human Rights* (Entebbe: Government Printer, 1994), 372.

76. Kasozi, *Social Origins of Violence*, 89. See also Samwiri Karugire, *The Roots of Instability in Uganda* (Kampala: Fountain Publishers, 1988), 71.

77. Omara-Otunnu, *Politics and the Military*, 79.

78. Ibid., 6. See also Aidan Southall, "Social Disorganization in Uganda: Before, During, and After Amin," *Journal of Modern African Studies* 18, no. 4 (1980): 630.

79. This is when Obote unveiled his Common Man's Charter, a new economic policy that would align the country with "African socialism."

80. Some observers suggest that Amin's nickname "Dada" comes from his cowardly or "sissy" behavior. See Martin, *General Amin*, 68; Allen, *Interesting Times*, 298–99, and *Days of Judgment*, 211; and Smith, *Ghosts of Kampala*, 64.

81. Omara-Otunnu, *Politics and the Military*, 89.

82. After Amin's coup, he ordered an investigation into the murder of Okoya. Brigadier Hussein spearheaded the commission of inquiry. The findings confirmed that Okoya and his wife were killed by "person or persons unknown," thus clearing Amin. The senior investigator, a Ugandan Asian named

Mohamed Hassan, was killed "while trying to escape." His Ugandan assistant was also killed. See Gwyn, *Idi Amin*, 42.

83. Brigadier Smuts Guweddeko and Major Geoffrey Kasule were arrested for the murder—allegedly on Amin's orders. Both men were awaiting trial in Luzira Prison and remained there until Amin's coup. See Rwehururu, *Cross to the Gun*, 25.

84. Hussein was one of the first casualties of Amin's coup. He was captured and then taken to Luzira Prison, where he was beaten to death on January 26, 1971. See Martin, *General Amin*, 130.

85. Omara-Otunnu, *Politics and the Military*, 90.

86. Martin, *General Amin*, 89. See also Jan Jelmert Jorgensen, *Uganda: A Modern History* (New York: St. Martin's Press, 1981), 268.

87. Obote had been supporting the southerners in their war against the Arab north. When General Gaafar Nimiery seized power in May 1969, promising to end the long civil war and to enact socialist reforms, Obote stopped supporting the southern "rebels." This was not in the best interests of Israel, which is why Israel supported Amin's coup. See Omara-Otunnu, *Politics and the Military*, 95–96.

88. See also Rolf Steiner, *The Last Adventurer* (Boston: Little, Brown, 1978).

89. Rwehururu, *Cross to the Gun*, 27. See also P. M. O. Onen, *The Diary of an Obedient Servant during Misrule* (Kampala: Janyeko Publishing, 2000), 51.

90. There is evidence to suggest that Onama was involved in the coup and may have even instigated it because of a falling-out with Obote. When Obote left for Singapore, he ordered all army officers with accumulated leave to take it at once or forfeit it. This meant that more than half of all officers were on leave on January 24 and 25, 1971. Although there were rumors that Onama would be given a top post, he soon retired to West Nile. See Onen, *Diary*, 55; and Jorgensen, *Uganda*, 268.

91. Listowel, *Amin*, 70.

92. Grahame, *Amin and Uganda*, 96.

93. Andrew Rice, *The Teeth May Smile but the Heart Does Not Forget: Murder and Memory in Uganda* (New York: Henry Holt, 2009), 89.

94. General and Administrative Order No. 2 (GAO 2/1971).

95. Ali Mazrui, "The Lumpen Proletariat and the Lumpen Militariat: African Soldiers as a New Political Class," *Political Studies* 21, no. 1 (1973): 6.

96. Quoted in Listowel, *Amin*, 76–77.

97. The death toll during Amin's rule is heavily contested. Jan Jorgensen estimates that approximately 50,000 people were killed. Tony Avirgan and Martha Honey suggest that 250,000–500,000 people died. Amnesty International claims that 300,000 were killed, while Winnie Byanyima puts the figure closer to 500,000. Louise Pirouet maintains that on the basis of population growth, or the lack thereof, there could be as many as 850,000 persons who were killed during Amin's rule. Although there is a substantial difference between 50,000 and 850,000, there is little doubt that many Ugandans died as a result of violence. See Jorgensen, *Uganda*, 314; Tony Avirgan and Martha Honey, *War in*

Uganda: The Legacy of Idi Amin (Westport, CT: Laurence Hill, 1982), 27; Amnesty International, *Human Rights in Uganda* (London: Amnesty International, June 1978), 13; Winnie Karagwa Byanyima, "Women in Political Struggle in Uganda," in *Women Transforming Politics: Worldwide Strategies for Empowerment*, ed. Jill M. Bystydzienski (Bloomington: Indiana University Press, 1992), 133; and M. Louise Pirouet, "Refugees in and from Uganda in the Post-Independence Period," in *Uganda Now: Between Decay and Development*, ed. Holger Bernt Hansen and Michael Twaddle (London: James Currey, 1988), 246.

CHAPTER 2: GENDER, PERFORMANCE, AND PAIN

1. Winnie Mugenyi [pseud.], interview by author, Kampala, June 25, 2005. Other women shared similar accounts. See also Evelyn Nyanzi [pseud.], interview by author, Kampala, July 23, 2005, and Rose Birungi [pseud.], interview by author, Mpererwe, July 28, 2005.

2. Samwiri Karugire makes a similar point about Ugandans in general. See Karugire, *The Roots of Instability in Uganda* (Kampala: Fountain Publishers, 1988), 68.

3. While this type of correspondence is hardly surprising, I did not expect so many of the congratulatory messages to come from women. This suggests one of three things: (1) women liked Amin and wanted to wish him success; (2) women wanted to appear as if they liked him; or (3) the government wanted to appear as if they had women's support. Determining which of the three options is most accurate is nearly impossible. These messages can be read, however, as evidence that women had a visible presence in public discourse. In other words, their voices mattered.

4. "General Amin the 'Savior': Deep Gratitude from Women," *Uganda Argus*, February 6, 1971.

5. "Common Man Saved from Jaws," *Uganda Argus*, February 9, 1971; "Women Thanks," *Uganda Argus*, May 3, 1971.

6. "General Amin Saved Uganda from Bloodshed," *Uganda Argus*, February 12, 1971. See also "'Take-Over Was the Power of God': Saza Level Teams to Be Formed," *Uganda Argus*, June 1, 1971.

7. "The General Dissolves Parliament," *Uganda Argus*, February 3, 1971.

8. Armed Forces Decree, Decree 1 of 1971. Amin amended this decree on April 4, 1972, to eliminate the position of chief of defense staff, to revise various military titles, and to establish the rules for courts-martial. He amended it again on January 23, 1973, to legalize trials by military tribunal. See Armed Forces (Amendment) Decree, Decree 4 of 1972 and Armed Forces (Amendment) Decree, Decree 3 of 1973.

9. Jan Jelmert Jorgensen, *Uganda: A Modern History* (New York: St. Martin's Press, 1981), 282; M. S. M. Kiwanuka, *Amin and the Tragedy of Uganda* (Munich: Weltforum, 1979), 82.

10. The ministers were occasionally sent for military training. See, for instance, "Ministers Train: Forces Act Now Covers Them All," *Uganda Argus*, August 7, 1971.

11. "Soldiers Appoint General Amin President," *Uganda Argus*, February 22, 1971.

12. Detention (Prescription of Time Limit) Decree, Decree 7 of 1971. This decree was amended on May 10, 1971, to remove the six-month limit on detention. Amin amended it again on September 11, 1971, to extend the period of detention through December 12, 1971. See Detention (Prescription of Time Limit) (Amendment) Decree, Decree 15 of 1971 and Detention (Prescription of Time Limit) (Amendment) (No. 2) Decree, Decree 31 of 1971.

13. "Good faith" refers to actions "done or purported to be done in the execution of duty or for the defense of Uganda or for the public safety or for the enforcement of discipline or law and order or otherwise in the public interest by a person holding office under or employed in the public service of Uganda or by a member of the Armed Forces of Uganda or any other person acting under the authority of a person so holding office or so employed." See Decree 7 of 1971.

14. Armed Forces (Powers of Arrest) Decree, Decree 13 of 1971 and Suspension of Political Activities Decree, Decree 14 of 1971. Although the former decree expired on March 17, 1972, Amin did not amend it until several months later. Decree 26 of 1972 indefinitely extended the armed forces' powers of arrest. It also made the decree effective retroactively from March 18, 1972. This meant that a person could be charged with a crime that was not illegal when they committed the so-called offense. See Armed Forces (Powers of Arrest) Decree, Decree 26 of 1972. The decree was eventually repealed on August 27, 1973. See Armed Forces (Powers of Arrest) (Repeal) Decree, Decree 21 of 1973.

15. Although arrested persons and their property were supposed to be transferred to the nearest police station within twenty-four hours, this rarely occurred. This decree also resulted in the militarization of prisons, meaning that the army took over the operation and authority of the prisons service. It was a "mechanism for horizontal spread of the machinery of terror in the interest of the regime." Republic of Uganda, *Report of the Commission of Inquiry into Violations of Human Rights* (Entebbe: Government Printer, 1994), 420.

16. Ibid., 124.

17. Military service in Uganda was historically associated with masculinity. In Buganda, for instance, those who showed cowardice in war were forced to dress as pregnant women or to perform "women's work" for more courageous warriors. This type of explicit gendering suggests that martial prowess was a valued masculine characteristic. Although a limited number of women may have served as military leaders before colonial rule, the vast majority of combat soldiers were men. Women did, however, play important roles as spies, cooks, and nurses, among others, both at home and on the front lines. For a brief overview of women in war in precolonial Uganda, see Richard Reid, *Political Power in Pre-Colonial Buganda* (Oxford: James Currey, 2002), 179 and Reid, *War in Pre-Colonial Eastern Africa* (Oxford: James Currey, 2007), 155–57. See also John Roscoe, *The Bakitara or Banyoro: The First Part of the*

Report of the Mackie Ethnological Expedition to Central Africa (Cambridge, UK: University Press, 1923) and Roscoe, *The Banyankole: The Second Part of the Report of the Mackie Ethnological Expedition to Central Africa* (Cambridge, UK: University Press, 1923).

18. A. B. K. Kasozi, *The Social Origins of Violence in Uganda* (Kampala: Fountain Publishers, 1994), 110. Numerous scholars and observers have written about the violence that accompanied the military takeover. See, for instance, Denis Hills, *The White Pumpkin* (New York: Grove Press, 1975), 118–19; Iain Grahame, *Amin and Uganda: A Personal Memoir* (London: Granada, 1980), 97–100; International Commission of Jurists, *Violations of Human Rights and the Rule of Law in Uganda* (Geneva: International Commission of Jurists, 1974), 27–31; Bernard Rwehururu, *Cross to the Gun: Idi Amin and the Fall of the Uganda Army* (Kampala: Monitor Publications, 2002), 31–35; David Martin, *General Amin* (London: Faber and Faber, 1974), 130–57; and Amii Omara-Otunnu, *Politics and the Military in Uganda, 1890–1985* (Basingstoke, UK: Macmillan, 1987), 102–12.

19. When one visited Singapore, he or she never returned. There was another infamous cell called "Dar es Salaam," so named for Obote's home in exile.

20. International Commission of Jurists, *Violations of Human Rights*, 30. This account is corroborated by Lt. Silver Tibihikwa, who was also imprisoned that night.

21. In his discussion of Latin American military dictatorships, Edelberto Torres-Rivas makes the point that terror is most useful to the state when it is publicly known. See Torres-Rivas, "Epilogue: Notes on Terror, Violence, Fear and Democracy," in *Societies of Fear: The Legacy of Civil War, Violence and Terror in Latin America*, ed. Kees Koonings and Dirk Kruijt (London: Zed Books, 1999), 293.

22. Martin, *General Amin*, 131–34.

23. Although estimates vary, Jorgensen suggests that at least one thousand Acholi and Langi soldiers died within the first six months of Amin's rule. Jorgensen, *Uganda*, 269. See also Karugire, *Roots of Instability*, 77; Holger Bernt Hansen, *Ethnicity and Military Rule in Uganda* (Uppsala, Sweden: Scandinavian Institute of African Studies, 1977), 104; Tony Avirgan and Martha Honey, *War in Uganda: The Legacy of Idi Amin* (Westport, CT: Laurence Hill, 1982), 7; Phares Mutibwa, *Uganda since Independence: A Story of Unfulfilled Hopes* (Trenton, NJ: Africa World Press, 1992), 87; and Morten Boas, "Uganda in the Regional War Zone: Metanarratives, Pasts and Presents," *Journal of Contemporary African Studies* 22, no. 3 (2004): 287.

24. Jorgensen, *Uganda*, 278.

25. Omara-Otunnu, *Politics and the Military*, 107–8.

26. Ibid., 108.

27. Ali Mazrui, *Soldiers and Kinsmen in Uganda: The Making of a Military Ethnocracy* (Beverly Hills, CA: Sage, 1975), 127.

28. Anthony Clayton and David Killingray, *Khaki and Blue: Military and Police in British Colonial Africa* (Athens: Ohio University Press, 1989), 84;

Peter Jermyn Allen, *Interesting Times: Uganda Diaries, 1955–1986* (Sussex, UK: Book Guild, 2000), 203, 210.

29. Republic of Uganda, *Report of the Commission of Inquiry (1994)*, 382, 6121, 6659.

30. "Israeli Embassy Told to Close," *Uganda Argus*, March 30, 1972.

31. V. Spike Peterson, "Gendered Identities, Ideologies, and Practices in the Context of War and Militarism," in *Gender, War, and Militarism: Feminist Perspectives*, ed. Laura Sjoberg and Sandra Via (Santa Barbara, CA: Praeger, 2010), 19.

32. Karugire, *Roots of Instability*, 80–81. For additional information on the collapse of the police force under Amin, see Peter Jermyn Allen, *Days of Judgment: A Judge in Idi Amin's Uganda* (London: William Kimber, 1987), 120.

33. Between 1971 and 1980, the Ugandan police force plummeted from 14,000 to 2,000 officers. Aidan Southall, "Social Disorganization in Uganda: Before, During, and After Amin," *Journal of Modern African Studies* 18, no. 4 (1980): 629.

34. Joyce Ondoga [pseud.], interview by author, Arua, July 8, 2008.

35. Patience Arube [pseud.], interview by author, Arua, July 10, 2008.

36. George Ivan Smith, *Ghosts of Kampala* (New York: St. Martin's Press, 1980), 114.

37. International Commission of Jurists, *Uganda and Human Rights: Report to the UN Commission on Human Rights* (Geneva: International Commission of Jurists, 1977), 150.

38. This meant that the organization—unlike the military and the police units—did not have a constitutional or a statutory basis. At first the unit was known as the Military Intelligence Unit. On March 16, 1972, Amin changed the name to the State Research Centre. Republic of Uganda, *Report of the Commission of Inquiry (1994)*, 396, 600, 9336.

39. Ibid., 402.

40. Ibid., 9302–3.

41. Throughout Amin's regime, the United States and Britain continued to provide SRC agents with training and equipment. Avirgan and Honey, *War in Uganda*, 18–19; Mahmood Mamdani, *Imperialism and Fascism in Uganda* (Nairobi: Heinemann, 1983), 78–83.

42. Republic of Uganda, *Report of the Commission of Inquiry (1994)*, 405.

43. Henry Kyemba estimates that there were 2,000 members. Kyemba, *A State of Blood: The Inside Story of Idi Amin* (New York: Paddington Press, 1977), 114. Commissioners estimate that there were 1,500 members. Republic of Uganda, *Report of the Commission of Inquiry (1994)*, 601.

44. Wycliffe Kato, *Escape from Idi Amin's Slaughterhouse* (London: Quartet Books, 1989), 4.

45. SRC agents were posted in pairs, known as "two-by-twos," to embassies around the world. Their purpose was to keep track of diplomats, exiles, and students. They also made reports on journalists and writers who criticized the regime. See Kyemba, *State of Blood*, 114, 235; and Smith, *Ghosts of Kampala*, 124–25.

46. Republic of Uganda, *Report of the Commission of Inquiry (1994)*, 403.

47. Kyemba, *State of Blood*, 115; Allen, *Days of Judgment*, 201; and Emmanuel Katongole, "Where Is Idi Amin? On Violence, Ethics, and Social Memory in Africa" (Uganda Martyr's University Working Paper no. 11, 2004), 17.

48. Kato, *Escape*, 3–4.

49. Republic of Uganda, *Report of the Commission of Inquiry (1994)*, 406, 601.

50. Kyemba, *State of Blood*, 114.

51. Kato, *Escape*, 40.

52. Jorgensen, *Uganda*, 315.

53. Republic of Uganda, *Report of the Commission of Inquiry (1994)*, 8585.

54. Elaine Scarry, *The Body in Pain: The Making and Unmaking of the World* (New York: Oxford University Press, 1985).

55. This unit replaced the Special Forces, which had been abolished in July 1971. See "Special Force Is Absorbed into Army," *Uganda Argus*, July 16, 1971; and "Public Safety Unit Formed," *Uganda Argus*, November 15, 1971.

56. Thomas Melady and Margaret Melady, *Idi Amin Dada: Hitler in Africa* (Kansas City, KS: Sheed Andrews and McMeel, 1977), 154.

57. Republic of Uganda, *Report of the Commission of Inquiry (1994)*, 3514.

58. Robbery Suspects Decree, Decree 7 of 1972.

59. Proceedings against the Government (Protection) Decree, Decree 8 of 1972. Several months later, Amin passed the Proceedings against the Government (Prohibition) Decree, which removed the military government's liability for any crimes or harms committed by the previous government. See Decree 19 of 1972.

60. See "Britain Hears Glowing Tribute to General Amin," *Uganda Argus*, January 30, 1971; "Britain Recognizes Amin Government," *Uganda Argus*, February 6, 1971; and "President Amin at Uhuru Event," *Uganda Argus*, April 30, 1971. Various scholars have also written about Amin's early relationship with Israel and Britain. See Jorgensen, *Uganda*, 272–73; Kasozi, *Social Origins of Violence*, 106; Dan Wadada Nabudere, *Imperialism and Revolution in Uganda* (London: Onyx Press, 1980), 280–81; Avirgan and Honey, *War in Uganda*, 9–10; Omara-Otunnu, *Politics and the Military*, 100; Mamdani, *Imperialism and Fascism*, 62; and Mutibwa, *Uganda since Independence*, 87.

61. The first Sudanese civil war raged from 1955 until 1972. Israel actively supported the southern separatist rebels during the late 1960s, using northern Uganda as a military supply corridor. Obote stopped supporting the rebels after Nimiery seized power in 1969. Amin, however, remained sympathetic to the Israelis and his Anya Anya kin. See Benjamin Beit-Hallahmi, *The Israeli Connection* (London: I. B. Tauris, 1987), 48; and Omara-Otunnu, *Politics and the Military*, 96.

62. Avirgan and Honey, *War in Uganda*, 10; Mamdani, *Imperialism and Fascism*, 61–67. See also "Ten Million Pounds from Britain," *Uganda Argus*, July 17, 1971; and "Minister Greets British Army Team," *Uganda Argus*, May 19, 1972.

63. Ade Adefuye, "The Kakwa of Uganda and the Sudan: The Ethnic Factor in National and International Politics," in *Partitioned Africans: Ethnic Relations across Africa's International Boundaries, 1884–1994*, ed. A. I. Asiwaju (New York: St. Martin's Press, 1985), 65.

64. For an official account of Amin's visit to Israel and Britain, see "President Amin in Israel," *Uganda Argus*, July 12, 1971; "President's Visit Has Good Start," *Uganda Argus*, July 14, 1971; and "Ten Million Pounds from Britain," *Uganda Argus*, July 17, 1971. See also Judith Listowel, *Amin* (Dublin: IUP Press, 1973), 93–96; and Avirgan and Honey, *War in Uganda*, 10–11.

65. Ochima was said to have been angry with Amin for putting a lower-ranking officer in charge while he was out of the country. See Listowel, *Amin*, 96–97.

66. "Uganda Not in Israeli Pockets," *Uganda Argus*, October 9, 1971; and "Uganda Take Over," *Uganda Argus*, December 10, 1971.

67. Like Amin, Gaddafi grew up poor and joined the military at a young age. As he rose through the ranks, he became increasingly inspired by the revolutionary political philosophy of Egyptian president Gamal Abdul Nasser. After seizing power in a military coup in 1969, he restructured the Libyan state to align with Nasserite principles—a process that political analysts dubbed "the Egyptianization of Libya." Toward this end, he nationalized the economy and implemented socialist reforms (e.g., free medical care, housing, education, etc.). Most important, he promoted gender equality, encouraging women to attend school and to serve in the armed forces. For additional information, see Mansour El-Kikhia, *Libya's Qaddafi: The Politics of Contradiction* (Gainesville: University of Florida Press, 1997); Rene Lemarchand, ed., *The Green and the Black: Qadhafi's Policies in Africa* (Bloomington: Indiana University Press, 1988); Yehudit Ronen, *Qaddafi's Libya in World Politics* (Boulder, CO: Lynne Rienner, 2008); and Dirk Vandewalle, *A History of Modern Libya* (Cambridge: Cambridge University Press, 2006).

68. After the death of Gamal Abdul Nasser in 1970, Gaddafi fashioned himself as guardian of the Egyptian president's legacy. Nasser's battle against imperialism and Zionism dated back to Egypt's defeat in the 1967 war against Israel.

69. Yehudit Ronen, "Libya's Intervention in Amin's Uganda—A Broken Spearhead," *Asian and African Studies* 26, no. 2 (1992): 175. See also Mamdani, *Imperialism and Fascism*, 64; and James Mittelman, *Ideology and Politics in Uganda: From Obote to Amin* (Ithaca, NY: Cornell University Press, 1975), 240.

70. "Uganda's Image Abroad Promoted," *Uganda Argus*, February 15, 1972.

71. "High-Powered Libyan Team Here," *Uganda Argus*, February 22, 1972; and "Uganda in Talks with Libya," *Uganda Argus*, February 23, 1972.

72. "Accord with Libya," *Uganda Argus*, February 28, 1972.

73. "President Amin Warns Israel," *Uganda Argus*, March 1, 1972.

74. "Go Back to Israel: No Renewal of Pacts," *Uganda Argus*, March 23, 1972; and "Embassy Staff Must Be Reduced," *Uganda Argus*, March 24, 1972.

75. "Israeli Embassy Told to Close," *Uganda Argus*, March 30, 1972.

76. "All Links with Israel Broken," *Uganda Argus*, April 10, 1972.

77. "Eban Sees Plot in Uganda Break," *New York Times*, April 11, 1972.

78. "Libya Offers to Build Hospitals," *Uganda Argus*, April 20, 1972.

79. Omara-Otunnu, *Politics and the Military*, 116–17. See also Omari Kokole, "Idi Amin, 'the Nubi' and Islam in Ugandan Politics, 1971–1979," in *Religion and Politics in East Africa: The Period since Independence*, ed. Holger Bernt Hansen and Michael Twaddle (London: James Currey, 1995), 47; Mamdani, *Imperialism and Fascism*, 64; and Avirgan and Honey, *War in Uganda*, 11.

80. James Mulira, "Soviet Prop to Idi Amin's Regime: An Assessment," *African Review* 13, no. 1 (1986): 112.

81. Mamdani, *Imperialism and Fascism*, 69.

82. "The Future of Asians in Uganda," *Uganda Argus*, August 5, 1972. The state newspaper reported that 80,000 Asians would be expelled. The actual number of Asians living in Uganda at the time may have been closer to 55,000. See Anneeth Kaur Hundle, "Exceptions to the Expulsion: Violence, Security and Community among Ugandan Asians, 1972–1979," *Journal of Eastern African Studies* 7, no. 1 (2013): 164–82.

83. "Asians Milked the Cow: They Did Not Feed It," *Uganda Argus*, August 7, 1972.

84. "These Asians Are Required to Report," *Uganda Argus*, August 15, 1972.

85. "All Asians Must Go," *Uganda Argus*, August 21, 1972.

86. "These Asians Can Stay," *Uganda Argus*, August 23, 1972.

87. For an interesting analysis of the experiences of Asians who remained in Uganda after the expulsion, see Hundle, "Exceptions to the Expulsion."

88. "Loan Action Frozen," *Uganda Argus*, August 30, 1972.

89. "Assassination Plot Denied by U.K.," *East African Standard* (Nairobi), September 6, 1972; "Britain Is Accused," *Uganda Argus*, September 6, 1972; and "They Must Get Out," *Uganda Argus*, September 12, 1972.

90. Ronen, "Libya's Intervention," 176; William J. Foltz, "Libya's Military Power," in *The Green and the Black: Qadhafi's Policies in Africa*, ed. Rene Lemarchand (Bloomington: Indiana University Press, 1988), 61–63. For an official account, see "President Welcomes Libyan Troops," *Uganda Argus*, September 25, 1972.

91. For more a detailed account of the invasion and its aftermath, see Listowel, *Amin*, 164–74; Martin, *General Amin*, 169–87; Avirgan and Honey, *War in Uganda*, 35–36; and Yoweri Kaguta Museveni, *Sowing the Mustard Seed: The Struggle for Freedom and Democracy in Uganda* (London: Macmillan, 1997), 59–71.

92. Rebecca Katumba and Chris Serunjogi, "Play an Effective Role, Women Told," *Uganda Argus*, November 23, 1972; "Malera Warns Gun Mongers while Towelli Nets More Saboteurs," *Voice of Uganda*, October 23, 1973; "Dangerous Religious Bodies Banned," *Voice of Uganda*, June 9, 1973; "Security Forces in Uganda Are on the Alert," *Voice of Uganda*, July 11, 1973. Samwiri Karugire argues that the invasion was an "excuse [for Amin] to unleash his murder squads on the population with renewed ferocity." Karugire, *Roots of Instability*, 80.

93. International Commission of Jurists, *Uganda and Human Rights*, 47.

94. Joseph Kamau [pseud.] and Andrew Cameron [pseud.], *Lust to Kill: The Rise and Fall of Idi Amin* (London: Transworld Publishers, 1979), 96.

95. D. A. Low, "The Dislocated Polity," in *Uganda Now: Between Decay and Development*, ed. Holger Bernt Hansen and Michael Twaddle (London: James Currey, 1988), 48.

CHAPTER 3: OF MINISKIRTS AND MORALITY

1. Lydia Balemezi, interview by author, Kampala, March 23, 2005.

2. Immy Wamimbi, "Minis Banned," *Uganda Argus*, May 29, 1972.

3. Joyce Mpanga, interview by author, Kampala, May 25, 2005; James Zikusoka, interview by author, Kampala, May 26, 2005; Joyce Ondoga [pseud.], interview by author, Arua, July 8, 2008. See also Denis Hills, *The White Pumpkin* (New York: Grove Press, 1975), 170; and M. S. M. Semakula Kiwanuka, *Amin and the Tragedy of Uganda* (Munich: Weltforum, 1979), 101.

4. Michael Schatzberg argues that in many parts of Africa, political legitimacy is established through the use of familial metaphors. It is based on a moral matrix that determines the various rights and obligations that a (male) leader has toward his citizens. As "father" of the nation, he is expected to provide for his "children," bestowing protection, guidance, and discipline whenever necessary. In exchange, he is able to command obedience, respect, and loyalty until his dying days. Schatzberg, *Political Legitimacy in Middle Africa: Father, Family, Food* (Bloomington: Indiana University Press, 2001), 1–4.

5. Eugene Burt, "Bark-Cloth in East Africa," *Textile History* 26, no. 1 (1995): 78.

6. Kefa Otiso, *Culture and Customs of Uganda* (Westport, CT: Greenwood Press, 2006), 76–77.

7. Lynn Thomas, *Politics of the Womb: Women, Reproduction, and the State in Kenya* (Berkeley: University of California Press, 2003), 170.

8. Floya Anthias and Nira Yuval-Davis, Introduction to *Women-Nation-State*, ed. Nira Yuval-Davis and Floya Anthias (London: Macmillan, 1989), 9–10.

9. For information on anti-miniskirt campaigns in Tanzania, see Andrew M. Ivaska, "'Anti-Mini Militants Meet Modern Misses': Urban Style, Gender, and the Politics of 'National Culture' in 1960s Dar es Salaam, Tanzania," in *Fashioning Africa: Power and the Politics of Dress*, ed. Jean Allman (Bloomington: Indiana University Press, 2004), 104–21. For information on campaigns in Zanzibar, see Thomas Burgess, "Cinema, Bell Bottoms, and Miniskirts: Struggles over Youth and Citizenship in Revolutionary Zanzibar," *International Journal of African Historical Studies* 35, no. 2–3 (2002): 287–313. And for information on bans in Malawi, see Audrey Wipper, "African Women, Fashion, and Scapegoating," *Canadian Journal of African Studies* 6, no. 2 (1972): 329–49; and Cyprian Kambili, "Ethics of African Tradition: Prescription of a Dress Code in Malawi, 1965–1973," *Society of Malawi Journal* 55, no. 2 (2002): 80–100. Although miniskirts were not formally banned in Zambia in the 1960s and 1970s, there was heated public debate over the issue. See Karen Tranberg Hansen, "Dressing Dangerously: Miniskirts, Gender Relations, and Sexuality

in Zambia," in *Fashioning Africa: Power and the Politics of Dress*, ed. Jean All-man (Bloomington: Indiana University Press, 2004), 166–85; and Ilsa Glazer Schuster, *New Women of Lusaka* (Palo Alto, CA: Mayfield Publishing, 1979).

10. Ali A. Mazrui, "Miniskirts and Political Puritanism," *Africa Report* 13, no. 7 (1968): 10. Audrey Wipper refers to these measures as "puritanical-authoritarianism." See Wipper, "African Women," 335.

11. Peace Nyenga, letter to the editor, *Uganda Argus*, November 12, 1971. Italics added.

12. Y. Serwanga, letter to the editor, *Uganda Argus*, January 10, 1972. See also Yowasi K. Buregyeya, letter to the editor, *Uganda Argus*, January 12, 1972; and Joseph W. Mukasa, letter to the editor, *Uganda Argus*, January 13, 1972. Many Ugandans wrote letters in defense of women's freedom of expression, however. See Irene R., letter to the editor, *Uganda Argus*, December 22, 1971; letter to the editor submitted by "A Guy Who Digs Girls in Minis," *Uganda Argus*, January 15, 1972; and Tereza Tibuliggwa-Kakooza, letter to the editor, *Uganda Argus*, March 30, 1972.

13. Christine Obbo suggests that when men feel like traitors to their culture for giving up their traditional customs and dress, "they yearn for the security and compensation of at least knowing that women are loyal to it." By ensuring that women remained the bearers of tradition, Ugandan men could enjoy the fruits of modernity without any of the guilt. Obbo, *African Women: Their Struggle for Economic Independence* (London: Zed, 1980), 11.

14. "Well Done, Zaire," *Uganda Argus*, December 22, 1971. Kibedi's appreciation for "natural beauty" among Zairian women is a bit odd given Amin's contemporaneous efforts to force the Karamojong to wear clothes. During an April 1971 visit to the remote northern region, Amin told members of the community that their standard of dressing was lower than the rest of the country: "I very strongly urge you to change your habits of dressing which are neither in your interest nor in the interest of the Republic." He said that their "standard of dressing was no longer benefiting modern times." See "Karamojong Are Advised to Dress Up Like Others," *Uganda Argus*, April 10, 1971; and "Karamo-jong Dress Up," *Uganda Argus*, April 27, 1971. There is evidence to suggest that the regime used significant force in their efforts to "dress up" the Karamo-jong. See Republic of Uganda, *Report of the Commission of Inquiry (1994)*, 11667–11693. Andrew Ivaska noticed a similar contradiction in Tanzania between state efforts to restore morality (Operation Vijana) and those to promote modernity (Operation Dress Up). See Ivaska, "Anti-Mini Militants." For information on antinudity campaigns in Ghana, see Jean Allman, "'Let Your Fashion Be in Line with Our Ghanaian Costume': Nation, Gender, and the Politics of Clothing in Nkrumah's Ghana," in *Fashioning Africa: Power and the Politics of Dress*, ed. Jean Allman (Bloomington: Indiana University Press, 2004), 144–65; and Benjamin Talton, "'All the Women Must Be Clothed': The Anti-Nudity Campaign of Northern Ghana," in *The Black Body: Imagining, Writing and (Re)Reading*, ed. Sandra Jackson (Pretoria: University of South Africa Press, 2008), 81–96.

15. N. P. Jolly, letter to the editor, *Uganda Argus*, January 6, 1972.

16. M. D. Kaggwa, letter to the editor, *Uganda Argus*, January 17, 1972. See also Willy Mukibi, letter to the editor, *Uganda Argus*, May 10, 1972.

17. Immy Wamimbi, "Minis Banned," *Uganda Argus*, May 29, 1972.

18. Penal Code Act (Amendment) Decree, Decree 9 of 1972. Although this decree could also be applied to men, the vast majority of those arrested were women.

19. Penal Code Act (Amendment) Decree, Decree 4 of 1973. See also "Kneeling Confusion," *Uganda Argus*, July 1, 1972; and John Katende, "Just Where Does the Knee Line Start?" *Uganda Argus*, July 14, 1972.

20. "Libya Offers Help to Uganda's Forces," *Voice of Uganda*, January 4, 1973. See also "Women's Trousers Banned in Offices," *Voice of Uganda*, January 15, 1973.

21. Penal Code (Amendment) Decree, Decree 4 of 1974.

22. Grace Bantebya Kyomuhendo and Marjorie Keniston McIntosh, *Women, Work, and Domestic Virtue in Uganda, 1900–2003* (Oxford: James Currey, 2006), 163. See also Aili Mari Tripp, *Women and Politics in Uganda* (Madison: University of Wisconsin Press, 2000), 49.

23. "Now Women Can Wear Trousers Again," *Voice of Uganda*, November 23, 1974. See also Penal Code Act (Amendment) (No. 2) Decree, Decree 26 of 1974.

24. "Keep Wigs Out of Office — Directive," *Voice of Uganda*, January 28, 1974. Less than two months after making this statement, Amin divorced his first three wives. There are several possible explanations as to why Amin divorced his first three wives, none of which involves wigs. One theory suggests that the women sought revenge on Amin by taking their own lovers. Once Amin found out about the affairs, he immediately divorced them. See Henry Kyemba, *A State of Blood: The Inside Story of Idi Amin* (New York: Paddington Press, 1977), 149–50. Another theory posits that Kay walked out of the marriage after learning that her husband had been implicated in the death of her cousin, Michael Ondoga (which I discuss in chapter 5). According to this version, Amin was so humiliated by her defection that he divorced his most "troublesome" wives. See International Commission of Jurists, *Uganda and Human Rights: Report to the UN Commission on Human Rights* (Geneva: International Commission of Jurists, 1977), 148. Both explanations are plausible. If Amin suspected any of his wives of infidelity, he would have lashed out harshly in an effort to assert his masculinity. He would have done the same if he believed that any of them were traitors. Both Malyam and Kay were related to so-called saboteurs. Perhaps he thought that it was only a matter of time before Norah — a cousin of the deposed president — would become a threat as well. Amin remained married to Madina Najjemba, a young Muganda woman whom he wed in March 1972. For official coverage of the divorces, see "General Amin Has One Wife and Others Are Out!" *Voice of Uganda*, March 26, 1974. For additional information on Amin's marital relationships, see Alicia C. Decker, "Militarismo, nazionalismo e matrimonio: Un ritratto

privato delle cinque mogli di Idi Amin" [Militarism, Nationalism, and Marriage: An Intimate Portrait of Idi Amin's Five Wives], *Afriche e Orienti* 14, no. 3–4 (2012): 124–38.

25. "Wigs May Be Banned Completely," *Voice of Uganda*, January 29, 1974.

26. This was part of the same decree that banned women's trousers.

27. "Decree Bans Women's Wigs and 'Trousers,'" *Voice of Uganda*, February 5, 1974. See also "Amin Hits Out at Cowboy Soldiers," *Drum Magazine*, May 1974, reprinted in Adam Seftel, ed., *Uganda: The Bloodstained Pearl of Africa and Its Struggle for Peace* (Lanseria, South Africa: Bailey's African Photo Archives Production, 1994), 143. Peter Jermyn Allen suggests that Amin learned about the "connection" between wigs and the Vietnam War from Roy Innis, chairman of the prominent African-American civil rights group CORE, or Congress for Racial Equality. See Allen, *Interesting Times: Uganda Diaries, 1955–1986* (Sussex, UK: Book Guild, 2000), 377.

28. "President Amin Scraps Mortgages on Land," *Voice of Uganda*, May 1, 1975.

29. "President Amin Bans Use of Skin Make-Up," *Voice of Uganda*, May 6, 1975.

30. "Mini Ban Backing Pours In," *Uganda Argus*, May 31, 1972. See also James Ntambi, letter to the editor, *Uganda Argus*, June 3, 1972; J. Maloba-Mahande, letter to the editor, *Uganda Argus*, June 3, 1972; and Gershom B. Bamanya, letter to the editor, *Uganda Argus*, June 5, 1972.

31. "Mini Ban Backing Pours In," *Uganda Argus*, May 31, 1972.

32. Historically, Ugandans did not think of nudity as "indecent." Nakedness has always had multiple social meanings. See Grace Akello, "Self Twice-Removed: Ugandan Woman," *Change International Reports: Women and Society* 8 (1982): 14.

33. Y. D. Okot-Omara, letter to the editor, *Uganda Argus*, June 3, 1972. See also "Minis Ban: President Amin Hailed," *Uganda Argus*, May 30, 1972.

34. Y. D. Okot-Omara, letter to the editor, *Uganda Argus*, June 3, 1972.

35. John Atwoki, letter to the editor, *Uganda Argus*, June 3, 1972.

36. Deti Nteeko, letter to the editor, *Uganda Argus*, June 3, 1972.

37. Rebecca Katumba, "But 'Don't Take Law into Your Own Hands' Plea," *Uganda Argus*, May 30, 1972.

38. Rebecca Katumba and Betty Nagadya, "Mini Girls Molested By Men," *Uganda Argus*, May 31, 1972. See also Jane Kagulasi, letter to the editor, *Uganda Argus*, June 3, 1972.

39. "Jinja Girl in Court on 'Mini Dress' Charge," *Uganda Argus*, June 12, 1972.

40. For examples of legal wrangling, see "Mini Dress Case—Prosecution Is Criticized," *Uganda Argus*, June 14, 1972; "Kneeling Confusion," *Uganda Argus*, July 1, 1972; John Katende, "Just Where Does the Knee Line Start?" *Uganda Argus*, July 14, 1972; and "Magistrate on Knee Line," *Uganda Argus*, July 26, 1972.

41. Margaret Ndawula, interview by author, Kampala, May 23, 2005.

42. Forum for Women in Democracy, *The Rising Tide: Ugandan Women's Struggle for a Public Voice* (Kampala: FOWODE, 2003), 81.

43. Recall that Amin did not revise the decree clarifying the knee-line until February 1973. See Penal Code Act (Amendment) Decree, Decree 4 of 1973. For reports on early arrests, see "Arua 'Mini' Roundup," *Uganda Argus*, June 20, 1972; "Girl Sentenced for Defying Mini Law," *Uganda Argus*, July 6, 1972; Harry Kasozi, "Two Women on Mini Charges," *Uganda Argus*, July 7, 1972; "Fined, Cautioned for Wearing Mini-Skirts," *Uganda Argus*, July 8, 1972; "Mbale Mini Skirt Fine," *Uganda Argus*, August 3, 1972; "Mini Dress Girls Are Fined," *Uganda Argus*, August 31, 1972; and "Woman Forfeits Dress," *Voice of Uganda*, December 13, 1972.

44. See "Mini Skirt Girls Warned, Hippies Banned," *Uganda Argus*, July 6, 1972; "Kantinti Angry over Minis," *Uganda Argus*, July 11, 1972; and "A Shame to Husbands—Prosecution," *Uganda Argus*, September 4, 1972.

45. "Mini-Dress Woman Sent to Prison," *Voice of Uganda*, April 5, 1973.

46. "State Registered Nurse Is Jailed," *Voice of Uganda*, April 7, 1973; "Mini Dresses: Women Jailed," *Voice of Uganda*, April 18, 1973; and "Women Sent to Jail for Wearing Minis," *Voice of Uganda*, April 21, 1973.

47. This is the first time that police records have been utilized to analyze morality campaigns in Uganda. This is hardly surprising, given the many difficulties that I had accessing the documents. See appendix A for additional information on my methodology and sources.

48. The file number of this case is missing. Maria Kikaziki was arrested on December 27, 1973.

49. Although the vast majority of persons arrested were women, a few men also violated the ban. See Harry Kasozi, "School Boy in Court for Wearing a 'Mini,'" *Uganda Argus*, July 19, 1972; "Shorts Man in Court," *Uganda Argus*, September 15, 1972; "White Man in Mini Shorts," *Voice of Uganda*, March 23, 1973; and "Student Charged," *Voice of Uganda*, December 5, 1973.

50. Francis Kutosi [pseud.], interview by author, Kampala, July 24, 2008.

51. Peter Jermyn Allen, a British-born colonial official, served as a police officer and High Court judge in Uganda for many years. See Allen, *Interesting Times*, 334.

52. Sam Echaku, interview by author, Kampala, July 29, 2008.

53. See "Uganda Girl Cautioned over Mini-Dress Charge," *Voice of Uganda*, April 13, 1974.

54. "Mini Wearers More Common Than Thieves," *Voice of Uganda*, 24 September 1974.

55. Rhoda Kalema, interview by author, Kampala, July 6, 2005.

56. Esther Ssengendo [pseud.], interview by author, Kanyanya, July 2, 2005.

57. Derek R. Peterson and Edgar C. Taylor, "Rethinking the State in Idi Amin's Uganda: The Politics of Exhortation," *Journal of Eastern African Studies* 7, no. 1 (2013): 59.

58. Ibid., 60.

59. Ibid., 60.

60. Hassifa Namboze [pseud.], interview by author, Bwaise, April 19, 2005.

61. Sarah Adroa [pseud.], interview by author, Arua, July 14, 2008.

62. Rebecca Katumba, "But 'Don't Take Law into Your Own Hands' Plea," *Uganda Argus*, May 30, 1972. See also Ray Maki, "Mini Skirt Girl Riles Crowd," *Uganda Argus*, May 5, 1972; Rebecca Katumba and Betty Nagadya, "Mini Girls Molested by Men," *Uganda Argus*, May 31, 1972; Jane Kagulasi, letter to the editor, *Uganda Argus*, June 3, 1972; "'Hooligans' Molest Girls after Miniskirt Ban," *East African Standard*, June 3, 1972; "Murder in the Mango Grove," by Godfrey Lule, *Daily Mirror*, July 6, 1977; and International Commission of Jurists, *Uganda and Human Rights*, 135. For evidence of violence against women wearing wigs, see "Omukazi Yasabye Wiigi Ye Eyokebwe," *Munno*, February 11, 1974; and "Security Man Swoops on Wig Lady," *Voice of Uganda*, June 3, 1974. Various scholars have noted the increase in violence against women following the bans. See Aidan Southall, "Social Disorganization in Uganda: Before, During, and After Amin," *Journal of Modern African Studies* 18, no. 4 (1980): 643; Obbo, *African Women*, 11; Mahmood Mamdani, *Imperialism and Fascism in Uganda* (Nairobi: Heinemann, 1983), 54; Christine Obbo, "Sexuality and Economic Domination in Uganda," in *Women-Nation-State*, ed. Floya Anthias and Nira Yuval-Davis (London: Macmillan, 1989), 81; and Winnie Karagwa Byanyima, "Women in Political Struggle in Uganda," in *Women Transforming Politics: Worldwide Strategies for Empowerment*, ed. Jill M. Bystydzienski (Bloomington: Indiana University Press, 1992), 133.

63. Concerned Ugandan Woman, "Tough for Us in Uganda," *Drum Magazine*, reprinted in Seftel, *Uganda*, 136.

64. "Mini Skirt Girls Warned, Hippies Banned," *Uganda Argus*, July 6, 1972. See also "Gen. Amin's Government Bans Hippies," *East African Standard*, July 7, 1972.

65. "Mini-Dress Girls To Be Arrested," *Voice of Uganda*, November 28, 1974.

66. Nakarema Kyolaba [pseud.], interview by author, Mukono, May 31, 2005.

67. International Commission of Jurists, *Uganda and Human Rights*, 135. Aidan Southall likewise claimed that soldiers shaved women's heads if they were dressed indecently. See Southall, "Social Disorganization in Uganda," 643.

68. Evelyn Nyanzi [pseud.], interview by author, Kampala, July 23, 2005.

69. Joyce Ondoga [pseud.], interview by author, Arua, July 8, 2008.

70. Florence Mubiru [pseud.], interview by author, Kampala, July 9, 2005.

71. Other scholars have written about public stripping as a form of humiliation and punishment. See Hansen, "Dressing Dangerously," 175, 182; Ivaska, "Anti-Mini Militants," 105; and Wipper, "African Women," 330.

72. Goretti Ssali [pseud.], interview by author, Bunamwaya, May 5 and 12, 2005.

73. Hassifa Namboze [pseud.], interview by author, Bwaise, April 19, 2005.

74. Mary Kyomukama [pseud.], interview by author, Lusanja, June 28, 2005. See also Jane Walusimbi [pseud.], interview by author, Kitende, July 19, 2005.

CHAPTER 4: AN ACCIDENTAL LIBERATION

1. Joyce Ondoga [pseud.], interview by author, Arua, July 8, 2008.

2. "'Asians Milked the Cow: They Did Not Feed It,'" *Uganda Argus*, August 7, 1972.

3. "They Will Go to Villages," *Uganda Argus*, November 3, 1972.

4. Immigration (Cancellation of Entry Permits and Certificates of Residence) Decree, Decree 17 of 1972.

5. "British Charter Plane Flies Out 150 Asians: Exodus Begins," *Uganda Argus*, August 12, 1972.

6. Bert Adams and Mike Bristow, "Ugandan Asian Expulsion Experiences: Rumor and Reality," *Journal of Asian and African Studies* 14, no. 3–4 (1979): 192. Anneeth Kaur Hundle suggests that only 300–500 Asians remained in Uganda after the expulsion and that most were men. Approximately 150 were citizens, while the rest were Indian nationals and contractors who had been long-term residents prior to the expulsion. Hundle, "Exceptions to the Expulsion: Violence, Security and Community among Ugandan Asians, 1972–1979," *Journal of Eastern African Studies* 7, no. 1 (2013): 167.

7. Bert Adams and Mike Bristow, "The Politico-Economic Position of Ugandan Asians in the Colonial and Independent Eras," *Journal of Asian and African Studies* 13, no. 3–4 (1978): 153; Benoni Turyahikayo-Rugyema, *Idi Amin Speaks: An Annotated Selection of His Speeches* (Madison: University of Wisconsin, 1998), 30.

8. Thomas Melady and Margaret Melady, *Idi Amin Dada: Hitler in Africa* (Kansas City, KS: Sheed Andrews and McMeel, 1977), 75; Turyahikayo-Rugyema, *Idi Amin Speaks*, 31.

9. Samuel Karugire, *The Roots of Instability in Uganda* (Kampala: Fountain Publishers, 1988), 82.

10. "Before Power Is Handed Over: New Constitution Pledge," *Uganda Argus*, May 4, 1971.

11. "The Big Count," *Uganda Argus*, October 18, 1971.

12. For a concise overview of Amin's anti-Asian policies, see Jan Jelmert Jorgensen, *Uganda: A Modern History* (New York: St. Martin's Press, 1981), 285–88. For a detailed account of Amin's address to the Asian elders, see Judith Listowel, *Amin* (Dublin: IUP Press, 1973), 116–18.

13. Cited in Listowel, *Amin*, 120.

14. The international press repeated this rumor. See Michael Hiltzik, "Powerful Dynasty: All in the Family Feud Rips Uganda," *Los Angeles Times*, April 4, 1989.

15. "Uganda Is Determined to Win the Economic War—General Amin," *Uganda Argus*, August 14, 1972. For an analysis of how Amin linked economic

exploitation to race (instead of class), see Mahmood Mamdani, *Imperialism and Fascism in Uganda* (Nairobi: Heinemann, 1983), 39.

16. James Mittelman, *Ideology and Politics in Uganda: From Obote to Amin* (Ithaca, NY: Cornell University Press, 1975), 245; Mahmood Mamdani, *Politics and Class Formation* (Portsmouth, NH: Heinemann, 1976), 302–13.

17. Mahmood Mamdani, "The Ugandan Asian Expulsion: Twenty Years After," *Journal of Refugee Studies* 6, no. 3 (1993): 271.

18. Mahmood Mamdani, *From Citizen to Refugee: Ugandan Asians Come to Britain* (London: Frances Pinter, 1973), 25; International Commission of Jurists, *Uganda and Human Rights: Report to the UN Commission on Human Rights* (Geneva: International Commission of Jurists, 1977), 5–7.

19. Declaration of Assets (Non-citizen Asians) (Amendment) Decree, Decree 29 of 1972. For additional information on the acquisition process, see the Properties and Businesses (Acquisition) Decree, Decree 32 of 1972.

20. "Businesses to Be Allocated," *Uganda Argus*, November 30, 1972.

21. Part of the reason that initial allocations were "too slow" was because civilian committee leaders required applicants to demonstrate their financial and occupational ability to take over businesses. This frustrated the military officers, who simply wanted to reward their compatriots. See Henry Kyemba, *A State of Blood: The Inside Story of Idi Amin* (New York: Paddington Press, 1977), 64. For another description of the acquisition process, see Denis Hills, *The White Pumpkin* (New York: Grove Press, 1975), 302.

22. Jorgensen, *Uganda*, 289.

23. For details on the government's obligation to compensate departing Asians for their properties, see the Properties and Businesses (Acquisition) Decree, Decree 32 of 1972.

24. Timothy Parsons, *The African Rank-and-File: Social Implications of Colonial Military Service in the King's African Rifles, 1902–1964* (Portsmouth, NH: Heinemann, 1999), chap. 3; Mark Leopold, *Inside West Nile: Violence, History and Representation on an African Frontier* (Oxford: James Currey, 2005), 70.

25. The literal translation of this Kiswahili phrase is "a large amount of cooking oil." It implies that one has enough money to overindulge or get fat. It signifies wealth and extravagance.

26. Phares Mutibwa, *Uganda since Independence: A Story of Unfulfilled Hopes* (Trenton, NJ: Africa World Press, 1992), 117.

27. Nakanyike Musisi, "Baganda Women's Night Market Activities," in *African Market Women and Economic Power: The Role of Women in African Economic Development*, ed. Bessie House Midamba and Felix Ekechi (Westport, CT: Greenwood Press, 1995), 135.

28. Irene Lubega [pseud.], interview by author, Kampala, June 25, 2005. For a similar account, see Grace Byandala [pseud.], interview by author, Kampala, July 31, 2005.

29. Christine Obbo, *African Women: Their Struggle for Economic Independence* (London: Zed, 1980), 49. Janet Bujra found that women traders in

colonial Nairobi opted to become Swahili Muslims for the same sense of kinship. Bujra, "Women Entrepreneurs of Early Nairobi," *Canadian Journal of African Studies* 9, no. 2 (1975): 215, 226–30.

30. Winnie Mugenyi [pseud.], interview by author, Kampala, June 25 2005.

31. Goretti Ssali [pseud.], interview by author, Bunamwaya, May 5 and 12, 2005.

32. Obbo, *African Women*, 103.

33. Victoria Mwaka, interview by author, Kampala, June 22, 2005.

34. James Zikusoka, interview by author, Kampala, May 26, 2005. See also David Martin, *General Amin* (London: Faber and Faber, 1974), 168.

35. Margaret Snyder, *Women in African Economies: From Burning Sun to Boardroom* (Kampala: Fountain Publishers, 2000), 18. For a detailed examination of labor patterns in colonial Uganda, see Thomas Fuller, "African Labor and Training in the Ugandan Colonial Economy," *International Journal of African Historical Studies* 10, no. 1 (1977): 77–95. See also Philip Geoffrey Powesland, *Economic Policy and Labour: A Study in Uganda's Economic History* (Kampala: East African Institute for Social Research, 1957).

36. Jorgensen, *Uganda*, 297–300.

37. Ibid., 296–98. For a similar statistical analysis, see Colin Legum, "Behind the Clown's Mask," *Transition* 75–76 (1975–76): 258.

38. Jane Walusimbi [pseud.], interview by author, Kitende, July 19, 2005.

39. Angela Mukasa [pseud.], interview by author, Kampala, April 19, 2005.

40. Florence Mubiru [pseud.], interview by author, Kampala, July 9, 2005.

41. Mary Kyomukama [pseud.], interview by author, Kitezi, June 28, 2005.

42. Agnes Kato [pseud.], interview by author, Bunamwaya, May 12, 2005. See also Grace Bantebya Kyomuhendo and Marjorie Keniston McIntosh, *Women, Work, and Domestic Virtue in Uganda, 1900–2003* (Oxford: James Currey, 2006), 155.

43. Kyomuhendo and McIntosh, *Women, Work*, 160.

44. M. S. M. Semakula Kiwanuka, *Amin and the Tragedy of Uganda* (Munich: Weltforum, 1979), 95; Peter Jermyn Allen, *Days of Judgment: A Judge in Idi Amin's Uganda* (London: William Kimber, 1987), 151.

45. Lydia Balemezi, interview by author, Kampala, March 23, 2005.

46. Kyemba, *State of Blood*, 253.

47. Hope Mwesigye, interview by author, Kampala, June 23 and 30, 2005.

48. Enid Kisembo [pseud.], interview by author, Kampala, May 13, 2005.

49. Margaret Mutibwa [pseud.], interview by author, Kampala, May 2, 2005.

50. Ritah Lukwago [pseud.], interview by author, Kitende, July 21, 2005.

51. Ibid. For a similar account, see Margaret Mutibwa [pseud.], interview by author, Kampala, May 2, 2005.

52. Economic Crimes Tribunal Decree, Decree 2 of 1975. In particular, see section 19(1).

53. Evelyn Nyanzi [pseud.], interview by author, Kampala, July 23, 2005. See also Josephine Kabalema [pseud.], interview by author, Kampala, May

1, 2005; Nakarema Kyolaba [pseud.], interview by author, Mukono, May 31, 2005; Florence Mubiru [pseud.], interview by author, Kampala, July 9, 2005; Jane Walusimbi [pseud.], interview by author, Kitende, July 19, 2005; and Grace Byandala [pseud.], interview by author, Kampala, July 31, 2005. See also Kyomuhendo and McIntosh, *Women, Work,* 155.

54. Kyomuhendo and McIntosh, *Women, Work,* 155–56.

55. Josephine Kabalema [pseud.], interview by author, Kampala, May 1, 2005; Consolata Lugudde [pseud.], interview by author, Kampala, August 6, 2005; Christine Godi [pseud.], interview by author, Arua, July 10, 2008; and Madina Abia [pseud.], interview by author, Arua, July 11, 2008.

56. Prior to the expulsion, most women worked as agricultural and domestic laborers. Few had the qualifications to enter the paid labor market. For a general history of Ugandan women's employment patterns, see Obbo, *African Women;* Snyder, *Women in African Economies;* and Kyomuhendo and McIntosh, *Women, Work.*

57. To qualify for international loans, President Museveni invited the Asian population back to Uganda in 1992. Within a short period of time, small numbers of Asians began trickling back into the country to reclaim their assets and properties. Today there is a substantial Asian community living in Uganda. Many of the women who remembered that "Amin taught us how to work" expressed frustration with the current economic climate. This confirms that their memories of Amin have been heavily mediated by present circumstances.

58. Margaret Mutibwa [pseud.], interview by author, Kampala, May 2, 2005.

59. Goretti Ssali [pseud.], interview by author, Bunamwaya, May 5 and 12, 2005.

60. Snyder, *Women in African Economies,* 17.

61. Miria Matembe, interview by author, Kampala, August 17, 2005.

62. Kyomuhendo and McIntosh, *Women, Work,* 177–79.

63. Irene Lubega [pseud.], interview by author, Kampala, June 25, 2005.

64. Winnie Karagwa Byanyima, "Women in Political Struggle in Uganda," in *Women Transforming Politics: Worldwide Strategies for Empowerment,* ed. Jill M. Bystydzienski (Bloomington: Indiana University Press, 1992), 134.

65. Sylvia Kategaya [pseud.], interview by author, Kampala, April 28, 2005.

66. Snyder, *Women in African Economies,* 20.

67. Kyomuhendo and McIntosh argue that most women who received shops got them during the second round of distributions. They suggest that most Asian shops were initially given to men. See Kyomuhendo and McIntosh, *Women, Work,* 172.

68. Patience Ssekandi [pseud.], interview by author, Bunamwaya, May 19, 2005.

69. Snyder, *Women in African Economies,* 19.

CHAPTER 5: NEITHER A PRIVILEGE NOR A CURSE

1. See United Nations General Assembly Resolution 3010 (XXVII) of December 18, 1972.

2. "Oyeru in for Peace at the UN," *Voice of Uganda*, December 6, 1975.

3. Most biographical details about Bagaya's life come from her autobiography. See Elizabeth Nyabongo, *Elizabeth of Toro: The Odyssey of an African Princess* (New York: Simon and Schuster, 1989).

4. "Liz Bagaya Gets Top Job," *Uganda Argus*, July 22, 1971.

5. Amina Mama suggests that military leaders often incorporate elite women into the state to normalize and legitimate military rule. Mama, "Khaki in the Family: Gender Discourses and Militarism in Nigeria," *African Studies Review* 41, no. 2 (1998): 4.

6. "Women's Biggest Step," *Uganda Argus*, July 28, 1971.

7. "Mothers Big Role," *Uganda Argus*, November 27, 1971.

8. "'Let Us Put More Emphasis on Women's Education' Plea," *Uganda Argus*, March 29, 1972. See also "Role of Modern Women in Our Society," *Uganda Argus*, April 27, 1972.

9. Nyabongo, *Elizabeth of Toro*, 135.

10. Ibid., 136.

11. Rebecca Katumba and Chris Serunjogi, "Play an Effective Role, Women Told," *Uganda Argus*, November 23, 1972.

12. Rebecca Katumba, "Uganda's Women Resolve to Unite," *Uganda Argus*, November 30, 1972.

13. Representatives came from the following organizations: Uganda Association of Women's Organizations, Young Women's Christian Association, Uganda Council of Women, Mothers' Union, Catholic Action, Muslim Women's Association, Association of University Women of Uganda, Federation of Community Development of Rural Clubs, and National Council of Social Services. "Women Meet in Camera," *Voice of Uganda*, January 5, 1973.

14. "First Woman Permanent Secretary," *Voice of Uganda*, March 24, 1973. Bagaya suggests that she had a direct hand in Mary Astles's promotion, although it was likely the product of patronage politics. Astles was married to Amin's right-hand man, a British man by the name of Bob Astles. In late February 1977, Amin appointed her minister of culture and community development, a position she held until the collapse of the regime. "Senkatuka Now Culture Minister," *Voice of Uganda*, February 23, 1977.

15. "Ambassador Bagaya Replaces Lt. Col. Ondoga," *Voice of Uganda*, February 20, 1974.

16. Etiang served as minister of foreign affairs (1973–74), minister of state in charge of African affairs (1974–76), and minister of transport, communication, and works (1976–78). Paul Etiang, interview by author, Kampala, July 26, 2005.

17. Barbet Shroeder, *General Idi Amin Dada: A Self Portrait*, DVD (New York: Criterion Collection, 1974).

18. Amin used similar rhetoric when announcing other high-level political appointments. For instance, when he named Helen Oyeru as permanent secretary in the Ministry of Provincial Administration, he said that "some women were proving to be better officers than a number of men officers

because a number of men in high ranking government and military positions indulge too much in heavy drinking." Later, when he announced the promotion of Ellen Pharas Awori to the rank of provincial commissioner for culture and community development in Karamoja District, he said women had become more hardworking than men. See "Oyeru Becomes Second Woman Permanent Secretary," *Voice of Uganda*, May 15, 1975; and "Dynamic Lady Promoted," *Voice of Uganda*, September 6, 1976.

19. "Challenge to Bagaya," *Voice of Uganda*, February 21, 1974.

20. "Thousands Mark Uganda's Uhuru Day," *Voice of Uganda*, October 10, 1974. The First Class award was reserved for heads of state.

21. Nyabongo, *Elizabeth of Toro*, 169–72.

22. Ibid., 175–76.

23. Declassified/Released US Department of State EO Systematic Review 30 JUN 2005, R 021341Z DEC 74.

24. "Miss Bagaya Loses Her Ministerial Post," *Voice of Uganda*, November 29, 1974.

25. "Radio Comment on Miss Bagaya," *Voice of Uganda*, January 24, 1975.

26. Photograph, *Voice of Uganda*, April 7, 1975.

27. Photograph, *Voice of Uganda*, January 21, 1975.

28. Paul Etiang, interview by author, Kampala, July 26, 2005. See also "Uganda Woman Official Named Our Bonn Envoy," *Voice of Uganda*, October 24, 1974.

29. "President Amin Scraps Mortgages on Land," *Voice of Uganda*, May 1, 1975.

30. Before Amin divorced his first three wives, they too played similar political roles. For additional information, see Alicia C. Decker, "Militarismo, nazionalismo e matrimonio: Un ritratto privato delle cinque mogli di Idi Amin" [Militarism, Nationalism, and Marriage: An Intimate Portrait of Idi Amin's Five Wives], *Afriche e Orienti* 14, no. 3–4 (2012): 124–38.

31. Madina Amin, Women's Day Speech, May 1, 1975 (translated from Luganda by Mary Senkatuka Astles). Italics added.

32. http://www.5wwc.org/conference_background/1975_WCW.html. See also Devaki Jain, *Women, Development and the UN: A Sixty-Year Quest for Equality and Justice* (Bloomington: Indiana University Press, 2005).

33. Joyce Mpanga, interview by author, Kampala, May 25, 2005. See also "Madina Urges Both Sexes to Take Part," *Voice of Uganda*, June 16, 1975.

34. "General Throws Ladies' Party at Entebbe," *Voice of Uganda*, June 14, 1975.

35. "Miss H. Oyeru Backs World Women's Year," *Voice of Uganda*, June 26, 1975.

36. "General Amin Appoints New Ministers," *Voice of Uganda*, July 12, 1975. He eventually transferred Doka to the Ministry of Tourism and Wildlife and moved Kateregga to the Ministry of Transport and Communications. Later, he sent her to the Ministry of Culture and Community Development.

37. International Commission of Jurists, *Uganda and Human Rights: Report to the UN Commission on Human Rights* (Geneva: International Commission of Jurists, 1977), 165.

38. Ibid., 165–66.

39. Joseph Kamau [pseud.] and Andrew Cameron [pseud.], *Lust to Kill: The Rise and Fall of Idi Amin* (London: Transworld Publishers, 1979), 182.

40. Peter Jermyn Allen, *Days of Judgment: A Judge in Idi Amin's Uganda* (London: William Kimber, 1987), 142.

41. For information on Amin's campaign to cover up the regime's "dirt," see Alicia C. Decker, "Idi Amin's Dirty War: Subversion, Sabotage and the Battle to Keep Uganda Clean, 1971–1979," *International Journal of African Historical Studies* 43, no. 3 (2010): 489–513.

42. Allen, *Days of Judgment*, 142. See also "Forces Promote President to Field Marshall," *Voice of Uganda*, July 16, 1975.

43. "The OAU Dress," *Voice of Uganda*, July 15, 1975.

44. "Governor Nasur Show [sic] Tailors How to Sew OAU Attire," *Voice of Uganda*, July 17, 1975.

45. "Beauty Pulls OAU Members to Kampala," *Voice of Uganda*, June 28, 1975.

46. Cartoon, *Voice of Uganda*, May 10, 1975.

47. Cartoon, *Voice of Uganda*, July 9, 1975.

48. "Margaret Miss OAU," *Voice of Uganda*, July 28, 1975.

49. "Marshal Gets New Bride," *Voice of Uganda*, August 2, 1975.

50. One such photograph was published in the *Voice of Uganda* on December 27, 1974.

51. Godfrey Lule, "Amin's Lust Is Deadly," *Daily Mirror* (London), July 5, 1977. Malyam Amin confirms this story. See Malyam Amin, "The Sad Story of 'Suicide' Sarah," *Daily Mirror* (London), July 31, 1979.

52. "Marshal Gets New Bride," *Voice of Uganda*, August 2, 1975; "Marshal's Wedding to Be Held Again," *Voice of Uganda*, August 5, 1975; and "Wedding of the Year," *Voice of Uganda*, August 8, 1975.

53. "Female Pilot Trainees Get a Word of Advice," *Voice of Uganda*, August 12, 1975.

54. See "Women to Prove Their Own Worth," *Voice of Uganda*, March 6, 1975; "Women Should Start Thinking Seriously," *Voice of Uganda*, March 19, 1975; "Do Women Understand the Term Equality," *Voice of Uganda*, March 31, 1975; "Owor Urges Women to Be Active," *Voice of Uganda*, July 26, 1975; and "Wasted Asset of Women's Rights," *Voice of Uganda*, September 22, 1975.

55. Cartoon, *Voice of Uganda*, December 1, 1975.

56. Cartoon, *Voice of Uganda*, January 6, 1976.

57. Cartoon, *Voice of Uganda*, February 19, 1976.

58. Rebecca Katumba, "Mawa Urges Workers to Be Practical," *Voice of Uganda*, May 1, 1976.

59. "Big Labor Day at Mbale," *Voice of Uganda*, May 3, 1976.

60. Rebecca Katumba, "Women Form National Council," *Voice of Uganda*, June 3, 1976.

61. "Conference for Women's Council Opens at Kyambogo," *Voice of Uganda*, September 2, 1976.

62. "Marshal Gives Women .5 Million/=," *Voice of Uganda*, September 4, 1976.

63. National Council of Women Decree, Decree 2 of 1978.

64. Aili Mari Tripp, *Women and Politics in Uganda* (Madison: University of Wisconsin Press, 2000), 49. See also Forum for Women in Democracy, *The Rising Tide: Ugandan Women's Struggle for a Public Voice* (Kampala: FO-WODE, 2003), 59.

65. Rebecca Katumba, "Mrs. Molly Okalebo Elected Chairman of Women's Council," *Voice of Uganda*, September 14, 1978.

CHAPTER 6: WIDOWS WITHOUT GRAVES

1. Republic of Uganda, *Report of the Commission of Inquiry into the Disappearances of People in Uganda since 25 January, 1971* (Entebbe: Government Printer, 1975), 282.

2. In an open letter, Amin's brother-in-law and the former minister of foreign affairs, Wanume Kibedi, claimed, "The expression 'disappearance' is a euphemism for Uganda's innocent dead—the thousands of people who, since the inception of your misrule, have been liquidated for personal, political or factional reasons, entirely outside the processes of law. The victims are said to have 'disappeared' because after their murders their bodies are clandestinely disposed of or mutilated beyond recognition, never to be recovered by their relatives." Kibedi, "Open Letter to General Idi Amin, Kampala," in *Uganda and Human Rights: Report to the UN Commission on Human Rights* (Geneva: International Commission of Jurists, 1977), 69.

3. Thomas Melady and Margaret Melady, *Idi Amin Dada: Hitler in Africa* (Kansas City, KS: Sheed Andrews and McMeel, 1977), 167.

4. "Stories of 'Killings' Work of Confusing Agents," *Uganda Argus*, March 23, 1971.

5. Republic of Uganda, *Commission of Inquiry into the Missing Americans* (Entebbe: Government Printer, 1972); Harry Kasozi, "Stroh, Siedle Report Out," *Uganda Argus*, July 25, 1972; and International Commission of Jurists, *Violations of Human Rights and the Rule of Law in Uganda* (Geneva: International Commission of Jurists, 1974), 34–38.

6. Rebecca Katumba and Chris Serunjogi, "Play an Effective Role, Women Told," *Uganda Argus*, November 23, 1972.

7. Joyce Mpanga, interview by the author, Kampala, May 25, 2005. Mpanga suggests that Mulindwa was later punished for speaking out. She lost her job as an educational officer and was "demoted" to her former position as headmistress of Jinja Secondary School.

8. Rugamayo was initially quoted anonymously. See International Commission of Jurists, *Violations of Human Rights*, 52. He later accepted responsibility for the statements. See International Commission of Jurists, *Uganda*

and Human Rights, 112. For official coverage of the event, see "Charred Body in Car of *Munno's* Editor," *Voice of Uganda*, January 15, 1973.

9. The missing included eleven former ministers, twenty-two army officers, twelve police officers, six former politicians, four prison officers, and thirty civil servants and other citizens.

10. Republic of Uganda, "Official Statement Relating to Disappearance of Persons," January 9, 1973 (available in US Institute of Peace, Truth Commission Digital Collection, hereafter cited as Truth Commission Collection).

11. "Disappearance of People Will Be Stamped Out," *Voice of Uganda*, December 5, 1973.

12. International Commission of Jurists, *Uganda and Human Rights*, ix.

13. Kibedi, "Open Letter," in ibid., 77.

14. Republic of Uganda, "President's Office Statement on Disappearances," June 30, 1974 (available in Truth Commission Collection).

15. Ibid.

16. Republic of Uganda, Legal Notice No. 2 of 1974, "Commission of Inquiry into the Disappearances of People in Uganda since 25 January, 1971: Charter," June 30, 1974 (available in Truth Commission Collection). The commissioners also had the authority to accept written memoranda at their discretion. They accepted a 63-page report from the International Commission of Jurists, although they refused to accept an affidavit from the former minister of foreign affairs, Wanume Kibedi.

17. Republic of Uganda, "President's Office Statement on Disappearances."

18. For an example of advertising, see *Voice of Uganda*, July 10, 1974.

19. "Saied Hands in Disappearance Inquiry Report," *Voice of Uganda*, June 26, 1975.

20. Richard Carver, "Called to Account: How African Governments Investigate Human Rights Violations," *African Affairs* 89, no. 356 (July 1990): 391–415; and Priscilla B. Hayner, *Unspeakable Truths: Confronting State Terror and Atrocity* (New York: Routledge, 2001).

21. US Institute of Peace, http://www.usip.org/publications/truth-commission-uganda-74 (accessed May 20, 2011). The institute uploaded a copy of the report in mid-2009 as part of a much larger initiative to develop a Truth Commission Digital Collection. Sadly, nearly one-third of this precious document is illegible. My analysis is based on the parts that I could read.

22. Republic of Uganda, *Report of the Commission of Inquiry* (1975), 620.

23. Ibid., 351–52.

24. Ibid., 635.

25. Ibid., 637.

26. On December 28, 1971, the government transferred 642 detainees from Luzira Prison to Mutukula Prison Farm on the Tanzanian border. All were Acholi or Langi. In mid-January 1972, the prison guards began brutally massacring the detainees. A small group managed to escape the slaughter and fled across the border into safety. For additional information on the "Mutukula massacre," see Judith Listowel, *Amin* (Dublin: IUP Press, 1973); David

Martin, *General Amin* (London: Faber and Faber, 1974); and International Commission of Jurists, *Violations of Human Rights.*

27. Republic of Uganda, *Report of the Commission of Inquiry* (1975), 639.

28. Ibid., 425.

29. Ibid., 406.

30. Ibid., 795. The commission reported that this practice was common.

31. David Gwyn [pseud.], *Idi Amin: Death-Light of Africa* (Boston: Little, Brown, 1977), 189.

32. Republic of Uganda, *Report of the Commission of Inquiry* (1975), 267.

33. Henry Kyemba, *A State of Blood: The Inside Story of Idi Amin* (New York: Paddington Press, 1977), 119.

34. Ibid., 119–20. For a gripping literary portrayal of this macabre new profession, see Moses Isegawa, *Snakepit* (New York: Random House, 2004), 132–39.

35. International Commission of Jurists, *Uganda and Human Rights*, 117. For additional information on these dump sites, see Peter Jermyn Allen, *Interesting Times: Uganda Diaries, 1955–1986* (Sussex, UK: Book Guild, 2000); George Ivan Smith, *Ghosts of Kampala* (New York: St. Martin's Press, 1980); Wycliffe Kato, *Escape from Idi Amin's Slaughterhouse* (London: Quartet Books, 1989); Melady and Melady, *Idi Amin Dada*; Joseph Kamau [pseud.] and Andrew Cameron [pseud.], *Lust to Kill: The Rise and Fall of Idi Amin* (London: Transworld Publishers, 1979); and P. M. O. Onen, *The Diary of an Obedient Servant during Misrule* (Kampala: Janyeko Publishing, 2000).

36. Republic of Uganda, *Report of the Commission of Inquiry* (1975), 777–78.

37. The women reported that this was not usually the case for police officers. Their property was often returned.

38. Republic of Uganda, *Report of the Commission of Inquiry* (1975), 680.

39. Estates of Missing Persons (Management) Decree, Decree 20 of 1973.

40. Republic of Uganda, *Report of the Commission of Inquiry* (1975), 162.

41. Néstor Kirchner, "Children of the Dirty War: Argentina's Stolen Orphans," *New Yorker*, March 19, 2012.

42. Republic of Uganda, *Report of the Commission of Inquiry* (1975), 705.

43. Ibid., 704.

44. Decree 13 of 1971 went into effect on March 15 and was supposed to expire in one year. Amin did not renew the decree until October 4, 1972. The Armed Forces (Powers of Arrest) Decree, or Decree 26 of 1972, extended the armed forces' power of arrest retroactively.

45. Republic of Uganda, *Report of the Commission of Inquiry* (1975), 715.

46. See Armed Forces (Powers of Arrest) (Repeal) Decree, Decree 21 of 1973 and Military Police (Powers of Arrest) Decree, Decree 19 of 1973. Amin promulgated these two decrees on the same day that he issued the Estates of Missing Persons (Management) Decree.

47. "Public Warned as Powers of Arrest Are Repealed," *Voice of Uganda*, August 28, 1973.

48. Republic of Uganda, *Report of the Commission of Inquiry* (1975), 728.

49. Ibid., 748.

50. Ibid., 710.

51. Ibid., 709.

52. Proceedings against the Government (Protection) Decree, Decree 8 of 1972.

53. Republic of Uganda, *Report of the Commission of Inquiry* (1975), 789.

54. International Commission of Jurists, *Uganda and Human Rights*, 123.

55. Peter Jermyn Allen suggests that Saied tried to resign after anonymous leaflets began circulating around Kampala calling for Amin to step down and turn over power to the chief justice. Amin suspected that the judiciary was involved and sent Mustafa Adrisi—by then minister of defense and minister of internal affairs—to talk to all judges and magistrates. Saied felt he had no choice but to resign because judicial autonomy had been compromised. However, Amin ignored his resignation. Allen, *Interesting Times*, 457–60.

56. "Uganda Elected to UN Commission on Human Rights," *Voice of Uganda*, May 19, 1976. The three-year term began on January 1, 1977.

57. "Election to Human Rights Commission," *Voice of Uganda*, May 20, 1976.

58. International Commission of Jurists, *Uganda and Human Rights*, vii–xii, 107.

59. Another notable example of Amin's strategic "concern" for public welfare was the movement to "Keep Uganda Clean." See Alicia C. Decker, "Idi Amin's Dirty War: Subversion, Sabotage and the Battle to Keep Uganda Clean, 1971–1979," *International Journal of African Historical Studies* 43, no. 3 (2010): 489–513.

60. My conceptualization of the commission as "political theater" comes primarily from the work of Adam Ashforth, *The Politics of Official Discourse in Twentieth-Century South Africa* (Oxford: Clarendon Press, 1990); and Derek R. Peterson, "Morality Plays: Marriage, Church Courts, and Colonial Agency in Central Tanganyika, ca. 1876–1928," *American Historical Review* 111, no. 4 (October 2006): 983–1010.

CHAPTER SEVEN: VIOLENCE IN THE SHADOWS

1. Republic of Uganda, *Report of the Commission of Inquiry into Violations of Human Rights* (Entebbe: Government Printer, 1994), 9220.

2. Ibid., 9225.

3. A. B. K. Kasozi, *The Social Origins of Violence in Uganda* (Kampala: Fountain Publishers, 1994), 121. For official coverage of the event, see "PFLP Commandos Hijack Plane," *Voice of Uganda*, June 29, 1976; "The Hijackers Make Strong Ultimatum," *Voice of Uganda*, June 30, 1976; "Ultimatum Stands," *Voice of Uganda*, July 1, 1976; "Hijackers Free 100 Hostages," *Voice of Uganda*, July 2, 1976; and "Israelis Invade Entebbe," *Voice of Uganda*, July 5, 1976.

4. For instance, see "Fadhul Warns Drunkards," *Voice of Uganda*, August 3, 1976; "Officers Advise the Public to Ignore Rumors," *Voice of Uganda*, March 3, 1977; "Colonel Ibrahim Warns Busoga on Rumors," *Voice of Uganda*, May 13, 1977; "Minister Condemns Rumor Mongers," *Voice of*

Uganda, May 16, 1977; "Do Not Write Dirty Letters," *Voice of Uganda,* September 10, 1977; Sam Wakoli, "Chief Chases the Jobless out of Mbale," *Voice of Uganda,* November 18, 1977; "Gowon Advises All God Fearing People," *Voice of Uganda,* May 6, 1978; "Rumor-Mongers Are Warned," *Voice of Uganda,* August 15, 1978; "Source of Dirty Plans Confirmed," *Voice of Uganda,* November 21, 1978; and "Lt. Wahib Warns," *Voice of Uganda,* December 18, 1978.

5. Kasozi, *Social Origins of Violence,* 121.

6. "4 Ministers Are Retired," *Voice of Uganda,* December 2, 1972.

7. Republic of Uganda, *Report of the Commission of Inquiry (1994),* 9047.

8. Ibid., 9048.

9. Ibid., 9050.

10. Ibid., 9057.

11. Ibid., 9165.

12. Amnesty International reported that approximately two hundred wives and children of Acholi and Langi soldiers who were murdered in Mubende and Mbarara Barracks were also killed upon their return to the north. See Amnesty International, *Human Rights in Uganda* (London: Amnesty International, 1978), 11.

13. Republic of Uganda, *Report of the Commission of Inquiry (1994),* 9229–9230.

14. Ibid., 9232.

15. Winnie Karagwa Byanyima, "Women in Political Struggle in Uganda," in *Women Transforming Politics: Worldwide Strategies for Empowerment,* ed. Jill M. Bystydzienski (Bloomington: Indiana University Press, 1992), 133.

16. International Commission of Jurists, *Uganda and Human Rights: Report to the UN Commission on Human Rights* (Geneva: International Commission of Jurists, 1977), 152.

17. George Ivan Smith, *Ghosts of Kampala* (New York: St. Martin's Press, 1980), 144.

18. International Commission of Jurists, *Uganda and Human Rights,* xii.

19. Henry Kyemba, *A State of Blood: The Inside Story of Idi Amin* (New York: Paddington Press, 1977), 127. See also Bryan Langlands, "Students and Politics in Uganda," *African Affairs* 76, no. 302 (January 1977): 18–19.

20. Kyemba, *State of Blood,* 123–24.

21. Smith, *Ghosts of Kampala,* 12. Smith's observation was corroborated by Wycliffe Kato, former director of Uganda's Civil Aviation Department, who was imprisoned but miraculously escaped in September 1977. See Kato, *Escape from Idi Amin's Slaughterhouse* (London: Quartet Books, 1989). See also WodOkello Lawoko, *The Dungeons of Nakasero* (Stockholm: Författares Bokmaskin, 2005).

22. Florence Wanaswa, "Train Tragedies," in *Looking Back: Tragedies of Uganda Women and Children, 1970–2000,* ed. Patricia Haward (Kampala: Fountain Publishers, 2009), 21.

23. Ibid., 22.

24. Ibid., 23.

25. International Commission of Jurists, *Uganda and Human Rights*, 151.

26. Hassifa Namboze [pseud.], interview by author, Bwaise, April 19, 2005.

27. Irene Lubega [pseud.], interview by author, Kampala, June 25, 2005.

28. Evelyn Nyanzi [pseud.], interview by author, Kampala, July 23, 2005.

29. Betty Mayiga [pseud.], interview by author, Kampala, April 26, 2005.

30. Rebekah Matua [pseud.], interview by author, Arua, July 10, 2008.

31. Catherine Asiimwe [pseud.], interview by author, Kitende, July 19, 2005.

32. Jane Walusimbi [pseud.], interview by author, Kitende, July 19, 2005.

33. Ritah Lukwago [pseud.], interview by author, Kitende, July 21, 2005.

CHAPTER EIGHT: MILITANT MOTHERHOOD

1. Esther Ssengendo [pseud.], interview by author, Kanyanya, July 2, 2005.

2. One of the most influential books written about the war—aptly titled *War in Uganda*, by Tony Avirgan and Martha Honey—does not include women, gender, rape, or violence in the index. In fact, in the entire 236-page book, only six sentences mention women at all. Avirgan and Honey, *War in Uganda: The Legacy of Idi Amin* (Westport, CT: Laurence Hill, 1982).

3. Ibid., 48–49.

4. For official coverage of this event, see "Mustafa Injured in Motor Accident," *Voice of Uganda*, April 20, 1978.

5. Avirgan and Honey, *War in Uganda*, 51.

6. "The Invasion That Went Wrong," *Drum*, April 1979, reprinted in Adam Seftel, ed., *Uganda: The Bloodstained Pearl of Africa and Its Struggle for Peace* (Lanseria, South Africa: Bailey's African Photo Archives Production, 1994), 222–29.

7. Avirgan and Honey, *War in Uganda*, 51–54.

8. "Tanzanian Troops Attack Uganda," *Voice of Uganda*, October 13, 1978.

9. "Ugandan Troops Won't Cross into Tanzania," *Voice of Uganda*, October 19, 1978.

10. Avirgan and Honey, *War in Uganda*, 60.

11. Ibid., 61.

12. "The Invasion That Went Wrong," *Drum*, April 1979, reprinted in Seftel, *Uganda*, 222–29.

13. Bernard Rwehururu, *Cross to the Gun: Idi Amin and the Fall of the Uganda Army* (Kampala: Monitor Publications, 2002), 96.

14. Avirgan and Honey, *War in Uganda*, 61.

15. "Boxing with Nyerere?" *Chicago Tribune*, November 4, 1978. See also "Amin Offers to Box with Enemy," *Los Angeles Times*, November 3, 1978.

16. Amin's propaganda machine claimed that Tanzanian soldiers had attempted to cross the river but were beaten back by Ugandan soldiers. See "Dr. Amin Orders Uganda Troops Back to the Recognized Border," *Voice of Uganda*, November 15, 1978.

17. Avirgan and Honey, *War in Uganda*, 68.

18. Ibid., 70.

19. Ibid., 78–86. See also Yoweri Museveni, *Sowing the Mustard Seed: The Struggle for Freedom and Democracy in Uganda* (London: Macmillan, 1997); and Rwehururu, *Cross to the Gun*.

20. "20 Ugandan Soldiers against 20,000 Forces," *Voice of Uganda*, February 26, 1979.

21. "Amin Family 'Flees as the End Nears,'" *Evening Standard* (London), February 28, 1979. See also Norman Kirkham, "Amin Family's Flight Confirmed," *Sunday Times* (London), March 4, 1979.

22. Avirgan and Honey, *War in Uganda*, 89–90, 93.

23. "Madam Sarah Amin Highly Commended," *Voice of Uganda*, March 5, 1979.

24. Robert McGowan, "Here Comes Suicide Sarah—Idi's Favorite Wife Leads His Troops in Battle," *Express* (London), March 5, 1979. See also "Suicide Sarah Wins Praise," *Daily Mail* (London), March 5, 1979.

25. Avirgan and Honey, *War in Uganda*, xiii.

26. Amin created a unit within the Police Air Wing called the Uganda Air Force Bravo Women's Squadron, but they did not participate in ground combat. For additional information on Amin's female pilots, see "Women in Air Force Advised," *Voice of Uganda*, March 2, 1976; "Women Told not to Be Cowards," *Voice of Uganda*, October 12, 1976; "Ugandan Women Prepare to Fly Combat MIGs," *Sarasota Herald-Tribune*, March 7, 1977; and "Women Pilots Receive Wings," *Voice of Uganda*, January 26, 1978.

27. Robert McGowan, "Here Comes Suicide Sarah—Idi's Favorite Wife Leads His Troops in Battle," *Express* (London), March 5, 1979.

28. Sylvia Kategaya [pseud.], interview by author, Kampala, April 28, 2005.

29. In *Waiting: A Novel of Uganda at War*, Goretti Kyomuhendo describes Amin's final weeks in power. The novel is told from the perspective of an adolescent girl who is waiting for the liberators to reach her village near Hoima. It describes the hardships experienced by rural communities during this time, particularly in terms of the violence and looting carried out by Amin's fleeing soldiers. Kyomuhendo, *Waiting: A Novel of Uganda at War* (New York: Feminist Press at CUNY, 2007).

30. Republic of Uganda, *Report of the Commission of Inquiry into Violations of Human Rights* (Entebbe: Government Printer, 1994), 9138–9148.

31. Ibid., 13188–13206.

32. Ibid., 8956.

33. Ibid., 8960–8961.

34. Ibid., 8959. Christine Grace Eperu, a prison wardress in Lira, testified that after the governor's rally, three prison officers and one police officer were arrested on charges of subversion. They were never seen again. She said that even before the meeting took place, she had heard rumors that many Acholi and Langi men would be arrested, particularly those who were associated with the security forces. It is very possible that Catherine Boyi's brother-in-law heard these rumors and decided *not* to attend the rally. Republic of Uganda, *Report of the Commission of Inquiry (1994)*, 9202–9215.

35. "Dusk to Dawn Curfew Declared," *Voice of Uganda*, March 26, 1979.

36. "Enemy Cuts Off Entebbe from Kampala," *Voice of Uganda*, March 27, 1979.

37. "Situation in Kampala Normal," *Voice of Uganda*, March 28, 1979.

38. Lydia Balemezi, interview by author, Kampala, March 23, 2005.

39. Sylvia Kategaya [pseud.], interview by author, Kampala, April 28, 2005. See also Florence Mubiru [pseud.], interview by author, Kampala, July 9, 2005.

40. Chance Kawuma [pseud.], interview by author, Kampala, April 8, 2005.

41. Fatima Musisi [pseud.], interview by author, Kampala, June 23, 2005.

42. Enid Musenyi [pseud.], interview by author, Kampala, July 9, 2005.

43. Theresa Mukiibi [pseud.], interview by author, Kampala, May 26, 2005.

44. Patience Ssekandi [pseud.], interview by author, Bunamwaya, May 19, 2005.

45. Rose Birungi [pseud.], interview by author, Mpererwe, July 28, 2005.

46. Miria Matembe, interview by author, Kampala, August 17, 2005.

47. Namuli Kasozi [pseud.], interview by author, Kampala, April 12, 2005.

48. Benoni Turyahikayo-Rugyema, *Idi Amin Speaks: An Annotated Selection of His Speeches* (Madison: University of Wisconsin, 1998), 114.

49. Avirgan and Honey, *War in Uganda*, 121.

50. Jane Walusimbi [pseud.], interview by author, Kitende, July 19, 2005.

51. Avirgan and Honey, *War in Uganda*, 122.

52. Ibid., 133.

53. Amin managed to escape into exile, taking a chartered flight from Arua to Tripoli in late April 1979, courtesy of his close friend and ally Muammar Gaddafi. One year later, his entire family resettled in Saudi Arabia as guests of the royal family. This is where Amin died on August 16, 2003. For additional information on Amin's life in exile, see Riccardo Orizio, *Talk of the Devil: Encounters with Seven Dictators* (New York: Walker, 2002), 9–32; and Jaffar Amin and Margaret Akulia, *Idi Amin: Hero or Villain? His Son Jaffar Amin and Other People Speak* (Charleston, SC: Millennium Global Publishers, 2010), 396, 452. For information on the fate of Amin's five official wives, see Alicia C. Decker, "Militarismo, nazionalismo e matrimonio: Un ritratto privato delle cinque mogli di Idi Amin" [Militarism, Nationalism, and Marriage: An Intimate Portrait of Idi Amin's Five Wives], *Afriche e Orienti* 14, no. 3–4 (2012): 124–38.

54. Avirgan and Honey, *War in Uganda*, 148. See also M. S. M. Semakula Kiwanuka, *Amin and the Tragedy of Uganda* (Munich: Weltforum, 1979), 194; A. B. K. Kasozi, *The Social Origins of Violence in Uganda* (Kampala: Fountain Publishers, 1994), 126–27; and Aidan Southall, "Social Disorganization in Uganda: Before, During, and After Amin," *Journal of Modern African Studies* 18, no. 4 (1980): 629.

55. Avirgan and Honey, *War in Uganda*, 148.

56. Ondoga ori Amaza, *Museveni's Long March: From Guerrilla to Statesman* (Kampala: Fountain Publishers, 1998), xiv.

57. Republic of Uganda, *Report of the Commission of Inquiry (1994)*, 4468–86.

58. Ibid., 4114–15.

CONCLUSION: GENDERED LEGACIES OF AMIN'S MILITARISM

1. Prossi Asumi [pseud.], interview by author, Arua, July 10, 2008.

2. Goretti Ssali [pseud.], interview by author, Bunamwaya, May 5 and 12, 2005.

3. Holger Bernt Hansen and Michael Twaddle, introduction to *Uganda Now: Between Decay and Development*, ed. Holger Bernt Hansen and Michael Twaddle (London: James Currey, 1988), 3.

4. John Njoroge and Ismail Musa, "Uganda Could Degenerate into Violence Next Year—US Report," *Daily Monitor*, April 7, 2013.

5. These include the Popular Resistance Army (1980), Uganda Freedom Fighters (1980), Former Uganda National Army (1980–?), Uganda National Rescue Front (1980–1985), National Resistance Army (1981–1986), Holy Spirit Movement (1986–1987), West Nile Bank Front (1986–1998), Uganda People's Army (1987–1992), Lord's Resistance Army (1987–present), National Army for the Liberation of Uganda (1988–?), Allied Democratic Forces (1996–present), Uganda National Rescue Front II (1996–2002), and People's Redemption Army (2004–?).

6. Global Network of Women Peacebuilders, *Women Count—Security Council Resolution 1325: Civil Society Monitoring Report 2012, Uganda* (New York: Global Network of Women Peacebuilders, 2012), 5.

7. Stockholm International Peace Research Institute Military Expenditure Database, http://www.sipri.org/research/armaments/milex/milex_database (accessed August 15, 2013).

8. Amina Mama and Margo Okazawa-Rey, "Militarism, Conflict and Women's Activism in the Global Era: Challenges and Prospects for Women in Three West African Contexts," *Feminist Review* 101 (2012): 100.

9. There is significant evidence to demonstrate that members of the Ugandan military forces have been complicit in perpetrating violence against women (and men). See IRIN, "Uganda: Government Soldiers Charged with Rape of IDPs," April 22, 2005, http://www.irinnews.org/printreport.aspx?reportid=54014; Olandason Wangama and Catherine Bekunda, "Uganda: Army Officers Fired over Gang Rape," *New Vision*, January 6, 2011; and "UPDF in Kony Hunt Accused of Rape, Looting," *Observer*, March 2, 2012.

10. Global Network of Women Peacebuilders, *Women Count*, 9. Estimated troop strength is based on the World Bank's World Development Indicators from 2011. See http://databank.worldbank.org/data/views/reports /tableview.aspx (accessed August 19, 2013).

APPENDIX: METHODS AND SOURCES

1. Republic of Uganda, *Report of the Commission of Inquiry into Violations of Human Rights* (Entebbe: Government Printer, 1994), 622. Grace Bantebya

Kyomuhendo and Marjorie Keniston McIntosh confirm that although Amin's rule had a profound impact on Ugandan women, their experiences have not been examined in much detail because of poor sources. See Kyomuhendo and McIntosh, *Women, Work, and Domestic Virtue in Uganda, 1900–2003* (Oxford: James Currey, 2006), 147.

2. Richard Carver, "Called to Account: How African Governments Investigate Human Rights Violations," *African Affairs* 89, no. 356 (July 1990): 391–415; and Priscilla B. Hayner, *Unspeakable Truths: Confronting State Terror and Atrocity* (New York: Routledge, 2001).

3. I had a similar problem when trying to access exhibits from the Commission of Inquiry into Violations of Human Rights. According to the commissioners' final report, these exhibits were located at the Uganda Human Rights Commission. Although the fifteen-volume report was housed in their library, no one seemed to know where the exhibits were kept. Someone eventually produced a key to a storage shed that purportedly contained the missing materials, but the contents were in a complete state of disarray. I did not have time to go through the boxes, although I am sure that there is valuable evidence hidden within them.

4. For an excellent discussion of violence and memory in Uganda, particularly in regard to the Amin era, see Andrew Rice, *The Teeth May Smile but the Heart Does Not Forget: Murder and Memory in Uganda* (New York: Henry Holt, 2009), 10–17, 154, 267–68.

5. Florence Mubiru [pseud.], interview by author, Kampala, July 9, 2005. See also Venereal Diseases Decree, Decree 16 of 1977.

6. Republic of Uganda, *Report of the Commission of Inquiry (1994)*, appendix 10, xxx.

Bibliography

ORAL INTERVIEWS

Henry Kyemba, interview by author, Kampala, February 2, 2005
Lucy Ndagire [pseud.], interview by author, Kampala, March 22, 2005
Lydia Balemezi, interview by author, Kampala, March 23, 2005
Khadija Kasume [pseud.], interview by author, Kampala, April 4, 2005
Chance Kawuma [pseud.], interview by author, Kampala, April 8, 2005
Namuli Kasozi [pseud.], interview by author, Kampala, April 12, 2005
Robinah Muwenda [pseud.], interview by author, Kampala, April 14, 2005
Hassifa Namboze [pseud.], interview by author, Bwaise, April 19, 2005
Angela Mukasa [pseud.], interview by author, Kampala, April 19, 2005
Sophie Sserunkuma [pseud.], interview by author, Kampala, April 22, 2005
Betty Mayiga [pseud.], interview by author, Kampala, April 26, 2005
Sylvia Kategaya [pseud.], interview by author, Kampala, April 28, 2005
Nalongo Naddima Mpanga, interview by author, Buganda Parliament, April 28, 2005
Ruth Nasolo, interview by author, Buganda Parliament, April 28, 2005
Josephine Kabalema [pseud.], interview by author, Kampala, May 1, 2005
Margaret Mutibwa [pseud.], interview by author, Kampala, May 2, 2005
Goretti Ssali [pseud.], interview by author, Bunamwaya, May 5 and 12, 2005
Agnes Kato [pseud.], interview by author, Bunamwaya, May 12, 2005
Enid Kisembo [pseud.], interview by author, Kampala, May 13, 2005
Patience Ssekandi [pseud.], interview by author, Bunamwaya, May 19, 2005
Margaret Ndawula, interview by author, Kampala, May 23, 2005
Joyce Mpanga, interview by author, Kampala, May 25, 2005
Night Kulabako, interview by author, Kampala, May 25, 2005
James Zikusoka, interview by author, Kampala, May 26, 2005
Janet Ssendaula [pseud.], interview by author, Kampala, May 26, 2005
Theresa Mukiibi [pseud.], interview by author, Kampala, May 26, 2005
Nakarema Kyolaba [pseud.], interview by author, Mukono, May 31, 2005
Aisha Ssebagala [pseud.], interview by author, Kampala, June 1, 2005
Melissa Masaazi [pseud.], interview by author, Kampala, June 2, 2005
Kevina Lutaaya [pseud.], interview by author, Kampala, June 3, 2005
Victoria Kiberu [pseud.], interview by author, Kampala, June 7, 2005
Claudia Mayengo [pseud.], interview by author, Kampala, June 8, 2005
Apolonia Lugemwa, interview by author, Buganda Parliament, June 10, 2005

George Mwenje [pseud.], interview by Denis Kakembo, Kampala, June 11, 2005

Abu Mayanja, interview by author, Kampala, June 13, 2005

Father John Mary Waliggo, interview by author, Kampala, June 13, 2005

James Lwasa [pseud.], interview by Denis Kakembo, Kampala, June 19, 2005

Norah Kawalya [pseud.], interview by author, Kampala, June 22, 2005

Susan Namuddala [pseud.], interview by author, Kampala, June 22, 2005

Victoria Mwaka, interview by author, Kampala, June 22, 2005

Henry Ssentongo [pseud.], interview by Denis Kakembo, Kampala, June 23, 2005

Alice Nakato [pseud.], interview by author, Kampala, June 23, 2005

Fatima Musisi [pseud.], interview by author, Kampala, June 23, 2005

Hope Mwesigye, interview by author, Kampala, June 23 and 30, 2005

Winnie Mugenyi [pseud.], interview by author, Kampala, June 25, 2005

Irene Lubega [pseud.], interview by author, Kampala, June 25, 2005

John Matovu [pseud.], interview by George Peter Ngogolo, Kampala, June 27, 2005

Cornelius Nkalubo [pseud.], interview by George Peter Ngogolo, Kampala, June 28, 2005

Mary Kyomukama [pseud.], interview by author, Kitezi, June 28, 2005

Milly Ddungu [pseud.], interview by author, Kitezi, June 28, 2005

Josephine Ssengendo [pseud.], interview by author, Kampala, July 1, 2005

Esther Ssengendo [pseud.], interview by author, Kanyanya, July 2, 2005

Rhoda Kalema, interview by author, Kampala, July 6, 2005

Herbert Mukomazi [pseud.], interview by George Peter Ngogolo, Kampala, July 6, 2005

William Banage, interview by author, Kampala, July 8 and August 22, 2005

Florence Mubiru [pseud.], interview by author, Kampala, July 9, 2005

Enid Musenyi [pseud.], interview by author, Kampala, July 9, 2005

Frank Nabwiso, interview by author, Kampala, July 14, 2005

Jane Walusimbi [pseud.], interview by author, Kitende, July 19, 2005

Catherine Asiimwe [pseud.], interview by author, Kitende, July 19, 2005

Martha Mugwanya [pseud.], interview by author, Kampala, July 20, 2005

Ritah Lukwago [pseud.], interview by author, Kitende, July 21, 2005

Jennifer Kiyingi [pseud.], interview by author, Kampala, July 21, 2005

Evelyn Nyanzi [pseud.], interview by author, Kampala, July 23, 2005

Paul Etiang, interview by author, Kampala, July 26, 2005

Joseph Ssekimpi [pseud.], interview by Suubi Sam, July 26, 2005

Hakim Naggaga [pseud.], interview by Suubi Sam, July 28, 2005

Rose Birungi [pseud.], interview by author, Mpererwe, July 28, 2005

Grace Byandala [pseud.], interview by author, Kampala, July 31, 2005

Joyce Mungherera, interview by author, Kampala, August 3, 2005

Consolata Lugudde [pseud.], interview by author, Kampala, August 6, 2005

Peter Njuki [pseud.], interview by Suubi Sam, Kampala, August 7, 2005

Miria Matembe, interview by author, Kampala, August 17, 2005

Joyce Ondoga [pseud.], interview by author, Arua, July 8, 2008

Abdu Onzima [pseud.], interview by author, Ayivu County, July 8, 2008

Johnson Mila [pseud.], interview by author, Arua, July 9, 2008
Robert Asega [pseud.], interview by author, Ombokoro Village, July 9, 2008
Moses Atiku [pseud.], interview by author, Arua, July 10, 2008
Patience Arube [pseud.], interview by author, Arua, July 10, 2008
Christine Godi [pseud.], interview by author, Arua, July 10, 2008
Prossi Asumi [pseud.], interview by author, Arua, July 10, 2008
Rebekah Matua [pseud.], interview by author, Arua, July 10, 2008
Benjamin Etukibu [pseud.], interview by author, Ayivu County, July 11, 2008
Madina Abia [pseud.], interview by author, Arua, July 11, 2008
Helen Okuonzi [pseud.], interview by author, Terego County, July 11, 2008
Jacob Aridru [pseud.], interview by author, Arua, July 12, 2008
Yudaya Obiga [pseud.], interview by author, Arua, July 12, 2008
Mohammed Atako [pseud.], interview by author, Arua, July 13, 2008
David Alima [pseud.], interview by author, Ayivu County, July 13, 2008
Hamida Kiiza [pseud.], interview by author, Arua, July 13, 2008
Sarah Adroa [pseud.], interview by author, Arua, July 14, 2008
Charles Ogama [pseud.], interview by author, Vurra County, July 14, 2008
Charity Ejua [pseud.], interview by author, Ayivu County, July 14, 2008
Stephen Malinga, interview by author, Kampala, July 18, 2008
Francis Kutosi [pseud.], interview by author, Kampala, July 24, 2008
Sam Echaku, interview by author, Kampala, July 29, 2008
Arnold Bisase, interview by author, Lafayette, Indiana, July 15–22, 2010
Bob Astles, interview by author, Wimbledon, UK, January 25–29, 2011

UNPUBLISHED AND ARCHIVAL SOURCES

BOB ASTLES, PERSONAL PAPERS, WIMBLEDON, UK

Assorted clippings from the following London newspapers: *Daily Mail, Daily Mirror, Evening Standard, Express, Sunday Telegraph, Sunday Times,* and *The Times*
BBC Summary of World Broadcasts, 1971–79
Untitled book manuscript by Bob Astles

CBS RADIO, BUGANDA PARLIAMENT, KAMPALA, UGANDA

Madina Amin, audio recording of interview with Medi Nsereko, 2005

CENTRAL POLICE STATION, KAMPALA, UGANDA

File number missing, Specious Namutebi, November 23, 1973
File number missing, Euniki Namusisi, November 23, 1973
File number missing, Joy Kobusirgye, November 26, 1973
File number missing, Margaret Namusoke Lunkuse, November 27, 1973
File number missing, Teddy Kizito, November 29, 1973
File number missing, Blandy Sebaggala, November 29, 1973
File number missing, Rosemary Nalima, December 2, 1973

File number missing, Eflasio Kabasita, December 3, 1973

File number missing, Sarah Kigozi, December 5, 1973

File number missing, Theody Nagudi, December 5, 1973

File number missing, Theodozia Mukasa Nakate, December 6, 1973

File number missing, Edith Nalubega, December 6, 1973

File number missing, Cissy Katumba, December 6, 1973

File number missing, Mary Gorreti Liyiga, December 6, 1973

File number missing, Rose Lovinsa Nankya, December 12, 1973

File number missing, Christin Kaye Mwebuza, December 19, 1973

File number missing, Maria Kikaziki, December 27, 1973

File number missing, Margaret Babirye, December 28, 1973

File number missing, Olwoth, May 17, 1974

File number missing, N. Naluwoza, May 20, 1974

File number missing, Hayama Margaret, May 21, 1974

File number missing, William Sempira, May 23, 1974

File 785/74, Tomson Kinara, May 23, 1974

File 786/74, John Niwamanya, May 23, 1974

File 787/74, Golet Nalusukusa, May 23, 1974

File 788/74, Murebwa Jolly, May 23, 1974

File 789/74, Mary Njingo, May 23, 1974

File 790/74, Kamida Lubwama, May 23, 1974

File number missing, Godfrey Kiwanuka, May 23, 1974

File number missing, William Ochan, May 24, 1974

File number missing, Frank Birungi, May 24, 1974

File 793/74, Sarah Nabwyiso, May 24, 1974

File 797/74, Christine Ndaula, May 24, 1974

File 798/74, Grace Namuddu, May 24, 1974

File 799/74, Florence Kajumba, May 24, 1974

File 801/74, Aurerio Bikanda-Gira, May 24, 1974

File 802/74, Sajjabi Kamida, May 25, 1974

File 811/74, Ayisa Nasanga, May 28, 1974

File number missing, John Tato, May 31, 1974

File 836/74, Mary Nambalirwa, June 4, 1974

File 840/74, Anna Mubiru, May 4, 1974

File 845/74, Esther Dambado, June 6, 1974

File 846/74, Vastina Rukunura, June 6, 1974

File 848/74, Unknown person, June 7, 1974

File 849/74, Marian Caruhanga, June 8, 1974

File 855/74, Mariam Naluwoza, June 11, 1974

File number missing, Leo Serwagi, June 14, 1974

File 869/74, Christine Dandi, June 17, 1974

File 890/74, Christine Gombe, July 2, 1974

File 908/74, Maduna Nsubuga, July 15, 1974

File number missing, Emanuel Bosa, July 15, 1974

File 948/74, Kanabi, August 1, 1974

File 949/74, Betty Mafabi, August 1, 1974
File 950/74, Justine Nantongo, August 1, 1974
File 951/74, Diana Mwesigye, August 1, 1974
File 952/74, Jane Nakaggwa, August 1, 1974
File 953/74, Jane Nakawuka, August 1, 1974
File 954/74, Gladys Keneeza, August 1, 1974
File 955/74, Nakate, August 2, 1974
File 956/74, Joy Maani, August 2, 1974
File 957/74, Mary Catherine Kyasimire, August 2, 1974
File 958/74, Betty Nakagga, August 2, 1974
File 960/74, Aida Nakaggwa, August 2, 1974
File 961/74, Ruth Lubega, August 2, 1974
File 962/74, Topista Kabunjuli, August 2, 1974
File 963/74, Agnes Nabwamu, August 2, 1974
Station Diary, February 23–March 20, 1976
Station Diary, March 9–March 28, 1978
Station Diary, June 1–June 19, 1978

MAKERERE UNIVERSITY LIBRARY, KAMPALA, UGANDA

East African Standard (English language regional daily newspaper), 1971–72
Munno (Luganda language daily newspaper), 1971–79
Uganda Argus (English language daily newspaper), 1971–72
Uganda Times (English language daily newspaper), 1979
Voice of Uganda (English language daily newspaper), 1972–79

MINISTRY OF INFORMATION AND BROADCASTING, PHOTOGRAPHIC SECTION, KAMPALA, UGANDA

Government photographs, 1971–79
Madina Amin, audio recording of Women's Day speech, May 1, 1975

NOTRE DAME UNIVERSITY LIBRARY, SOUTH BEND, INDIANA

Africa: A Semi-Weekly Inter-African News Survey (Agence France Presse), 1979–80
Africa Contemporary Record: Annual Survey and Documents, 1979–80

PARLIAMENTARY LIBRARY, KAMPALA, UGANDA

Armed Forces Decree, Decree 1 of 1971
Detention (Prescription of Time Limit) Decree, Decree 7 of 1971
Armed Forces (Powers of Arrest) Decree, Decree 13 of 1971
Suspension of Political Activities Decree, Decree 14 of 1971
Detention (Prescription of Time Limit) (Amendment) Decree, Decree 15 of 1971
Detention (Prescription of Time Limit) (Amendment) (No. 2) Decree, Decree 31 of 1971

Armed Forces (Amendment) Decree, Decree 4 of 1972
Robbery Suspects Decree, Decree 7 of 1972
Proceedings against the Government (Protection) Decree, Decree 8 of 1972
Penal Code Act (Amendment) Decree, Decree 9 of 1972
Immigration (Cancellation of Entry Permits and Certificates of Residence) Decree, Decree 17 of 1972
Proceedings against the Government (Prohibition) Decree, Decree 19 of 1972
Armed Forces (Powers of Arrest) Decree, Decree 26 of 1972
Declaration of Assets (Non-citizen Asians) (Amendment) Decree, Decree 29 of 1972
Properties and Businesses (Acquisition) Decree, Decree 32 of 1972
Armed Forces (Amendment) Decree, Decree 3 of 1973
Penal Code Act (Amendment) Decree, Decree 4 of 1973
Military Police (Powers of Arrest) Decree, Decree 19 of 1973
Estates of Missing Persons (Management) Decree, Decree 20 of 1973
Armed Forces (Powers of Arrest) (Repeal) Decree, Decree 21 of 1973
Penal Code (Amendment) Decree, Decree 4 of 1974
Penal Code Act (Amendment) (No. 2) Decree, Decree 26 of 1974
Economic Crimes Tribunal Decree, Decree 2 of 1975
Venereal Diseases Decree, Decree 16 of 1977
National Council of Women Decree, Decree 2 of 1978

UNITED NATIONS GENERAL ASSEMBLY

Official Records of the 2113th Plenary Meeting, December 18, 1972

US INSTITUTE OF PEACE, TRUTH COMMISSION DIGITAL COLLECTION

Republic of Uganda, Legal Notice No. 2 of 1974, "Commission of Inquiry into the Disappearances of People in Uganda since 25 January, 1971: Charter," June 30, 1974
———. "Official Statement Relating to Disappearance of Persons," January 9, 1973
———. "President's Office Statement on Disappearances," June 30, 1974

US DEPARTMENT OF STATE

Declassified/Released US Department of State EO Systematic Review 30 JUN 2005, R 021341Z DEC 74

PUBLISHED PRIMARY AND SECONDARY SOURCES

Achebe, Nwando. "'And She Became a Man': King Ahebi Ugbabe in the History of Enugu-Ezike, Northern Igboland, 1880–1948." In *Men and Masculinities in Modern Africa*, edited by Lisa A. Lindsay and Stephan F. Miescher, 52–68. Portsmouth, NH: Heinemann, 2003.
Adams, Bert, and Mike Bristow. "The Politico-Economic Position of Ugandan

Asians in the Colonial and Independent Eras." *Journal of Asian and African Studies* 13, no. 3–4 (1978): 151–66.

——. "Ugandan Asian Expulsion Experiences: Rumor and Reality." *Journal of Asian and African Studies* 14, no. 3–4 (1979): 191–203.

Adefuye, Ade. "The Kakwa of Uganda and the Sudan: The Ethnic Factor in National and International Politics." In *Partitioned Africans: Ethnic Relations across Africa's International Boundaries, 1884–1994*, edited by A. I. Asiwaju, 51–69. New York: St. Martin's Press, 1985.

Akello, Grace. "Self Twice-Removed: Ugandan Woman." *Change International Reports: Women and Society* 8 (1982): 1–19.

Allen, Peter Jermyn. *Days of Judgment: A Judge in Idi Amin's Uganda.* London: William Kimber, 1987.

——. *Interesting Times: Uganda Diaries, 1955–1986.* Sussex, UK: Book Guild, 2000.

Allman, Jean. "'Let Your Fashion Be in Line with Our Ghanaian Costume': Nation, Gender, and the Politics of Clothing in Nkrumah's Ghana." In *Fashioning Africa: Power and the Politics of Dress*, edited by Jean Allman, 144–65. Bloomington: Indiana University Press, 2004.

Amadiume, Ifi. *Male Daughters, Female Husbands: Gender and Sex in an African Society.* London: Zed Books, 1987.

Amaza, Ondoga ori. *Museveni's Long March: From Guerrilla to Statesman.* Kampala: Fountain Publishers, 1998.

Amin, Jaffar, and Margaret Akulia. *Idi Amin: Hero or Villain? His Son Jaffar Amin and Other People Speak.* Charleston, SC: Millennium Global Publishers, 2010.

Amnesty International. *Human Rights in Uganda.* London: Amnesty International, 1978.

Anthias, Floya, and Nira Yuval-Davis. Introduction to *Women-Nation-State*, edited by Nira Yuval-Davis and Floya Anthias, 1–15. London: Macmillan, 1989.

Ashforth, Adam. *The Politics of Official Discourse in Twentieth-Century South Africa.* Oxford: Clarendon Press, 1990.

Avirgan, Tony, and Martha Honey. *War in Uganda: The Legacy of Idi Amin.* Westport, CT: Laurence Hill, 1982.

Beit-Hallahmi, Benjamin. *The Israeli Connection.* London: I. B. Tauris, 1987.

Boas, Morten. "Uganda in the Regional War Zone: Metanarratives, Pasts and Presents." *Journal of Contemporary African Studies* 22, no. 3 (2004): 283–303.

Bujra, Janet. "Women Entrepreneurs of Early Nairobi." *Canadian Journal of African Studies* 9, no. 2 (1975): 213–34.

Burgess, Thomas. "Cinema, Bell Bottoms, and Miniskirts: Struggles over Youth and Citizenship in Revolutionary Zanzibar." *International Journal of African Historical Studies* 35, no. 2–3 (2002): 287–313.

Burt, Eugene C. "Bark-Cloth in East Africa." *Textile History* 26, no. 1 (1995): 75–88.

Butler, Judith. "Performative Acts and Gender Constitution: An Essay in Phenomenology and Feminist Theory." *Theater Journal* 40, no. 4 (December 1988): 519–31.

Byanyima, Winnie Karagwa. "Women in Political Struggle in Uganda." In *Women Transforming Politics: Worldwide Strategies for Empowerment*, edited by Jill M. Bystydzienski, 129–42. Bloomington: Indiana University Press, 1992.

Carver, Richard. "Called to Account: How African Governments Investigate Human Rights Violations." *African Affairs* 89, no. 356 (July 1990): 391–415.

Clark, Yaliwe. "Security Sector Reform in Africa: A Lost Opportunity to Deconstruct Militarized Masculinities?" *Feminist Africa* 10 (2008): 49–66.

Clayton, Anthony, and David Killingray. *Khaki and Blue: Military and Police in British Colonial Africa*. Athens: Ohio University Press, 1989.

Cock, Jacklyn. Introduction to *Society at War: The Militarization of South Africa*, edited by Jacklyn Cock and Laurie Nathan, 1–13. New York: St. Martin's Press, 1989.

——. "Keeping the Fires Burning: Militarization and the Politics of Gender in South Africa." *Review of African Political Economy* 45/46 (1989): 50–64.

——. *Women and War in South Africa*. Cleveland, OH: Pilgrim Press, 1993.

——. "Women in the Military: Implications for Demilitarization in the 1990s in South Africa." *Gender and Society* 8, no. 2 (June 1994): 152–69.

Decker, Alicia C. "Idi Amin's Dirty War: Subversion, Sabotage and the Battle to Keep Uganda Clean, 1971–1979." *International Journal of African Historical Studies* 43, no. 3 (2010): 489–513.

——. "Militarismo, nazionalismo e matrimonio: Un ritratto privato delle cinque mogli di Idi Amin" [Militarism, Nationalism, and Marriage: An Intimate Portrait of Idi Amin's Five Wives]. *Afriche e Orienti* 14, no. 3–4 (2012): 124–38.

El-Kikhia, Mansour. *Libya's Qaddafi: The Politics of Contradiction*. Gainesville: University of Florida Press, 1997.

Enloe, Cynthia. *Does Khaki Become You? The Militarization of Women's Lives*. Boston: South End Press, 1983.

——. *Maneuvers: The International Politics of Militarizing Women's Lives*. Berkeley: University of California Press, 2000.

Foltz, William J. "Libya's Military Power." In *The Green and the Black: Qadhafi's Policies in Africa*, edited by Rene Lemarchand, 52–69. Bloomington: Indiana University Press, 1988.

Forum for Women in Democracy. *The Rising Tide: Ugandan Women's Struggle for a Public Voice*. Kampala: FOWODE, 2003.

Fuller, Thomas. "African Labor and Training in the Ugandan Colonial Economy." *International Journal of African Historical Studies* 10, no. 1 (1977): 77–95.

Global Network of Women Peacebuilders. *Women Count—Security Council Resolution 1325: Civil Society Monitoring Report 2012, Uganda*. New York: Global Network of Women Peacebuilders, 2012.

Gould, Loyal N., and James Leo Garrett, Jr. "Amin's Uganda: Troubled Land of Religious Persecution." *Journal of Church and State* 19, no. 3 (1977): 429–36.

Grahame, Iain. *Amin and Uganda: A Personal Memoir*. London: Granada, 1980.

Gwyn, David [pseud.]. *Idi Amin: Death-Light of Africa*. Boston: Little, Brown, 1977.

Hansen, Holger Bernt. *Ethnicity and Military Rule in Uganda*. Uppsala, Sweden: Scandinavian Institute of African Studies, 1977.

——. "Pre-Colonial Immigrants and Colonial Servants: The Nubians in Uganda Revisited." *African Affairs* 90 (1991): 559–80.

Hansen, Holger Bernt, and Michael Twaddle. Introduction to *Uganda Now: Between Decay and Development*, edited by Holger Bernt Hansen and Michael Twaddle, 1–25. London: James Currey, 1988.

Hansen, Karen Tranberg. "Dressing Dangerously: Miniskirts, Gender Relations, and Sexuality in Zambia." In *Fashioning Africa: Power and the Politics of Dress*, edited by Jean Allman, 166–85. Bloomington: Indiana University Press, 2004.

Hattersley, C. W. *The Baganda at Home*. London: Frank Cass, 1908.

Hayner, Priscilla B. *Unspeakable Truths: Confronting State Terror and Atrocity*. New York: Routledge, 2001.

Hills, Denis. *The White Pumpkin*. New York: Grove Press, 1975.

Hundle, Anneeth Kaur. "Exceptions to the Expulsion: Violence, Security and Community among Ugandan Asians, 1972–1979." *Journal of Eastern African Studies* 7, no. 1 (2013): 164–82.

Hutchful, Eboe, and Abdoulaye Bathily, eds. *The Military and Militarism in Africa*. Dakar: CODESRIA, 1998.

International Commission of Jurists. *Uganda and Human Rights: Report to the UN Commission on Human Rights*. Geneva: International Commission of Jurists, 1977.

——. *Violations of Human Rights and the Rule of Law in Uganda*. Geneva: International Commission of Jurists, 1974.

Isegawa, Moses. *Snakepit*. New York: Random House, 2004.

Ivaska, Andrew M. "'Anti-Mini Militants Meet Modern Misses': Urban Style, Gender, and the Politics of 'National Culture' in 1960s Dar es Salaam, Tanzania." In *Fashioning Africa: Power and the Politics of Dress*, edited by Jean Allman, 104–21. Bloomington: Indiana University Press, 2004.

Jain, Devaki. *Women, Development and the UN: A Sixty-Year Quest for Equality and Justice*. Bloomington: Indiana University Press, 2005.

Jamison, Martin. *Idi Amin and Uganda: An Annotated Bibliography*. Westport, CT: Greenwood Press, 1992.

Jorgensen, Jan Jelmert. *Uganda: A Modern History*. New York: St. Martin's Press, 1981.

Kamau, Joseph [pseud.], and Andrew Cameron [pseud.]. *Lust to Kill: The Rise and Fall of Idi Amin*. London: Transworld Publishers, 1979.

Kambili, Cyprian. "Ethics of African Tradition: Prescription of a Dress Code in Malawi, 1965–1973." *Society of Malawi Journal* 55, no. 2 (2002): 80–100.

Karugire, Samwiri. *The Roots of Instability in Uganda*. Kampala: Fountain Publishers, 1988.

Kasozi, A. B. K. *The Social Origins of Violence in Uganda*. Kampala: Fountain Publishers, 1994.

Kato, Wycliffe. *Escape from Idi Amin's Slaughterhouse*. London: Quartet Books, 1989.

Katongole, Emmanuel. "Where Is Idi Amin? On Violence, Ethics, and Social Memory in Africa." Uganda Martyr's University Working Paper no. 11, 2004.

Kibedi, Wanume. "Open Letter to General Idi Amin, Kampala." In *Uganda and Human Rights: Report to the UN Commission on Human Rights*, 65–85. Geneva: International Commission of Jurists, 1977.

Kirby, Paul, and Marsha Henry. "Rethinking Masculinity and Practices of Violence in Conflict Settings." *International Journal of Feminist Politics* 14, no. 4 (2012): 445–49.

Kiwanuka, M. S. M. Semakula. *Amin and the Tragedy of Uganda*. Munich: Weltforum, 1979.

Kleinschmidt, Harold. *Amin Collection: Bibliographical Catalogue of Materials Relevant to the History of Uganda under the Military Government of Idi Amin Dada*. Heidelberg: Kivouvou, 1983.

Kokole, Omari H. "Idi Amin, 'the Nubi' and Islam in Ugandan Politics, 1971–1979." In *Religion and Politics in East Africa: The Period since Independence*, edited by Holger Bernt Hansen and Michael Twaddle, 45–55. London: James Currey, 1995.

———. "The 'Nubians' of East Africa: Muslim Club or African 'Tribe'? The View from Within." *Journal of the Institute of Muslim Minority Affairs* 6, no. 2 (1985): 420–48.

Kyemba, Henry. *A State of Blood: The Inside Story of Idi Amin*. New York: Paddington Press, 1977.

Kyomuhendo, Goretti. *Waiting: A Novel of Uganda at War*. New York: Feminist Press at CUNY, 2007.

Kyomuhendo, Grace Bantebya, and Marjorie Keniston McIntosh. *Women, Work, and Domestic Virtue in Uganda, 1900–2003*. Oxford: James Currey, 2006.

Langlands, Bryan. "Students and Politics in Uganda." *African Affairs* 76, no. 302 (January 1977): 3–20.

Lawoko, WodOkello. *The Dungeons of Nakasero*. Stockholm: Författares Bokmaskin, 2005.

Legum, Colin. "Behind the Clown's Mask." *Transition* 75–76 (1975–76): 250–58.

Lemarchand, Rene, ed. *The Green and the Black: Qadhafi's Policies in Africa*. Bloomington: Indiana University Press, 1988.

Leopold, Mark. *Inside West Nile: Violence, History and Representation on an African Frontier*. Oxford: James Currey, 2005.

————. "Legacies of Slavery in North-West Uganda: The Story of the 'One-Elevens.'" *Africa* 76, no. 2 (2006): 180–99.

————. "Sex, Violence and History in the Lives of Idi Amin: Postcolonial Masculinity as Masquerade." *Journal of Postcolonial Writing* 45, no. 3 (September 2009): 321–30.

Liebowitz, Daniel, and Charles Pearson. *The Last Expedition: Stanley's Mad Journey through the Congo*. New York: W. W. Norton, 2006.

Listowel, Judith. *Amin*. Dublin: IUP Press, 1973.

Low, D. A. "The Dislocated Polity." In *Uganda Now: Between Decay and Development*, edited by Holger Bernt Hansen and Michael Twaddle, 36–53. London: James Currey, 1988.

————. "The Making and Implementation of the Uganda Agreement of 1900." In *Buganda and British Overrule, 1900–1955: Two Studies*, edited by D. A. Low and R. Cranford Pratt, 3–159. London: Oxford University Press, 1960.

Luckham, Robin. "The Military, Militarization, and Democratization in Africa: A Survey of Literature and Issues." *African Studies Review* 37, no. 2 (1994): 13–75.

MacDonald, Kevin. *The Last King of Scotland*, DVD. Los Angeles: Fox Searchlight Pictures, 2006.

Mama, Amina. "Feminism or Femocracy? State Feminism and Democratization in Nigeria." *Africa Development* 20, no. 1 (1995): 37–58.

————. "Khaki in the Family: Gender Discourses and Militarism in Nigeria." *African Studies Review* 41, no. 2 (1998): 1–17.

Mama, Amina, and Margo Okazawa-Rey. "Militarism, Conflict, and Women's Activism." *Feminist Africa* 10 (2008): 1–8.

————. "Militarism, Conflict and Women's Activism in the Global Era: Challenges and Prospects for Women in Three West African Contexts." *Feminist Review* 101 (2012): 97–123.

Mamdani, Mahmood. *From Citizen to Refugee: Ugandan Asians Come to Britain*. London: Frances Pinter, 1973.

————. *Imperialism and Fascism in Uganda*. Nairobi: Heinemann, 1983.

————. *Politics and Class Formation*. Portsmouth, NH: Heinemann, 1976.

————. "The Ugandan Asian Expulsion: Twenty Years After." *Journal of Refugee Studies* 6, no. 3 (1993): 265–73.

Martin, David. *General Amin*. London: Faber and Faber, 1974.

Mazrui, Ali A. "The Lumpen Proletariat and the Lumpen Militariat: African Soldiers as a New Political Class." *Political Studies* 21, no. 1 (1973): 1–12.

————. "Miniskirts and Political Puritanism." *Africa Report* 13, no. 7 (1968): 9–12.

————. "Religious Strangers in Uganda: From Emin Pasha to Amin Dada." *African Affairs* 76, no. 302 (January 1977): 21–38.

————. "The Resurrection of the Warrior Tradition in African Political Culture." *Journal of Modern African Studies* 13, no. 1 (1975): 67–84.

————. "The Social Origins of Ugandan Presidents: From King to Peasant Warrior." *Canadian Journal of African Studies* 8, no. 1 (1974): 3–23.

————. *Soldiers and Kinsmen in Uganda: The Making of a Military Ethnocracy.* Beverly Hills, CA: Sage, 1975.

————. "Soldiers as Traditionalizers: Military Rule and the Re-Africanization of Africa." *Journal of Asian and African Studies* 12, no. 1–4 (1977): 236–58.

Mba, Nina. "Kaba and Khaki: Women and the Militarized State in Nigeria." In *Women and the State in Africa*, edited by Jane L. Parpart and Kathleen Staudt, 69–90. Boulder, CO: Lynne Rienner Publishers, 1989.

McFadden, Patricia. "Plunder as Statecraft: Militarism and Resistance in Neocolonial Africa." In *Security Disarmed: Critical Perspectives on Gender, Race, and Militarization*, edited by Barbara Sutton, Sandra Morgen, and Julie Novkov, 136–56. New Brunswick, NJ: Rutgers University Press, 2008.

Melady, Thomas, and Margaret Melady. *Idi Amin Dada: Hitler in Africa.* Kansas City, KS: Sheed Andrews and McMeel, 1977.

Middleton, John. "Some Effects of Colonial Rule among the Lugbara." In *Colonialism in Africa, 1870–1960*, edited by Victor Turner, 6–48. Cambridge: Cambridge University Press, 1971.

Miescher, Stephan F., and Lisa A. Lindsay. "Introduction: Men and Masculinities in Modern African History." In *Men and Masculinities in Modern Africa*, edited by Lisa A. Lindsay and Stephan F. Miescher, 1–29. Portsmouth, NH: Heinemann, 2003.

Mittelman, James. *Ideology and Politics in Uganda: From Obote to Amin.* Ithaca, NY: Cornell University Press, 1975.

Moghal, Manzoor. *Idi Amin: Lion of Africa.* Central Milton Keynes, UK: Author House, 2010.

Moyse-Bartlett, Lt. Col. Hubert. *King's African Rifles: A Study in the Military History of East and Central Africa, 1890–1945.* Aldershot, UK: Gale and Polden, 1956.

Mulira, James. "Soviet Prop to Idi Amin's Regime: An Assessment." *African Review* 13, no. 1 (1986): 105–22.

Museveni, Yoweri Kaguta. *Sowing the Mustard Seed: The Struggle for Freedom and Democracy in Uganda.* London: Macmillan, 1997.

Musisi, Nakanyike. "Baganda Women's Night Market Activities." In *African Market Women and Economic Power: The Role of Women in African Economic Development*, edited by Bessie House Midamba and Felix Ekechi, 132–40. Westport, CT: Greenwood Press, 1995.

Mutibwa, Phares. *Uganda since Independence: A Story of Unfulfilled Hopes.* Trenton, NJ: Africa World Press, 1992.

Nabudere, Dan Wadada. *Imperialism and Revolution in Uganda.* London: Onyx Press, 1980.

Nyabongo, Elizabeth. *Elizabeth of Toro: The Odyssey of an African Princess.* New York: Simon and Schuster, 1989.

Obbo, Christine. *African Women: Their Struggle for Economic Independence.* London: Zed, 1980.

————. "Sexuality and Economic Domination in Uganda." In *Women-Nation-State*, edited by Floya Anthias and Nira Yuval-Davis, 77–91. London: Macmillan, 1989.

Ofcansky, Thomas P. *Uganda: Tarnished Pearl of Africa*. Boulder, CO: Westview Press, 1996.

Okazawa-Rey, Margo. "Warring on Women: Understanding Complex Inequalities of Gender, Race, Class, and Nation." *Affilia* 17 (2002): 371–83.

Omara-Otunnu, Amii. "The Currency of Militarism in Uganda." In *The Military and Militarism in Africa*, edited by Eboe Hutchful and Abdoulaye Bathily, 399–428. Dakar: CODESRIA, 1998.

———. *Politics and the Military in Uganda, 1890–1985*. Basingstoke, UK: Macmillan, 1987.

Onen, P. M. O. *The Diary of an Obedient Servant during Misrule*. Kampala: Janyeko Publishing, 2000.

Orizio, Riccardo. *Talk of the Devil: Encounters with Seven Dictators*. New York: Walker, 2002.

Otiso, Kefa M. *Culture and Customs of Uganda*. Westport, CT: Greenwood Press, 2006.

Oyěwùmí, Oyèrónkẹ́. *The Invention of Women: Making an African Sense of Western Gender Discourses*. Minneapolis: University of Minnesota Press, 1997.

Parsons, Timothy. *The African Rank-and-File: Social Implications of Colonial Military Service in the King's African Rifles, 1902–1964*. Portsmouth, NH: Heinemann, 1999.

———. *The 1964 Army Mutinies and the Making of Modern East Africa*. Westport, CT: Praeger, 2003.

Peterson, Derek R. "Morality Plays: Marriage, Church Courts, and Colonial Agency in Central Tanganyika, ca. 1876–1928." *American Historical Review* 111, v. 4 (October 2006): 983–1010.

Peterson, Derek R., and Edgar C. Taylor. "Rethinking the State in Idi Amin's Uganda: The Politics of Exhortation." *Journal of Eastern African Studies* 7, no. 1 (2013): 58–82.

Peterson, V. Spike. "Gendered Identities, Ideologies, and Practices in the Context of War and Militarism." In *Gender, War, and Militarism: Feminist Perspectives*, edited by Laura Sjoberg and Sandra Via, 17–29. Santa Barbara, CA: Praeger, 2010.

Pirouet, M. Louise. "Refugees in and from Uganda in the Post-Independence Period." In *Uganda Now: Between Decay and Development*, edited by Holger Bernt Hansen and Michael Twaddle, 239–53. London: James Currey, 1988.

Powesland, Philip Geoffrey. *Economic Policy and Labour: A Study in Uganda's Economic History*. Kampala: East African Institute for Social Research, 1957.

Reid, Richard. *Political Power in Pre-Colonial Buganda*. Oxford: James Currey, 2002.

———. *War in Pre-Colonial Eastern Africa*. Oxford: James Currey, 2007.

Republic of Uganda. *Commission of Inquiry into the Missing Americans*. Entebbe: Government Printer, 1972.

———. *Report of the Commission of Inquiry Appointed to Inquire into Certain Allegations Made in Parliament on 4th February, 1966.* Entebbe: Government Printer, 1966.

———. *Report of the Commission of Inquiry into the Disappearances of People in Uganda since 25 January, 1971.* Entebbe: Government Printer, 1975.

———. *Report of the Commission of Inquiry into Violations of Human Rights.* Entebbe: Government Printer, 1994.

Rice, Andrew. *The Teeth May Smile but the Heart Does Not Forget: Murder and Memory in Uganda.* New York: Henry Holt, 2009.

Richards, Audrey. *East African Chiefs: A Study of Political Development in Some Uganda and Tanganyika Tribes.* London: Faber and Faber, 1959.

Ronen, Yehudit. "Libya's Intervention in Amin's Uganda—A Broken Spearhead." *Asian and African Studies* 26, no. 2 (1992): 173–83.

———. *Qaddafi's Libya in World Politics.* Boulder, CO: Lynne Rienner, 2008.

Roscoe, John. *The Bakitara or Banyoro: The First Part of the Report of the Mackie Ethnological Expedition to Central Africa.* Cambridge, UK: University Press, 1923.

———. *The Banyankole: The Second Part of the Report of the Mackie Ethnological Expedition to Central Africa.* Cambridge, UK: University Press, 1923.

Rowe, John A. "Islam under Idi Amin: A Case of Déjà Vu?" In *Uganda Now: Between Decay and Development,* edited by Holger Bernt Hansen and Michael Twaddle, 267–79. London: James Currey, 1988.

Rwehururu, Bernard. *Cross to the Gun: Idi Amin and the Fall of the Uganda Army.* Kampala: Monitor Publications, 2002.

Scarry, Elaine. *The Body in Pain: The Making and Unmaking of the World.* New York: Oxford University Press, 1985.

Schatzberg, Michael. *Political Legitimacy in Middle Africa: Father, Family, Food.* Bloomington: Indiana University Press, 2001.

Schuster, Ilsa Glazer. *New Women of Lusaka.* Palo Alto, CA: Mayfield Publishing, 1979.

Scott, Joan Wallach. Introduction to *Gender and the Politics of History,* 1–11. New York: Columbia University Press, 1999.

Seftel, Adam, ed. *Uganda: The Bloodstained Pearl of Africa and Its Struggle for Peace.* Lanseria, South Africa: Bailey's African Photo Archives Production, 1994.

Segal, Lynne. "Gender, War and Militarism: Making and Questioning the Links." *Feminist Review* 88 (2008): 21–35.

Shroeder, Barbet. *General Idi Amin Dada: A Self Portrait.* DVD. New York: Criterion Collection, 1974.

Smith, George Ivan. *Ghosts of Kampala.* New York: St. Martin's Press, 1980.

Snyder, Margaret. *Women in African Economies: From Burning Sun to Boardroom.* Kampala: Fountain Publishers, 2000.

Southall, Aidan. "General Amin and the Coup: Great Man or Historical Inevitability?" *Journal of Modern African Studies* 13, no. 1 (1975): 85–105.

———. "Social Disorganization in Uganda: Before, During, and After Amin." *Journal of Modern African Studies* 18, no. 4 (1980): 627–56.

Steiner, Rolf. *The Last Adventurer*. Boston: Little, Brown, 1978.

Talton, Benjamin. "'All the Women Must Be Clothed': The Anti-Nudity Campaign of Northern Ghana." In *The Black Body: Imagining, Writing and (Re)Reading*, edited by Sandra Jackson, 81–96. Pretoria: University of South Africa Press, 2008.

Tandon, Yash. *Militarism and Peace Education in Africa: A Guide and Manual for Peace Education and Action in Africa*. Nairobi: African Association for Literacy and Adult Education, 1989.

Thomas, Lynn. *Politics of the Womb: Women, Reproduction, and the State in Kenya*. Berkeley: University of California Press, 2003.

Torres-Rivas, Edelberto. "Epilogue: Notes on Terror, Violence, Fear and Democracy." In *Societies of Fear: The Legacy of Civil War, Violence and Terror in Latin America*, edited by Kees Koonings and Dirk Kruijt, 285–300. London: Zed Books, 1999.

Tripp, Aili Mari. *Women and Politics in Uganda*. Madison: University of Wisconsin Press, 2000.

Turyahikayo-Rugyema, Benoni. *Idi Amin Speaks: An Annotated Selection of His Speeches*. Madison: University of Wisconsin, 1998.

Twaddle, Michael. "The Emergence of Politico-Religious Groupings in Late Nineteenth-Century Buganda." *Journal of African History* 29 (1988): 81–92.

Vandewalle, Dirk. *A History of Modern Libya*. Cambridge: Cambridge University Press, 2006.

Wanaswa, Florence. "Train Tragedies." In *Looking Back: Tragedies of Uganda Women and Children, 1970–2000*, edited by Patricia Haward, 21–23. Kampala: Fountain Publishers, 2009.

Whitehead, Major E. F. "A Short History of Uganda Military Units Formed during World War II." *Uganda Journal* 14, no. 1 (March 1950): 1–14.

Wipper, Audrey. "African Women, Fashion, and Scapegoating." *Canadian Journal of African Studies* 6, no. 2 (1972): 329–49.

Woodward, Peter. "Ambiguous Amin." *African Affairs* 77, no. 307 (April 1978): 153–64.

Worker, J. C. "With the 4th (Uganda) K.A.R. in Abyssinia and Burma." *Uganda Journal* 12, no. 1 (March 1948): 52–56.

Index

Aate, Aisha Chumaru, 23–25
Abacha, Sani, 8
Abandoned Property Custodian Board, 80
Acha, Lydia, 123
Achebe, Chinua, 94
Achebe, Nwando, 6
Acholi: Amin's coup, aftermath, 43, 192n23;
    "enemies" of the state, 44, 124, 127, 140,
    216n34; Moroto massacre, 124; Mutukula
    massacre, 211n26; violence against, 44–
    45, 116, 121, 135, 138, 140, 192n23, 211n26,
    214n12; "warrior tradition," 4
Acilo, Margaret, 121
Adoko, Akena, 34
Adrisi, Mustafa, 35, 149, 213n55
Adroa, Kay, 17–19, 199n24, 208n30, 217n53
African National Congress, 8
Ahmad, Mohammed, 21
Air Force Detention Center, 125
Akello, Nakaliya, 127
Akoko, Catherine, 121–22
Akurut, Mary, 128–29
Albert Nile, 22, 185n11
Ali, Moses, 150
Allen, Peter Jermyn, 29–30, 34, 69, 200n27,
    201n51, 213n55
Allied Democratic Forces, 218n5
Alur, 46, 54
Amadiume, Ifi, 6
Amin, Idi
    assassination attempt on Obote, 35
    boxing, 4, 152
    childhood, 24–25, 186n27
    commissioned as officer, 26
    Congo scandal, 32–33
    coup, 36–38, 40–41, 43–48, 190nn2–3,
        189n84, 189n87, 189n90, 191n18
    death toll during his rule, 189n97
    education, 17, 25, 186n29
    escape into exile, 154, 217n53
    family history, 23–25, 185n26
    as "father of the nation," 1, 2, 10, 60, 63, 137,
        151, 197n4
    gendered rhetoric, use of, 6, 47, 48, 64,
        92–93, 96–98, 100, 149, 151, 207n18
    insulting women on Women's Day, 111

as *kijambiya*, 73, 137, 146
    marriages, 16, 17, 19, 106–9, 199n24, 208n30
    as mentally ill, 3–4
    origins of "Dada," 188n80
    performative aspects of his rule: to create
        a sense of normalcy, 159; to emasculate
        perceived enemies, 96–97, 152–53, 155;
        to foster national unity, 76–77; media,
        strategic use of, 70, 96–97, 215n16;
        political capital, cultivating, 117–18,
        132–33, 137; as political theater, 105, 119,
        133, 155, 209n41, 213n59–60
    recruitment into military, 25, 30, 186n29,
        186n30
    as resurrection of the "warrior tradition," 4–5
    as sadistic, 4
    violence, allegations of, 3, 18–19, 25, 26–27,
        210n2
    "women's empowerment" used by for
        political advantage, 100–101, 141
Amin, Jaffar, 186n29
Amin, Kay, 17–19, 199n24, 208n30, 217n53
Amin, Madina, 101–2, 109, 113, 179, 199n24,
    217n53
Amin, Malyam, 16–19, 199n24, 208n30,
    209n51, 217n53
Amin, Norah, 18–19, 184n6, 199n24, 208n30,
    217n53
Amin, Sarah, 106–9, 154–55, 169, 217n53
Amin nvaako, 73
Amnesty International, 189n97, 214n12
Amori (aunt of Amin), 23
Anguduru, E., 35
Anthias, Floya, 60
Anti-smuggling Unit, 86, 179
Anya Anya, 36, 54–55, 166, 194n61
Anywar, Christine, 124
Anywar, Wilson, 125
Apio, Grace, 128
Apunyo, Constance, 114–15
Arach, Mitolesi, 139
Argentina, 129
Armed Forces (Amendment) Decree (1972),
    190n8
Armed Forces (Amendment) Decree (1973),
    190n8

Mazrui, Ali, 4–5, 9, 46, 62, 181n12
Mba, Nina, 8
Mbarara Barracks, 56, 116, 120, 123, 214n12
Mbuya Barracks, 48
McFadden, Patricia, 9, 183n23
McGowan, Robert, 155
McIntosh, Marjorie Keniston, 88, 206n67, 218n1
Melady, Margaret, 116
Melady, Thomas, 51, 116
memory, 11–15, 20–21, 177–78, 206n57, 219n4
Miescher, Stephan, 6
militarism: definition of, 2, 7, 182n19; as legacy of Amin's rule, 171, 173; relationship to citizenship, 9; relationship to gender, 2–3, 5–11, 19–20, 29, 39, 43, 46, 134, 149, 153, 172, 183n23, 183n31, 191n17, 207n5; relationship to patriarchy, 7; relationship to violence, 2, 44, 48, 149
militarism-masculinity nexus, 39
militarization of Ugandan state, 7, 8, 34, 43, 190n10, 191n15
militarized femininity, 7
militarized masculinity, 7, 9, 20
military. See Uganda Armed Forces
Military Commission, 158
Military Intelligence, 48, 131, 193n38
Military Police (Powers of Arrest) Decree, 130
Military Police Force, 35, 44, 51, 122, 125, 130–31. See also Makindye Barracks
military spending, 15, 36, 84–85, 173
Minawa, Farouk, 49
miniskirts: Amin posing with mini-clad women, 61; Amin's efforts to establish political legitimacy, 60; arrest of men for being "idle and disorderly," 201n49; banning order, 63–64, 67–68, 201n43; Malawi, 197n9; militarization of women's bodies, 60; relationship to African "authenticity," 62–63; relationship to morality, 61–62; relationship to violence against women, 67, 71, 202n67, 202n71; resistance to the ban, 66–67, 69; support for the ban, 66, 176; Tanzania, 197n9, 198n14; Zambia, 197n9. See also morality decrees
missionaries, 60–61
Miss OAU, 105–7
Mogadishu Agreement, 56–57, 150
morality decrees, 60, 63–64, 65, 71, 201n49, 202n62, 202n67, 202n71
Moshi Conference, 158
Mothers' Union, 207n13
Moyo Barracks, 125
Mpanga, Joyce, 103, 210n7
Mubende Barracks, 127, 139–40, 214n12
Mulago Hospital, 109, 142, 168
Mulindwa, Thereza, 41, 117, 210n7

Mulira, Rebecca, 41
Musa, Juma, 36
Musa, Sergeant Major (soldier who mobilized start of coup), 37
Museveni, Yoweri Kaguta, 172, 174, 178, 206n57
Musisi, Nakanyike, 81
Muslim Women's Association, 207n13
mutiny (1897), 28
mutiny (1964), 31, 187n60
Mutukula massacre, 124, 211n26
Muwanga, Paulo, 158
Mwaka, Victoria, 82
Mwesigye, Hope, 86
Mzee Ibrahim (husband of Amin's mother), 24

Naguru Barracks, 35, 44, 51, 122, 125, 130, 131, 142
Najembe Forest, 126, 129
Najjemba, Madina, 101–2, 109, 113, 179, 199n24, 217n53
Nakakande, Yudaaya, 166–67
Nakasero, 50, 136, 142, 214n21
Namaganda, Irene Druscilla, 24
Nasawuli, Margaret, 106
Nasser, Gamal Abdel, 36, 195nn67–68
Nasur, Abdullah, 105
National Army for the Liberation of Uganda, 218n5
National Consultative Council, 158
National Council of Social Services, 207n13
National Council of Women, 112
National Council of Women Decree, 112
National Executive Committee, 158, 165
National Parents' Association, 66
National Resistance Army, 172, 218n5
NCC (National Consultative Council), 158
Ndagano, Evasta, 129
Ndawula, Marget, 67
NEC (National Executive Committee), 158, 165
Nekyon, Adoko, 33
Ngobi, Mathias, 33
Nigeria, 6, 8, 9, 182n14, 183n28, 207n15
Nile Mansions, 106, 166
Nimiery, Gaafar, 53, 56, 189n87, 194n61
nostalgia, 11–15, 20–21, 177–78, 206n57, 219n4
Nsereko, Medi, 179
Ntambi, Mathias, 51–52
Nteeko, Deti, 66
Nubian identity, 20, 30, 46, 49, 80–81, 82, 166, 185n10
Nubianization, 81–82, 91, 204n29
nudity, 198n14, 200n32
Nyabongo, Elizabeth, 93–99, 207n3, 207n14
Nyenga, Peace, 62
Nyerere, Julius, 53, 56–57, 60, 104–5, 152–53, 154, 158